Big Bend Schoolhouse

A Surprise in the Park

Pat Seawell

First published by Dog Ear Publishing
4010 W. 86th Street, Ste H
Indianapolis, IN 46268
www.dogearpublishing.net

ISBN: 978-1-4575-1926-0

This book is printed on acid-free paper.

Printed in the United States of America

For my students and their parents,
happy memories everlasting.

ACKNOWLEDGEMENTS

This story has many authors, and I am grateful to them all. Thank you to my husband, John P. Seawell. After I retired he presented me with his "Big Bend Postcards." I knew he had been emailing family and friends during our sojourn in the wilderness, but I had no idea how comprehensive his emails had been. "I made these notes for your book," said he. Book? He persisted until I edited the emails and filled in the blanks.

Thank you to my friend and fearless leader, Shirley Coleman. The weekly letters she wrote to keep parents informed of school events provided an amazing chronological record of my four years at San Vicente Elementary School. She also answered my many questions and gave encouraging words as I wrote.

Thank you to my dear friend and avid cheerleader, Lisa Spier. The summaries of the yearly highlights and the farewell tribute she composed for my scrap book gave me the courage to sit down at my word processor and begin.

Thank you to my students, my delightful muses: Elena, Allison, Wyatt, Buck, Tristan, Don, Kassandra, Tanya, Garrett, Anna, Erik, Francella, Lauren, Apryl, Destiny, Andrea, Jonathan, Gabriel, Alex, Alicia, Jessie, Abbey, Jessica, Scott, Edgar, Quincy, and Bryan. Their stories, essays, reports, and letters added sugar and spice to this tale.

Thank you to my high school English teacher and enduring inspiration, John Henry Irsfeld. Authors and poets he introduced during his one semester at my school left their indelible marks, and without him random lines from T.S. Eliot's *The Lovesong of J. Alfred Prufrock* would not have been rattling around in my head for the past 50 years.

Thank you to Peggy Lipscomb for providing information relating to the history and social life of south Brewster County, and to my *comadre* Adamina Molina-Morlock and her second and third grade math class for spending a hot, buggy morning taking measurements of the school buildings for me. Adamina also served as my Border Culture consultant. Thank you to Noami Acosta for retrieving javalina information, and to Janelle Brady for providing details when my mind went blank.

Thank you to Claudia Arberger, Interpretive Staff Assistant at BBNP, who answered my questions while remaining cheerful throughout the inquisition, and to Don Corrick, Vidal Davila, Rob Dean, Mark Flippo, Raymond Skiles, Mark Spier, Tom VanderBerg, and David VanInwagen who shared their knowledge of numerous park features and details.

Thank you to Shelia Cox, Andy Cloud, Jody Davila, Melissa Forsythe, Doug Karr, and Paul and Chris Seawell who read all or parts of early drafts, asked questions, made suggestions, corrected errors, and shared their enthusiasm when mine waned.

And thank you to Sandy Bogus who provided expert instruction and cheerful support when the mysteries of technology left me clueless.

To each of you I am grateful. It takes a village.

A pproximately thirty-seven million American children attend elementary school, but only 20 of these children do so in one of the most remote national parks in the lower 48. From the fall of 2002 through the spring of 2006 my husband and I lived and taught in Big Bend National Park, Texas. This is the story of our experience in this remarkable school. One hundred miles from a supermarket, a hospital, or a Pizza Hut, my students and I laughed, learned, and flourished.

When my husband and I embarked on this adventure we stepped into a rare world which moves at a pace and is imbued with a serenity of an earlier time. The park children became our children, their parents became our friends. No dull moments and many amazing escapades developed as we followed the children through four years of bus trips, video conferences, school plays, river voyages, re-vegetation projects, and desert hikes. Woven through these events is the bigger story of the children growing, maturing, expanding their knowledge, and exploring possibilities.

This account also includes glimpses into some behind-the-scenes activities and events that occurred in this particular national park. Whether attending presentations of the scientists who conduct research in the park, hunting down a mountain lion that has attacked a tourist, or relocating a rattlesnake retrieved from the school playground, the park rangers and interpreters stayed busy. Yet they took time to share their expertise with my students whenever called upon.

Some of the history of the Big Bend region, along with its geology, flora, and fauna is also included. This area of the State retains echoes of earlier times – times when this vast, rugged, remote, and hauntingly beautiful part of Texas was indeed, the last frontier.

This is a book with many authors. I incorporated excerpts from emails my husband sent to friends, letters my superintendent wrote to parents, excerpts a parent composed for a scrapbook, lines from a T.S. Eliot poem, and compositions created by my students. Linking these authors' contributions is the love song that I sing for the children, the community members, my husband, a moment in time, and an enduring, enchanting place. It is my fond wish that through these pages you will experience some of the laughter and joy that enriched my life during my years in Big Bend National Park.

Pat Seawell
June 2013

CHAPTER 1

The Unsettling

Teaching. I made my career choice the year I turned three, and opened my first school the summer I was six. Four students, four wooden apple crates for desks, a chalkboard and three stubs of pink chalk. My classroom was in the original ranch house. Vacant, by then. The house consisted of two large square rooms with wide covered porches on two sides. It was built of rock chiseled from hills not so far away. Mortared with red clay. Covered with white plaster. The walls were three feet thick.

My oldest student, Maria, was four that summer. Roger and Dora were two. Yolie was a toddler. Ours was a multi-level class, and monolingual. All Spanish. All the time. Attendance was mandatory. When I rang the cow bell, the children had to come. No choice. I was the oldest, the ranch foreman's daughter, the *maestra*. I had to be obeyed. Besides, summer mornings in Texas are long and my students were happy for a diversion.

Those 1940's and 50's summers tumbled along, and as the babies in the *vaqueros'* families got old enough to walk, my enrollment grew. With my allowance I bought Big Chief tablets, crayons, water color books. My record player and records found their way to my classroom, as did all my children's books. *National Geographic* maps lined the walls. Somewhere I acquired a globe. Thus it was. My multi-level, monolingual school. My bliss. All Spanish. All the time.

The summer after my freshmen year of college my father outlined a proposal. A new program was being piloted in our county. Head Start. He said it sounded like a fine idea, and he had encouraged the parents of our five-year-olds and the parents of the five-year-olds on the two adjoining ranches to allow their children to attend.

So, how would I like to drive the five-year-olds to Laredo every morning? Seventy miles away. Over mostly unimproved dirt roads. Across cattle guards and through pasture gates. Oh, and in order to get all the children picked up and in Laredo by eight, he expected I'd need to be up by four.

Or ... or ... maybe ... I'd prefer his other idea, a possible option. He had made some inquiries, had worked out an alternate plan. If I spent a few days volunteering and observing at the Head Start school, bingo! I could teach a Head Start program of my own. In my old classroom. Where the chalkboard, the children's books, and the record player were waiting still. Our school district would loan us desks, furnish our supplies. And he'd already ordered the booklet for me. The one with the 600 English words the Spanish-speaking children were supposed to learn.

What nineteen-year-old can get up at four a.m.? Besides, summer mornings in Texas are long. I would enjoy a diversion.

"Plan B, Daddy. I'll take Plan B."

The resident six and seven-year-olds could think of no reason to while away their mornings at home, and the five-year-olds from the adjoining ranches had younger siblings eager for excitement. Who could say no to young children seeking an education?

It was set then. Our Head Start mornings would be multi-level; our session would last for eight-weeks; our enrollment would be ten. And, as always, our class would be monolingual. But our one language would change.

All English. All the time. The children were stunned. Horrified. Their silence was absolute. I dressed like a professional teacher. I followed my innovative lesson plan. I was dynamic and spirited. Three days passed.

"Daddy, I don't know what to do. I can't make the five-year-olds and the little kids say a word. They just stare at me ... like I've betrayed them or something."

"Well, give them time. It's all new."

The next morning I took my big red teddy bear to school. The one I'd won at a carnival that spring. I held it in my arms. I hugged it. I smiled at my class.

"Bear!"

A few of the children grinned. Everyone's eyes sparkled. I tried again.

"Bear!"

The bravest of the five-year-olds gathered her courage. Then came her shy whisper.

"Bear."

I handed her the big red teddy bear. If "bear" wasn't on the 600 English words list, it should have been. From "bear" we went immediately to "red bear." The race was on. 598 words to go. We were taking turns holding a big red teddy bear, and from that day forth, we were all laughing and learning.

After that summer there were to be many other students, many other classrooms, much more laughing, much more learning. I completed my Bachelor's degree at The University of Texas and began teaching at a middle school in Freeport. I had chosen this position for two reasons. First, it was the highest-paying district in Texas; second, I could live in a beach house at Surfside.

I had hardly begun fueling my idea of remaining at this school until I became a legend, or at least a character, when I shocked myself by marrying my university sweetheart.

John P. Seawell had chosen the military for his career, and in short order we were off to Korea. I switched from teaching Spanish to twelve-year-olds to teaching conversional English (or was that conversional Texan?) to post-graduate students at Seoul National University. All my students were U.S. bound to further their studies.

After Korea we lived here, there, everywhere. In most of these places I was able to find a teaching position, and in most of these places, we stayed only one year. Time after time, I began again. New city, new school, new grade level. But teaching was never dull, and I became an expert at being a first-year teacher. To my astonishment, during this enthusiasm for all experiences educational, thirty years raced by.

With my teaching days behind me, I began reveling in the wonders of leisure time. More reading. More gardening. More late breakfasts on our deck.

"This is interesting."

"Mmmm…"

The first queen of the morning was hovering over a bed of blue mist-flowers. Lifting my binoculars I watched it insert its amazing proboscis into a lavender puff. *Eupatorium greggi.* I love it when I can remember these scientific names. Amazing new sounds that tangle my brain and tease my tongue. Native plants. I'm all about natives now.

"The legislature has voted to allow retired teachers to return to the classroom."

"Mmmm…

Today I'll finish setting out the flame acanthus. *Anisacanthus quadrifidus.* I amaze myself!

"With full salary."

"Mmmm … more coffee?"

"And continue drawing full retirement."

"Mmmm … oh, you mean they'll get both a full salary plus their retirement checks?"

Retirement checks. What a concept. I get paid every month. For *staying at home*! I'm on Retirement Check #61 already. I *love* retirement checks.

"Right."

"The State is obviously desperate for teachers."

"I guess. But … such a deal."

"Yeah, such a deal for *some* retired teacher, maybe. Not this one. I wouldn't even consider it. I *love* retirement."

Black chinned hummingbirds were arriving to nectar at the fall sage. *Salvia greggi.* Up went my binoculars. John finished the section of the paper he'd been reading and moved on to the next.

4

"Well, okay ... I would consider it ... but there's only one school I would consider."

"San Vicente. Right?"

"Right."

San Vicente Elementary. Big Bend National Park. Desert. Mountains. River. 801,000 acres of wild. 1,250 square miles of majestic desolation. Tucked into the southernmost tip of the western arm of Texas. Touched on three sides by the Rio Grande. *El Río Bravo del Norte.* After running southeast along the Texas border for some 450 miles, the Rio Grande makes a big bend and runs northeast for the next 150. Finally it loops southeast again and travels the remaining 650 miles to the Gulf of Mexico. Since 1944 the region inside the tip of the river's bend has been a national park. Big Bend National Park. A hundred miles from a supermarket. A hundred miles from a hospital. It is in this vast, isolated wilderness, legend whispers, that the rainbow waits for rain.

Many times I had visited the park. With my husband. With my friend Amy. Like a magnet this rugged, untamed land drew me in. Its geology careened through my head with rhyolite dikes and basalt-crowned mesas. Laccolith domes. Alluvial fans. Its black nights shimmered with other worlds and overpowering wonder. Its sunsets stunned me with brilliant oranges and golds, then brought tears to my eyes with every gentle shade of peace and mauve and contentment.

And in the middle of this park, San Vicente Independent School District. No one can live in the park unless he or she works in the park. I could work in the park. I could be one of those four teachers who teaches those seventeen students. (Busted! I peek at the San Vicente website. Sometimes.)

But we're so *settled* here. Family. Friends. Doctors, dentist, vet. Taekwondo class. Theaters. Restaurants. Movies. Museums. Dozens of trips to the stable and the shred site to turn this little back yard into a butterfly garden. No mortgage. No worries.

"We still have too many pets."

"Just four geriatric kitties and a puppy."

"Yeah, well, it's the puppy I'm worried about. Eighty-eight pounds of energy! Look at her! She's toppling the birdbath again! Mandy! Come!"

I had contacted San Vicente once. A long time ago. In another life. I'd been invited for an interview. But when I asked about pets I learned there was a two-pet limit. We had seven. Five cats. Two dogs. Not regular dogs. Giant dogs. Newfoundland dogs. Hard to hide a Newfoundland dog. I had graciously declined the interview.

But John and I had thought about it and wondered about it and occasionally even talked about it ever since. Living in the park. Being a part of something unique. Unusual. Out of the ordinary.

Opportunity missed. Gone. Last chance forever.

But we're so *settled* here.

In a minute there is time

For decisions and revisions which a minute will reverse.

I had been retired from the classroom for eight years. Retirement was a joy. The possibilities that had been presenting themselves to me in San Antonio seemed endless. I was content. And yet ...

"I'm gonna write to them anyway. Who'll know about the kitties? They're happy staying inside."

"I'm not sure. I don't want to move out there just to get evicted."

"That's what you said last time. Nobody's going to get evicted. Anyway, we'll probably have to live in a tent."

"More likely a trailer."

"Four kitties and a wild Newfy puppy in a trailer?"

"We're not going unless they'll let us have a yard fence built for Mandy."

"Okay ... but you know, Sweetheart, we're really comfortable here. We're so ... *settled.*"

A few days later I mailed a letter of inquiry to the superintendent at San Vicente Elementary School. I must be crazy. I completed and returned the application that was sent in reply. I *am* crazy.

Then nothing happened. Weeks passed. Finally I forgot about being unsettled, forgot about being crazy. Peace returned to the butterfly garden.

"Pat, phone for you."

I was in the garage packing Mandy's crate into the Jeep. We were almost off for a long weekend in West Texas.

"Let me call them back."

"It's San Vicente. They want to know if you're still interested?"

Am I still interested? Am I ... still ... interested? A totally perturbing, utterly unnerving question. I took the call.

I was invited for a visit. To meet the superintendent. See the children. Have a look around. I added a dress to the jeans already in my bag. Projecting a professional image is important, even for an unsettled crazy person. I tried to calm myself. No pressure. No decisions. We were already West Texas bound. We were just adding a little side trip. Big Bend National Park. Tranquility. All that geology. But my head was spinning and I was not calm.

The next morning, leaving John and Mandy snoozing at a hotel in Alpine, I drove the 108 miles to the park. The superintendent greeted me in the parking lot and together we walked to the school building.

The guest chair in Shirley's office is a rocker. I had never interviewed from a rocker. I wondered what psychological messages Shirley was reading from my interactions with the rocker. Should I rock back and forth? Quickly, to highlight my abundant energy and enthusiasm? Slowly, to show I was poised and relaxed? I decided to sit still in the rocker. I wondered what sitting still might mean. Lethargy? Insufficient motivation? Lack of work ethic? I took a deep, gentle, yogic breath and rocked forward ... slowly.

Shirley grew up in San Antonio, but she had done her undergraduate work at Sul Ross State University in Alpine. With a population of 5,786 Alpine is the largest town in Brewster County and the county seat. Brewster County is the largest of Texas's 254 counties. 6,204 square miles. It's approximately the combined size of Rhode Island and Connecticut. Big Bend National Park fills its southern tip.

Few other settlements are found in Brewster County. Lajitas, population estimated at 200; Marathon, population 455; Study Butte, and Terlingua. Study Butte and Terlingua tend to run together in a strange version of rural sprawl, *south county*. Terlingua includes a ghost town and an international chili cook-off. The official population of this area is undetermined; 392 names are listed in the Study Butte/Terlingua phone directory.

After graduating, Shirley stayed in West Texas. She had a thing for cowboys. Maybe it was the hats. Or the boots. It could have been the starched Levis with the razor-sharp creases. Sul Ross is, after all, the birthplace of the Intercollegiate Rodeo Association. Since 1949 the rodeo team has won eight national championships and placed in the top ten thirty-three times. Talented cowboys and girls are awarded rodeo scholarships at Sul Ross State University.

Shirley's office walls were covered with plaques and certificates. She belonged to all the state and national professional education organizations and had served as an officer in many. I began to rock slowly backward as she described the upcoming vacancy. It was a multi-level position that included kindergarten through second grade plus pre-kindergarten two mornings a week. The teacher for this position could expect about a dozen children.

Then Shirley told me about the children. Each one of them. Thumbnail sketches of their backgrounds and abilities. Their strengths and their weaknesses. Their laughter and their tears. She talked about her hopes and expectations for them and the goals she and her teachers had for them. She called each child by name.

"If you take this position, it will be the hardest job you have ever had."

I had had hard jobs. My husband is, after all, a retired Army officer. We relocated many times while he was on active duty. Most of our moves included a promotion and a career-building advancement. For him. I remained a Second Lieutenant. I didn't actually have a career. I had a series of interesting teaching jobs. I had taken whatever was left over when we got there.

I rocked forward. And smiled.

"I like challenges."

"This will be your greatest challenge."

Although my graduate work had been in early childhood education, my first years in the classroom and most of my experience had been at the secondary level. Yet I love the awe and astonishment that characterizes the early elementary grades. I love the joy. Working with young children is exciting. Exhilarating. But the demands at the pre-kindergarten through second grade level are many and immediate. The needs are extensive and wide-ranging. Elementary teachers meet with all their clients, simultaneously, six or seven hours a day, five days a week, ten months a year. It is exhausting work, mentally and physically draining. In addition to giving their hearts, most elementary teachers give their souls.

During my twenty-plus years in the classroom I had taught pre-kindergarten for four years, first grade for one year, third grade for two. At the age of forty-five I had concluded that teaching young children was a young person's job, and I had returned to the secondary level. Now I was on the very far side of forty-five.

But I'd been retired for eight years. I'd just had a long rest.

"We're looking for someone who can commit for three to five years."

... *"Do I dare?" and, "Do I dare?"*

I knew the teacher for whose position I was being considered had held it for only one year, but I wasn't aware that the three teachers who had preceded her had also held it for only one year. Legitimate circumstances had led each of them to resign. Still, teaching young children in a multi-level class *is* a hard job.

I had good credentials. Endorsements in kindergarten, general elementary, reading K–12, English as a Second Language, and secondary English and Spanish. I could get a bilingual endorsement in a heartbeat. I even had a PhD in Education, Curriculum and Instruction, my accidental PhD. (Accidental, as in "I'm just taking classes here while John P. Seawell prepares for his post-retirement career." Accidental, as in, "Pat, you've completed more than half the course work toward a degree, and we just happen to have this fellowship available.") But even though I had a plethora of official documents, I didn't have enough certifications for Shirley.

"You'll need to pick up your gifted and talented hours and pass the State ExCET for special education. How are your technology skills? All our students have laptops. We're thoroughly committed to computer literacy."

My weakness. Computers had just begun creeping into classrooms and email was just becoming a part of our popular culture when I retired. I was eight years behind in computer skills. Eight light years.

"You would have to scramble. We have a trainer who comes out from Region 18. Also, I can send you to workshops."

A tour of the school was next on the agenda. That's when I meet the kindergarteners and first graders. They were outside for recess. The children were gleeful over something their teacher had just given them. Glo-Gurt!

"Come on, Dr. Seawell! Look! It *glows*! It *glows in the dark!*"

Then a gaggle of animated, confident, giggling little girls propelled me into the girls' restroom and turned out the light so I could observe the magic of yogurt sticks glowing in the dark. I'd been with the children for less than a minute and I was smitten.

Then we were back in Shirley's office to answer questions I might have. She had invited Edgar to bring his new story in to read to me. Edgar was a first grader who had come to San Vicente late in the year after beginning school in Mexico. His mother worked as a housekeeper at the lodge in the park. English was Edgar's second language, but it had served him well for his story about a monster. His illustrations were lively and exuberant with color and imagination. And they were *scary*. Edgar had big brown eyes, the sweetest of faces, and a contented little smile that appeared quickly and lingered.

Although I had thought this meeting with the school superintendent was a job interview, I finally understood that it really was only a visit. Just as it had been described in the phone call. But I had made my decision. I wanted this job! However, my official interview with Shirley and the members of the site-based committee was scheduled for 7:30 a.m., June 19, a full month away. It was going to be a long wait.

After leaving Shirley's office I sat for a minute in my car gazing across the small parking lot at the igneous intrusions of Pummel, Wright, and Panther Peak. Evidence of the region's turbulent, volcanic activity some 35 million years ago. A red-tailed hawk drifted in a lazy circle above the playground. And I drifted into a gray cloud of melancholy so intense it took my breath away.

Whoa! What emotion is this that arrives without warning? What secret so deep it comes with no words? A memory lost? Shadow of a leftover dream? Unfamiliar feelings for Miss Mary Sunshine. A curious reaction for this cheerful gal. Astonished and not a little bit baffled, I struggled to shove the feelings aside. I may be an unsettled, crazy person, but why should wanting this job make me all gloomy and weepy-eyed. Especially when I can't fathom a cause.

My father had a proverb for every occasion and I had learned them well. I excel at letting sleeping dogs lie, leaving Pandora's box closed, and not rushing in where angels fear to tread. But now something was rocking the boat. My boat. And although I couldn't identify the problem, it felt like something huge. Something beyond wanting this job. For a woman who has been playing her cards close to her chest for decades and looking before she leaps for a lifetime, this "something" had me up the creek without a paddle.

By the day of the interview I had thought of many excellent reasons why I wouldn't be offered the job and I had fixated on two. My experience. My education. I was at the top of the salary scale. Expensive for a Texas teacher. Too bad, too sad. I had rung my hands, shed my tears, accepted my disappointment, and gotten a grip. Then with the melancholy and awkward emotional outburst of my last visit safely at bay, I drove out to the park and was outrageously merry during my interview.

I was offered the position. Amazing. A shocking surprise.

John and I divided the tasks and began the scramble. To put our home on the market, to attend the thirty-hour seminar for the gifted and talented certification, to separate the possessions we would keep from those we would let go, and to wonder about that really critical question: what is this new Big Bend teacher to wear?

It had taken eight years and two household moves, but I had finally disposed of all my teacher clothes. A painful task. It had required courage. And discipline. All those pretty dresses. Dresses that I would never wear again. Ever. Periodically I had stood at my closet door. Stood there until I had chosen three of those dresses for recycling, reincarnation, regeneration. And now? Oh, what is this new Big Bend teacher to wear?

Washable cotton slacks and T-shirts? I went boldly forth seeking teacher clothes for the new, low-maintenance me.

How we hustled! A chance reading of a chance article in a newspaper three months ago had catapulted our lives from tranquil to tumult, from peaceful to pandemonium. Yet bouncing high above the occasional frustration was the excitement, the anticipation, the thrill. Have John P. Seawell and I always been vagabonds at heart?

Most amazing of all, I would be in a classroom again. Endless possibilities. Endless opportunities to ignite that ephemeral shooting star. And, although I'd had many teaching experiences – four states, three continents, pre-k to post-graduate students – I had forever longed to follow my grandmother's footsteps into that one-room school house where she had taught and my fantasies had lingered. My Big Bend school would not be one room, but it came close. And there was another echo. Floating through the decades was the contented murmur of a carefree little *maestra*. Teaching her multi-level class. In an old rock house. On a ranch. In the middle of nowhere.

In addition to our other pre-move preparations I was giving my husband a crash course in early childhood education. True, he had completed some twenty-four hours of education classes during his post-retirement foray into public school teaching, but he had been preparing for high school students. Ultimately, he had decided secondary teaching was not for him, but he had had many years of teaching experience, both in the military and in adult basic education classes. He had also been a guest speaker in my high school classes many times. It had not occurred to me that he would be apprehensive about interacting with young children. I was surprised when he told me he felt anxious.

Too late! No dragging of feet! During my job interview I had claimed my husband as one of my assets. I had announced that he would be my classroom volunteer, always available, always eager to assist. Perhaps he should have been consulted before I made such a claim. Even my promises of extensive on-the-job-training didn't leave him reassured. I stepped up my tutoring efforts. In a multi-level class of young children, I would need his help. Refusal was not an option.

My concerns about living in a tent ended when we were shown the cozy three-bedroom house that came with the job. Two-car garage. Dishwasher. Laundry room with a sink. We would be comfortable beyond expectations. John began inviting our friends to come for a visit. But he urged them to consult their maps, and he warned them that Big Bend National Park lay at the far end of an exceptionally long and lonely road.

Even though we were busy during the month before our move, I would sometimes stand back and observe our behavior. We were so excited, so thrilled. It was fascinating to watch these two senior citizens, whom I knew so very well, react to this unforeseen change in their lives. Maybe they had thought they were established, settled, set. Maybe they supposed they had already had their last great adventure. Could they even have imagined they would linger quietly in their butterfly garden until they rested in peace? The buoyancy of the human spirit is astounding, and the magnitude of our excitement filled me with awe.

We had only one concern. It had to be resolved.

"Hello, Ms. Coleman? Shirley? Thanks for returning my call. I just have one question. It's about … it's about our pets. And, well, I'm prepared to lie about them if I have to. But I'm not going to lie to you. We have four old cats – old cats – seventeen, fifteen, thirteen, and twelve. And we have a puppy. A *big* puppy. She's a Newfoundland. The cats always stay inside, but … if there's ever an inspection or anything … "

"I'm the only person authorized to inspect your house, and I won't be doing any inspecting."

"Okay, I just wanted you to know."

"Good! Now I know."

"And Shirley? We're very pleased with the house, and we're really, really happy about the fenced back yard."

"Good! See you in three weeks!"

Three weeks. Goodbye leisure time. Goodbye quiet days. Goodbye butterflies. See you later retirement. This well-ordered, predictable interlude is over, and we are racing full speed ahead to our next adventure.

CHAPTER 2

The Beginning

I shall forever be grateful to my dear friend Amy for making that crazy pre-move trip with me. We brought kitties, house plants, sleeping bags, food, and cleaning supplies, then spent four days organizing either the house or the classroom. Unlike our previous trips to the park, we didn't take time for hiking or stargazing. Our wildlife viewing was limited to the rattlesnake being chased out of the back yard by three determined cactus wrens and the scores of scorpions that appeared on our driveway every night. On the fifth day, the moving van arrived. John and Mandy couldn't be far behind.

When John and the puppy arrived I put them both to work. John's job was unpacking boxes and shelving books. Mandy's was splashing in her wading pool and stalking the giant tarantulas in her new back yard. Most of my waking hours were spent at school, becoming familiar with the curriculum and preparing my classroom.

Realizing that John P. Seawell, my nervous apprentice, might feel more comfortable if he were familiar with his new environment, I took a morning off and invited him over for a tour of the school.

The original concrete-block building was constructed in 1951 when the park headquarters was moved from the Basin in the Chisos Mountains to its present location at the mountains' base. This building consisted of two classrooms plus a tiny efficiency apartment to house the teacher.

Over the years, as populations and requirements changed, the original building was expanded to include a small library. Eventually more buildings were added. In addition to the original structure, the present school includes two free-standing classrooms, a building that houses the school offices and another classroom, a large multi-purpose building called "the gym," and a screen-enclosed shade ramada with picnic tables inside referred to with affection as "the cafeteria." Sidewalks, porches, and covered breezeways hold this maze of buildings together.

Then, there's the school greenhouse. This building was made possible through a grant written by a couple of the teachers, and was built five years ago by the students, the teachers, and several community members with some professional help. Now the students work with park botanists on re-vegetation projects. Among other things, they propagate native grasses and transplant them to disturbed areas in the park. Public service in action.

During our first days in the park we familiarized ourselves with the other buildings in the community. They include the national park offices and visitor center as well as housing for park personnel, the other San Vicente teachers, concession employees, and members of the U. S. Border Patrol. All the buildings are within walking distance of each other. Spaces where park volunteers can secure their mobile housing are also located in this area.

A post office, the Big Bend Natural History Association office, and a service station/small convenience store complete the picture. Altogether, this section of the park is home to approximately 200 people. The community is called Panther Junction. PJ for short.

In many ways life in the park reminded John and me of our time in Frankfurt, Germany, and Asmara, Ethiopia. In both cases we lived in a self-contained "village" where we all knew each other and everyone walked to work and walked home for lunch. The difference here is that there is no city outside the gate. Much like the military, some National Park Service personnel move every two or three years, but unlike the military, park personnel get to choose when and where to go. Name any national park in the inventory and the chances are good that at least one person here has been stationed there.

Mandy Watching for Mom

We soon learned that there is a strong community spirit among the park residents. A few days before school began a potluck supper was held at the headquarters building to celebrate the arrival of a new academic year. We were delighted with the outpouring of friendliness and good food, and pleased to hear that potlucks are held often.

Within two weeks we were feeling very much at home, and Mandy was enjoying her new life immensely. From our back door she could watch javelinas, deer, rabbits, and an occasional skunk roaming just outside our yard. One evening she had an encounter with a small javelina at the fence. She even licked the snout it stuck through a missing slat. Fortunately, the only reaction of the two young animals was mutual surprise. Yet with all this wildlife activity, the true highlight of Mandy's busy days is the morning walk we take as the sun is coming up over the Sierra del Carmen Mountains in Mexico, twenty miles to the east. Nothing is more exciting to a puppy than an excursion with the pack.

A few things about living here will take some getting used to. The electricity is notoriously unreliable, although they are upgrading the lines. Power goes off, at random and for no apparent reason, but it seldom stays off more than an hour or two. Mail takes two to three days longer to reach us, and some of it never arrives at all. This postal service glitch has given rise to rumors of a "black hole" somewhere in the El Paso area into which occasional parcels enigmatically fall.

And on a more personal level, there is the matter of housekeeping. Not a Molly Maid in sight. I've begun pushing my own vacuum cleaner and trying hard to be a good martyr about it. Also, we must involve ourselves in the infamous monthly "grocery run." John made his first trip into Alpine yesterday – one hour and 45 minutes each way, but he reported that the dramatic scenery (and the audio book) made it seem like less. Still, this jaunt to town is an investment of time and gas, so we plan ahead and have multiple purposes for each trip. This time, in addition to shopping for the August groceries, he had a hardware store shopping list, got a haircut, changed the address on his driver's license, registered to vote, and had lunch in a nice restaurant. After this successful trip, he feels like a true West Texan.

On Monday, the third week of August, school started. Ready or not. Mr. John P. Seawell and I began the year with eleven children: two kindergartners, seven first graders, and two second graders. On Wednesday and Friday mornings two pre-kindergarten children joined this group. The thirteen pre-k–2nd graders were the "little kids," not to be confused with the eight 4th–8th grade "big kids." We had no 3rd graders that fall. Somewhere along the way another kindergartner arrived and toward the end of the year a third grader joined us. ("A *third* grader, Shirley? You're giving me a *third* grader?")

Fortunately I was sharing the little kids with a second teacher that first year. After beginning the day with PE, John and I would take half the children for reading and language arts while the second teacher took the other half for math. At a given point, we would switch children.

In the afternoons John would be dismissed and I would take the whole group for social studies and Spanish, then the second teacher and I kept the group together for science. At 2:45 we walked the children to one or the other of the big kids' teachers for art or music. On the way back to my classroom I would swing by the school office for a handful of Milky Way and Snickers fun bars from the never-empty candy dish. For the next ten minutes I would nibble chocolate and collapse ...*a patient etherised upon a table*...

Finally, inspired by a sugar buzz, I would begin the real work ... putting the room in order, accessing the children's progress, preparing for tomorrow's lessons, planning for next week, completing required paperwork and/or the questionnaires and surveys that never ceased popping up online, conferencing with parents.

John and I had long honored "the six o'clock rule." At six o'clock the one of us who was not yet home would check in by phoning home. After a few days at San Vicente we changed our six o'clock rule to a seven o'clock rule because I rarely got everything done by six and saw no point in interrupting my work with a six o'clock phone call. On those occasions when I was still in my classroom at eight, John would call me. He would ask if I were planning to spend the night and offer to bring my pillow.

Shirley had been right. This was the hardest job I had ever had.

By the end of August I was beginning to get a clue about multi-level classrooms. The reason this job was so difficult was because *all* of my children were young. A one-room school house always had a few big kids. The big kids helped with the little kids. My grandmother had told me all about it. At noon she had dismissed the younger children and devoted the afternoons to the older students. But that was long before the No Child Left Behind days. Addressing the requirements and documenting the progress for additional students in additional grade levels would be a nightmare I didn't even want to contemplate.

While I was attempting to sort out this multi-level challenge, my husband began experiencing an identity crisis. For the first time ever he was feeling old! Years ago, when he was a company commander, his people called him "the old man," but that was just military tradition and was not true since many of the unit's NCO's were older than he was. But now it is true. He is the oldest person in our community of over 200 people. Since many of the people here work for the Park Service or the Border Patrol, with a mandatory retirement at age 62, and the rest work for Park concessions and tend to be 20-something kids on a lark, this makes John the village elder. This has given him a real jolt.

To distract him from his preoccupation with age, I increased John's volunteer time from two mornings a week to three. His reservations about teaching young children are gone; he is learning how to support each child's special wants and needs; and, he is discovering that young children appreciate his wisdom and value his friendship. The hours he spends in the classroom are enriching for him, helpful for the children, and give me opportunities to work more closely with those children who are not with him. It's an arrangement that benefits us all.

Yet even with John's additional volunteer hours, I wasn't getting everything done. Life took on a strange, surrealistic quality. There weren't enough hours in my days. Try as I might, the scope and sequence of my classes seemed always to develop gaps. Instead of moving along in the smooth, well-organized patterns I had achieved in the past, I seemed to be lurching along in fits and starts. I agonized. I worried. When the second graders were on track, the first graders derailed. When the first graders were smoothly sailing, the second graders had a man overboard. When the kindergartners got ahead of schedule, the pre-k children fell behind. Working long hours had paid off in all of my previous schools. Working long hours had kept me organized and on top of things. But long hours were not doing the trick here. Not at San Vicente.

During my previous forays into elementary schools I had sometimes felt like a high school English teacher pretending to be an elementary teacher. But this time it was worse. I began to feel like a genuine imposter. Had taking this job been a grave mistake? Could I complete the year? More immediately, would I make it to the end of the first semester? The responsibility of teaching young children can be overwhelming. Each time I was successful in one area, something startling and unexpected would pop up somewhere else.

"Pat, you need your PDAS training."

"PDAS?"

"Professional Development and Appraisal System. You remember, the tool TEA uses for teacher evaluation. You had the training before you retired, but the TEKS and TAKS objectives have been revised since then so the PDAS has been revised to reflect the changes. You need training for the new version."

"Oh."

"You can get the training in Presidio next week. You'll need to spend the night. Check with Kathy. She'll take care of the reservations. She'll give you the credit card and the keys to the truck."

"Oh."

I had already spent one night away from home for teacher training. I'd gone with the whole staff to Ft. Stockton the week before school began.

Teachers from throughout the region had attended this training. Ft. Stockton, 130 miles to our north, huddles on a huge, wind-swept desert plateau along Interstate 10. Cabeza de Vaca and his three companions reportedly wandered through this area in 1535. The last survivors of a shipwreck on the Texas coast, they were attempting to join their countrymen in Mexico City. Or find gold. Or both. A dependable water source, a life-giving, life-saving spring, was located in the Ft. Stockton area. Perhaps water from the spring saved their lives.

"Oh, and Pat," Shirley was at my door again. "One of the new Terlingua teachers needs the PDAS training, also. You can pick him up on your way."

"Oh."

Our school district shares a high school with the school district in Terlingua. Big Bend High School is only seven years old and has a unique background. Prior to its construction, getting to school was an ordeal for our secondary school students. They had a 28-mile car ride to Terlingua, followed by an 80-mile school bus ride to Alpine. According to an article in *The New York Times* in December, 1994, this was the longest school bus ride in the nation. After several years of lobbying the Texas Education Agency for a high school in south Brewster County, our previous superintendent finally succeeded in getting some TEA representatives to come down from Austin in the spring of 1995 to assess the situation.

The superintendent simply drove the TEA people to Terlingua, put them on the big yellow school bus, and drove them to Alpine. Then he drove them back to Terlingua, transferred them back to the car, and returned them to the park. At the end of these six hot hours of nightmare travel, they agreed, unanimously, that south Brewster County needed its own high school.

TEA would facilitate the opening of a San Vicente/Terlingua joint high school, but it did not provide funds for its construction. This was left to the two school districts and the Big Bend Education Corporation, a non-profit organization established to support the building and running of the school. (After the article appeared in the *NY Times*, contributions began coming in – a man in Dallas donated 320 acres of land in West Texas; a company in Ohio donated a septic system; a hardware store in Ft. Stockton donated fencing.)

During the following year public meetings were held to plan the new school. Members of the community, the Terlingua and San Vicente Boards of Trustees, the Big Bend Education Foundation, TEA, and members of the Sul Ross State University staff were all involved.

By then Shirley had arrived at San Vicente and Terlingua had a new superintendent, also. By late August of 1996, these two women had somehow rounded up a few temporary buildings, a mobile home, some furniture, and a high school faculty. After classes began in the temporary quarters, the foundation for the new building was poured – by a highway contractor who just happened to be working in the area that fall and, when approached, agreed to charge a reasonable fee.

Later an architect willing to design a building to fit on the existing foundation was located, construction began, and by the fall of 1997, the new building opened its doors to the 33 high school students in south Brewster County.

Dedication, persistence, hard work, imagination, a wing, and a prayer had put an end to the long commutes. As this current school year begins, five of our park students are car pooling to Big Bend High School.

Classes at San Vicente had only been in session for two weeks, but I had already fallen months behind. And now I had been instructed to pick up a new Terlingua teacher and attend PDAS training. Fortunately this training was scheduled for the evening. If I left Panther Junction immediately after science class and got back to school before eight the next morning I wouldn't lose any class time. I'd only lose precious hours of prep time. I'd only be a few more months behind.

But I would be visiting Presidio. That legendary port of entry on the Rio Grande. Throughout my childhood I'd heard about Presidio. Almost daily. In my child's mind, it grew more fascinating with each report. Details crept into my head. Heroines emerged. Castles materialized. Imagination is an astonishing thing.

My father told me Presidio was a town way out in Far West Texas. On the Rio Grande. I was growing up on a ranch on the Rio Grande. The ranch was 400 miles southeast of Presidio, but it was on the same river. In some magical, cosmic, serendipitous way, I was *connected* to this mythical place way out in Far West Texas.

In those days Presidio was all about weather, and weather is of vital importance to ranching families. They pray for rain and listen to daily weather reports with religious fervor. Throughout the devastating drought of my childhood, the hot spot of the State was announced daily. And the hot spot of the State was *always* Presidio. Presidio was famous.

I was an adult before I actually visited Presidio. Some twenty-six years ago John and I had driven the River Road from the park and arrived in Presidio after dark. We found only one motel. Our room had a bare, concrete floor, six single beds, and smelled of disinfectant. During dinner John announced he felt the motel was unsafe. He reported he'd seen "creeps" and "unsavory characters" lurking about. He was certain we'd both be murdered as we slept. I begged to drive on. I studied our map. I promised I would find another town. But he wouldn't hear of it. He said we'd already paid our eleven dollars. Eleven dollars. John P. Seawell is a generous man. Money had never, ever, been an issue with him. Yet now we were to risk our lives. Because we'd already paid our eleven dollars.

When we returned to the eleven-dollar motel, I dragged one of the six beds across the door and propped myself up in another bed on the opposite side of the room. Throughout the night I kept my eyes on the door and listened breathlessly to every ominous sound.

John slept in another bed. Like a baby. He awoke the next morning with great joy and an enthusiastic yearning for a breakfast of huevos rancheros. As it turned out, we had not been murdered in our beds. It came to me years later to consider a possible link between the Lone Star beers my husband had downed while I was careening our new truck along the River Road and the eleven dollar value he had placed on our lives.

But now I needed PDAS training, and asking Shirley for a description of my motel room seemed wimpy and inappropriate. She wouldn't send me into harm's way, right? This was official business, right? I wondered if a village of 2,000 could support a Motel 6.

On PDAS day I climbed into the school pick-up truck promptly at 2:46, set the cruise control at the park speed limit of 45 mph, and followed the afternoon sun out of the park. I was slightly apprehensive, and looping through my brain were ...*half-deserted streets, The muttering retreats Of restless nights in one-night cheap hotels.*

Twenty-eight miles west of Panther Junction I turned south onto Roadrunner Circle, bounced over a cattle guard, and got my first look at Big Bend High School.

The school building itself, with its tan stucco walls and gray metal roof, fits well into the landscape. In this wild, untamed place, surrounded by buttes, mesas, and mountains, it sits low to the ground and only hints at civilization.

It took only a few minutes to locate the new Terlingua teacher who was to accompany me, and after augmenting water and snack supplies, we set out for Presidio. That town in Far West Texas. That parallel universe that had preoccupied my childhood and established my monetary value as an adult.

This trip provided more evidence of the teacher shortage Texas is experiencing. I was back in the classroom because of the rehire-a-retiree program, but the new Terlingua teacher's story was more colorful. He had gotten his job two weeks before school started. On the last day of his annual vacation in Big Bend he'd gotten gas at a service station in Terlingua prior to beginning his long drive back to the Dallas metroplex. He'd mentioned to the attendant that he wished he could find a way to stay in the area permanently.

"Can you teach math?"

"Teach math?"

"They're still looking for a math teacher at the high school."

"There's a high school here?"

"Go on over and talk to the superintendent. I'll call and let her know you're coming."

"I can't interview in shorts and Tevas."

"I'll call and let her know you're coming."

The River Road, Texas Ranch Road 170, Terlingua to Presidio, is one of the most geologically satisfying 65-mile drives in the State. It skirts the Rio Grande, sometimes at river level, sometimes on hills high above the river. It celebrates yellow limestone deposits laid down when Texas was covered by a shallow sea, dark brown intrusions and extrusions and black lava flows layered between gray ash beds from the volcanic period, and whimsical white hoodoos sculpted from volcanic ash by water and wind during the ensuing eons. Mexico is on the south side of the river. Texas, on the north side, is a whole other country.

As with most of the Ranch Roads in this part of the state, the chances of meeting more than a vehicle or two along the way are slim, and meeting no vehicle at all is a real possibility. On the mesas the country lies flat. Pale umber earth and low gray-green scrub unroll to the horizon. In all directions. Nothing moves. Nothing makes a sound. This part of the State could seem daunting, could seem intimidating. Edged with heartbreak. Traversed by spirits long abandoned and lost. But these stark, desolate landscapes ignite my compassion. Stoic and unpretentious in their loneliness, they endure. My heart opens to them and I embrace their unassuming beauty. They lie serene and I am soothed by their stillness.

In keeping with border hospitality, when we arrived at the school in Presidio we were treated to refreshments. That's when we met the Filipino teachers. All nine of them.

"Pardon me? You're from where?"

Presidio Independent School District, like many isolated Texas districts, must actively seek teachers. Texas school administrators recruit in Utah, Iowa, Kansas, Wisconsin, and many other places both inside and outside the State. They recruit in Germany and search in Spain. The Filipino teachers had arrived in Presidio via an international placement service.

On impact, Presidio shocks. It's third world. In 1913 a journalist described it as "a straggling and indescribably desolate village." At first glance, the description holds. My sympathy went out to the Filipino teachers. I feared they were in despair.

But the outcome has been good. The extensive paperwork involved in hiring the Filipino teachers has been worth the effort. Most adapt to Presidio's unique setting and are excellent teachers. When the school district began paying a recruiting incentive to their employees, the Filipino teachers responded. Like one notorious Presidio resident of yesteryear, they became bounty hunters. Their recruitment of family and friends brings a steady stream of teachers to the school district.

If you're a teacher, you're wanted in Presidio. If you're a teacher, Presidio has placed a bounty on your head.

Incidentally, except for its lack of a coffee maker, my room at the Three Palms Motel was absolutely and completely conventional, and San Vicente ISD paid more than eleven dollars for my one-night stay. I awoke the next morning with great joy and an enthusiastic yearning for a breakfast of huevos rancheros.

Before sunrise I walked across the parking lot to the motel restaurant, and while eating the eggs and tortillas, I realized that in some magical, cosmic, serendipitous way I am *connected* to Presidio. I always will be.

CHAPTER 3

Laughter and Love

Teaching eleven-plus-two young students isn't easy, but John and I took great pleasure in our mornings with the "little kids." The children were enthusiastic about life in general and about learning to read and write in particular. They were eager and lively. As with any group of young children, each was at a unique developmental level. Their abilities ranged from eight-year-old Edgar, who was still acquiring English as he was learning to read, to five-year-old Erik, who was reading at the second grade level. Our reading groups were fluid and flexible and we usually had three or four groups running simultaneously.

While I attempted to follow the lessons outlined in the kindergarten, first, and second grade state-adopted reading program, which focused on reading comprehension, vocabulary development, phonics and spelling, John presided over something he called Story Writing 101. With his journalism background it was no surprise that the children's story maps and graphic organizers always included the famous five W's and "how." As the stories were completed, John would key and print them and the children would illustrate them. Then they would be published in various ways, sometimes on classroom walls or breezeway bulletin boards, sometimes gathered together as a class anthology for the library shelf, sometimes sent with their authors to be read to Shirley, or Kathy our secretary, or Beth our business manager, or to any other willing adult who happened to be in the area. Occasionally they would be placed in an envelope and mailed to someone in a place far away.

By mid-September John was volunteering five mornings a week and had cancelled the cruise to South America he had planned for January. I was working twelve hours a day and spending full days at school on the weekends. This little one-room schoolhouse adventure was proving to be a formidable undertaking, and I sometimes wondered how long I could maintain such a pace.

But teaching is a performing art. The show must go on. I wasn't accomplishing everything I wanted to accomplish and I was horrified and humbled by the disorganized manner in which I seemed to be stumbling along. Yet, despite my concerns over all matters academic, the children remained astonishing cooperative, high-spirited, and cheerful. We were experiencing an abundance of laughter and love in our classroom, and there is much to be said about the power of laughter and love. The Russian-born surrealist Marc Chagall said *everything* is possible if it is based on love. Does that include learning to read? I had to believe it did. Teaching is also an act of faith. I had to believe.

It was my students themselves who sustained me. Throughout the days. In many ways. Often we sat on the floor during science period, the last class of the day I had with the children. At some point during the session, five-year-old Lauren would manage to climb onto my lap and whisper "I love you, Dr. Seawell." On one difficult day she put her two little hands on my cheeks, smiled up into my eyes, and whispered, "Dr. Seawell, every time I see you, I just want to hug you." For affection so generously given I could make it through another day.

And there was Gabriel. At noon I would walk across the playground and half a block up the street to our house for lunch. When I walked back, Gabriel always saw me coming. Shouting, "Dr. Seawell! Dr. Seawell!" he would tear across the playground to meet me. At his cue, all the other little kids would begin shouting my name and racing across the playground behind him. Then there would be greetings and great laughing and hugging all around. This happened every day. This happened even though it had been less than thirty minutes since we'd last seen each other. For welcoming committees so genuinely cordial I could make it through another day.

Coming Back From Lunch

I remember you coming back from lunch on a warm summer day wearing that big floppy hat and a short sleeve shirt. I was playing on the playground. I saw you and came running with the other children. I remember hugging you and saying hello and feeling excited and happy. I remember going back to playing and you going inside. I love you, Dr. Seawell!

By Erik 3/16/2006

Each child was enchanting and I cherished them all. Jessica took my hand at the end of every recess and walked me to the classroom. Edgar's bear hugs came spontaneously and often. Abbey's bright blue eyes flashed with enthusiasm no matter what my question or assignment. Scott's sweet, gentle, kindness toward us all left me calm and reassured. Andrea's spunky, "can-do" attitude inspired me. Destiny's merry little giggle lifted my spirits. Jonathan's astonishing quest for knowledge, coupled with his little boy playfulness made me chuckle. Erik's comments were always outside the box, over the top, and wonderful. Lauren and Gabriel loved me. And it took but a wink in her direction to set Apryl's whole being dancing with a joy that could fill a room. And a teacher's heart.

Erik's Essay "Coming Back From Lunch"

The children were happy and I knew most of the parents were happy because they told me so. This parental support, openly and generously given, was invaluable. It helped keep me going through those early and somewhat desperate weeks. Often it was a parent's casual, yet encouraging, remark that made my day. When I confessed to Jonathan's mom that I felt disorganized she said, "Well, *they* don't know that! They're first graders! Don't worry about it. They're doing fine." Of course I continued struggling to become organized, but many times throughout that year I would take a deep breath and replay Susie's mantra. "They-don't-know-that! They're-first-graders!" It always made me smile.

In October Melissa and her 6th–8th graders, with some help from a few community volunteers, sponsored a baby-sitting night for the little kids. Although most park get-togethers are attended by entire families, the baby-sitting nights usually coincide with a farewell party for a park staff member and are often organized at the request of the moms. Rather than feeling forsaken or left out, the little kids adore these events and view them as their own private parties. And well they should! The gym is set up with a cornucopia of entertaining games and crafts activities, juice and snacks are served, and the evening culminates with the children stretched out on mats in front of a big TV screen watching a favorite movie.

The money generated by these events is used for the end-of-school trips the big kids take, often to Corpus Christi. In addition to visiting the various museums and the State aquarium in Corpus Christi, they also participate in science projects with the 8th graders from London. No, not what you're thinking. London is our K–8th grade sister school on the Gulf Coast near Corpus Christi. Every fall, the London ISD 8th graders spend a week camping and participating in educational activities here in the park. Although the little kids don't take part in hosting the London students, they usually have an opportunity to show them around our classroom during their tour of our school. And like most young children, my students enjoy having an audience for the various performances and activities in which they participate throughout the day.

No matter what performances and activities are scheduled for the day, we always begin our mornings with the time-honored activity, first circle. This consists of the children sitting on the floor in front of a big calendar for what Mr. John P. Seawell calls "the morning briefing." In addition to learning the names of the days, the months, and the passing seasons, all sorts of other important information is shared during this first ten minutes of our day.

In my past incursions into early childhood classrooms I had used Maurice Sendak's amusing *Chicken Soup With Rice* during first circle. For each month of the year Sendak created a poem and an illustration to highlight some traditional, or not-so-traditional, aspect: ice for January, wind for March, and so on. He linked the poems together by ending the last verse of each with some variation of "stirring once, stirring twice, stirring chicken soup with rice." With a previous class I had set the poems to music and motion and we would begin each calendar session by singing the tune of the month and carrying out the motions.

Throughout the day, when children had a free minute, they would drop by the calendar area, pick up the book, turn to the pages of past months, and sing the poems to themselves while pretending to read them. Pretending to read is a good thing. Pretending to read is the step that immediately precedes reading. Since including Sendak's poems in the calendar routine had been successful in the past, I was using it again with the younger members of this multi-level group.

The poems of August and September swept by in a flurry of getting children tested, grouped, settled, and reacquainted with school. Suddenly October arrived. October, that exhilarating interlude of skeletons and jack-o-lanterns. October, that electrifying month that culminates with the intoxicatingly mysterious and scary event we call Halloween.

To say the children were excited about Halloween from the first week in October would be an understatement. "High screech" more aptly describes their level of anticipation. From the moment they saw the new calendar stapled to the bulletin board and realized what was in store for the 31st day of that month, my entire class was on high screech.

Sendak's illustration for October features traditional Halloween fare. The poem begins "In October I'll be host to witches, goblins, and a ghost. I'll serve them chicken soup on toast." It ends with the phrase now familiar to the children, "Whoopy once, whoopy twice, Whoopy chicken soup with rice."

I'm not sure how it started, probably with some teasing remark from John, but the children became fascinated by the whimsical notion that the treat given at our house on Halloween evening would consist of chicken soup with rice. Destiny, in particular, seemed mesmerized by the concept.

"But, Dr. Seawell, how will we take it home? How are we going to carry soup?"

I'd wink at her, and smile. She'd go back to Sendak's book and study his October illustration.

"And what about toast? Are you going to give us toast? How are we going to hold hot soup? Will it be in a bowl? Do we get to keep the bowl? It's going to spill, Dr. Seawell. We'll be spilling chicken soup with rice all over the place. Oh, I get it! You're going to tell us to come in and eat it at the table. Dr. Seawell, we won't have time to sit down and eat chicken soup with rice while we're trick-or-treating."

A wink. And a smile.

October could not have been more exciting. Conversations focused on costumes and costuming, we read dozens of stories about Halloween, we watched Halloween videos, we decorated our classroom with bats and spider webs. Mr. John P. Seawell even bought us a real pumpkin on his October grocery run. And … the logistics of managing a treat of chicken soup with rice continued to haunt Destiny.

The week before Halloween the gym was declared off limits to the little kids so the big kids, with the help of their teachers and their sponsor group, could turn it into an elaborate and spooky haunted house. The sponsor group consists of adult volunteers from the community who meet with the big kids once a month for social and/or recreational events. This gives the big kids some contact with adults other than their parents or teachers, and working together on the haunted house project, which always includes a pizza party or two, is one of the favorite sponsor activities.

At last October shrieked to an end. Children rushed home from school. Dinners were wolfed down. Costumes flew off hangers and onto energized bodies. Flashlights and goodie bags were assembled. Then moms and dads walked squealing little kids back to school.

Slowly and with dramatic foreboding, the door of the Haunted House creaked open. Halloween had arrived.

The big kids scared the socks off the little kids in the gym – round after round because the little kids just couldn't take in all the delicious terror at one go, besides, their parents were happy to accompany them through the haunted house "just one more time."

Finally, the full hour of frightening the little kids ended in triumph. The big kids stopped their screeching, screaming, wailing, and gnashing of teeth. They emerged from their coffins, swamps, and creepy attics, and closed the doors of the Haunted House. Halloween in the Park, Phase One, ended.

Then, in groups of three or four, often accompanied by as many adults, the students of San Vicente Independent School District began their stroll through Panther Junction. Phase Two, trick-or-treating, began.

Campbell's makes a rather nice can of chicken soup with rice. If you wrap the can in orange shrink wrap and include it in your bag of traditional Halloween goodies, little kids think it's the perfect treat. They ask their moms or dads to serve it up after a cool evening of trick-or-treating. They announce that it's the best soup they've ever eaten and offer to share it with their families. Thus traditions are born. There is a small group of children in this world who will link together chicken soup with rice and Halloween. Forevermore. Wouldn't Maurice Sendak chuckle?

November began and I was still struggling. Language Arts, with its flexible groupings and John in the classroom to assist, was almost manageable, and Spanish class, because it was oral and interactive, seemed to work most of the time. The second teacher was handling math, and the two of us were piecing together a fairly comprehensive and engaging science program.

But my social studies class was a disaster. The few social studies books available were in their last year prior to new adoptions. After seven years in the little hands of six-year-olds the books were depressed and exhausted, and much of the teacher resource material that had originally accompanied the series had vanished. I read and re-read the scores of specific social studies learning objectives that were to be taught in grades K–2, the TEKS, the Texas Essential Knowledge and Skills. How do I structure a social studies class for five-through-eight-year-olds? Where are the extra hours in my day to pull social studies rabbits out of my hat?

I needed more moments to sort this out. In the interim, during our designated social studies period the children took turns choosing the fabulous fragrance wall plug of the day and I'd plug it in. We'd dim the lights and gather in a circle on the floor. Then with the scent of Warm Vanilla Sugar, Sun-kissed Raspberry, or Juniper Breeze wafting through the room, I'd read a story to the class about far-away people in a far-away land. Afterward we'd turn up the lights, locate the far-away land on our globe and wall maps, draw pictures based on the story we'd just read, and write a couple of pertinent sentences at the bottom of the illustration. Yup, my social studies class was a disaster. I needed to read those TEKS again.

I am confident, maybe overly so, about teaching English to secondary school students. No insecurities there. But teaching young children has always been a mystery. How does one do it? How does one teach eleven (or twenty-five!) young children whose abilities stretch out on a continuum from Maine to Mexico?

The findings of the prominent psycholinguist and educational researcher, Frank Smith, had been my salvation in the past. He concludes that one difficult way to make learning to read easy is to follow the lead of the child. I had tried to follow the lead of my young students as they learned to read, and I had tried to follow their lead in other areas of learning, as well. My classroom had been a cheerful, productive place. My students had learned. Easily.

However, following the lead of a child is difficult for teachers. It takes time. It brings surprises. It gets us off schedule and leads us to places we were not expecting to go. Simply telling students what they need to know, then checking to see if they've gotten it, seems much more efficient. Deliver information. Question. Answer. Deliver information. Question. Answer. Push, poke, prod, prompt. Check a few TEKS off the list. Move on to the next page.

But human beings learn best by constructing their own meaning, making their own sense of things, connecting with new ideas in ways that appeal to them on a personal level.

Look at the magic of a child acquiring language. He or she is not "taught" language. Moms never say, "Today, my dear, I'll be presenting verbs and adverbs. Listen closely. There will be a quiz." No, moms, dads, and all the other members of a child's speech community simply immerse the child in a steady stream of meaningful chunks of language, including verbs and adverbs.

The child listens to all this language, experiments with it, ferrets out the structure, discerns the system, and figures out for him or herself how verbs and adverbs work. By the age of five the project is finished. Done. Children will learn more vocabulary, more subtleties, but they've already internalized the rules. They can communicate. They have language.

How can I take advantage of this easy way of learning? Should I immerse my students in a steady stream of social studies? Should I provide enriching materials and determine which materials capture the children's interests and imaginations? How can I support these interests? How can I follow the lead of the child?

What, Frank Smith? Tell me. What am I to do with my social studies class? I'm going crazy here.

Group projects? Would group projects be a solution to this multi-level conundrum? If we did lots of hands-on activities and followed-up with a field trip, each child would have a way to be engaged and involved according to his or her interests and abilities. All I'd need to do is correlate the projects and activities with the learning objectives mandated by the TEKS. Then I'd need to document this correlation in my lesson plan book and devise a method for assessing whether or not each child mastered each TEKS. Oh, my. Difficult.

But I had to give group projects a try. The oil in our fabulous fragrance wall plugs was running low.

Ft. Davis National Historic Site in Ft. Davis, Texas, is 120 miles northwest of our school. During the mid-1800's soldiers stationed at the post played a key role in defending immigrants, freighters, mail coaches, and travelers on the San Antonio to El Paso road. Parts of the post were preserved, parts have been restored, parts are undergoing restoration. Ft. Davis is one of the best examples we have of a frontier military post. It's an important piece of history. History is an important piece of social studies. Our first group project began to unfold.

There are at least five hundred things K–2nd grade youngsters can do to learn some history and prepare for a field trip. We did about a hundred of them. In addition to reading and writing stories, visiting websites, plotting bus routes on maps, considering why Texas is divided into 254 counties, creating itineraries and estimating times of departures and arrivals, reviewing museum manners, discussing geological and botanical changes we'd encounter on our journey, planning nutritious snack and sack lunch menus, studying bus safety and practicing bus evacuation procedures, we also used many of the teaching materials sent to us from Ft. Davis by the National Park Service.

The children were engaged and interested. Each child's Ft. Davis packet was growing plumper, and I was checking TEKS off the list by the dozens. This was real social studies, I was following the lead of the child, and Frank Smith would be proud.

In addition to studying the mission and historical context of Fort Davis, we were also learning about the everyday life of the soldiers stationed there, including the food they ate. A few days before the field trip, five-year-old Lauren informed her mother immediately after finishing her lunch that she needed to hurry back to school.

"What's the big rush today?"

"We're having our heart attacks right after lunch. I don't want to be late!"

"You're having *what*? Lauren, tell me more!"

"Our heart attacks. When the soldiers were at the fort they ate regular bread. But when they went out on horse trips for six days, they ate heart attacks. It was easier to carry on the horses."

"Heart attacks."

"We made them yesterday and they were baking all night long in Dr. Seawell's oven. She's bringing them for us to eat right after lunch."

See there? Told you! Children construct meaning in their own way and at their own pace. I'm sold on group projects.

The "heart attacks," that 19th century field ration made solely of flour, water, and salt, proved to be one of the most delicious taste sensations the children in my class had ever sampled. Because these children are thoughtful and kind, they asked to include the recipe in their Ft. Davis packets. They want to produce this mouth-watering treat at home for their parents and siblings. They are truly generous children.

Hardtack Recipe
(sufficient for 12 small soldiers)

Ingredients: $4\frac{1}{2}$ cups flour
$\frac{1}{4}$ teaspoon salt
2 cups water

Mix flour and salt together. Add water. Knead. Roll dough to a thickness of $\frac{1}{4}$ inch. Cut into $2\frac{3}{4}$ " x $3\frac{1}{4}$ " biscuits. Place biscuits on greased cookie sheets. Punch 8 holes in each biscuit with a nail or a Philips screwdriver. Bake at 175 – 200 degrees for 24 hours flipping biscuits occasionally so they bake evenly. Pack biscuits in a canvas bag. Saddle up!

Our experience at Ft. Davis exceeded my expectations. After we watched a lively film depicting the historical background of the fort, the education director helped divide my little group into four teams, provided each team with a list of questions, then sent us out to explore the fort while finding the answers to the questions.

Locating the box of hardtack on the commissary shelf, deciding how many offenders the guardhouse could hold, and imagining ways to help the Buffalo Soldiers spiff up the barracks were among the activities that tickled the children's fancies. But the sight that most astounded and amazed them was unrelated to this reconnaissance mission. It was a feature they discovered when we carried our sack lunches down to the picnic tables under the giant cottonwood trees in front of the fort.

"Dr. Seawell! Look! *Grass!* Look at all this *grass!*"

"Can we sit on it, Dr. Seawell? Can we eat lunch on the grass?"

"Look how *green* it is! Can we just roll around on it?"

"Dr. Seawell! Feel how soft it is! Here! Touch it! Put your hand right here!"

Grass. Green grass. This enriching material had captured the imaginations of my students. Now they were *immersing* themselves in it. I sat down on the grass with my young desert dwellers, my children of the rocky terrain. I was supporting their interest, following their lead. And it wasn't difficult at all.

Although most of our waking moments were focused on our students, John made some time every week for the two of us. Perhaps because the magic has never gone out of our marriage, perhaps to provide a semblance of our former, retired selves, he reserved Friday evenings for our "date." My former Army officer, the master planner, scheduled this event to begin promptly at five o'clock. Therefore, Fridays, and Fridays only, I'd give myself the evening off, leaving my classroom no later than 4:45.

That first year most of our dates consisted of a drive to the Basin of the Chisos Mountains for dinner at the Lodge Restaurant. This was the nearest place we could get a meal, and by the end of the week a ten-mile trip was usually as far as my energy would expend.

The Chisos Mountains are near the middle of the park and are completely surrounded by the Chihuahuan Desert. The mountains have been described as a sky island anchored in a desert sea. It has been said, and it is supported by the geologic record, that the volcanic birth of the Chisos would have made Mount St. Helens look like a birthday candle. Yet these mountains are inviting and driver-friendly. With only a couple of switchbacks and hairpin curves, the road climbs from cactus and lechuguilla into oaks and conifers, a complete eco-change including a temperature drop of 10 degrees, in less than twenty minutes.

At road's end lies the Basin, a rocky bowl just over a mile high and six miles in diameter. Red peaks and pinnacles 2,500 feet and higher surround the Basin, but a V-shaped gap in this massive circle of rock is visible on the west side. The Window. Through the Window all the water from the surrounding mountains drains, and it is this draining water, over millennia, that separated the yielding rock from the unyielding rock and created the basin.

Often John and I would walk the short Basin Loop Trail, sit on a bench at its center, hold hands, inhale the sweet mountain air, and watch the sun go down.

Let us go then, you and I,
When the evening is spread out against the sky…

On certain days in spring, the sunsets are framed by The Window. At certain times in summer, the sunsets are obscured by dramatic desert thunderstorms framed by The Window. Each hour, each day, each season has its splendor. Sun and shadow, sun and shadow. Ever changing sun and shadow.

I cherished our Friday night dates and looked forward to them. The hours from five p.m. Friday until nine a.m. Saturday were ours, John's and mine, and I chose not to mar them with a single worry.

The menu at the Lodge Restaurant isn't extensive and the quality of the food isn't consistent, but the views from the dining room are magnificent and a leisurely meal, with a glass of West Texas sauvignon blanc, make for a pleasant evening.

We would relax over dinner and engage in a bit of non-classroom related conversation. Like old times. Like the friends we have always been. Occasionally it would occur to me that we were surrounded by tourists. Tourists, whose visits were limited and whose homes were many miles away. Poor tourists. I couldn't help but feel a little smug. *I live here. This is my home.*

Sometimes other families from PJ would be dining at the Lodge. Our neighbors, our students, our friends. The children would always drop by our table for a conversation and a hug. One evening we were visited and hugged over the course of our meal by no fewer than seven children. It made the tourists wonder. It made John P. Seawell and me feel loved.

In addition to the restaurant, there are cabins, a motel, a campground, and a convenience store in the Basin. We have noticed that few of the people who work at these places are Texans, and we are always curious to know where everyone is from and what brought them to Big Bend. One week the young woman who waited on us in the restaurant told us her story.

She had never heard of Big Bend until six months earlier when she found an offer of immediate employment on the concessionaire's website. A few days later she got on an Amtrak train to Alpine. Now she waits tables at the restaurant and lives in the dorm for single employees in the Basin. When I asked her if she had been particularly drawn to this wild, isolated area she said, "No, I just wanted to get out of Ohio!"

Back at school I continued lurching along until December brought the end of our first semester. December also brought many holiday activities to our little community and many pleasant surprises. Our school secretary set my festive mood by initiating the merrymaking.

Quilting is Kathy's thing, her passion. She'd tell me about quilts she was creating. She'd bring a finished block in to show. In early December she said she was hosting a quilters and crafters gathering for her girlfriends. I am neither quilter nor crafter, but she invited me anyway.

The evening of the get-together I discovered Kathy's second passion. Christmas. Every year this creative woman, with the help of her skillful husband, hurls herself into a whirlwind of decorating that turns her home into a wonderland. Elaborate department store displays, eat your hearts out! Professional holiday decorators, fuhgeddaboutit! Kathy wins. Hands down. "Angels" was her theme and every room had been touched by celestial wings. Gentle lightning. Hand-crafted wreaths. Quilted wall-hangings. And *dozens* of angels.

To the middle of nowhere, to the back of beyond, Kathy had summoned Christmas. With elegance and charm. I made new acquaintances and giggled with the girls. When I left the party the sky was black velvet and the stars within reach. My soul had been nourished and my spirits soared.

A few days later we attended the Community Dinner. It was held at park headquarters and was catered by a company from Alpine. The dinner was preceded by a social hour which included a visit from Santa with gifts for all the children. After-dinner entertainment was provided by the Big Bend Community Choir. Led by the band director at Big Bend High School, these singers presented a beautiful program. Almost everyone who lives in the park was present for this enjoyable evening.

Next came Shirley's Christmas party. We'd been hearing about it since August. Consensus promised an amazing event that highlighted Shirley's twin passions, cooking and baking. Over the nine years she'd been in the park, this annual affair had grown, swelled, expanded, and taken on a life of its own. She collected and tested recipes all year and began assembling ingredients in October. November was a blur of baking, and in December all afternoons and weekends were devoted to preparations.

Throughout the day of the party Panther Junction had floated and drifted amid damp, milky clouds. As John and I left our house that evening the fog that had grown softer, denser, ...*Curled once about the house, and fell asleep.* Through the haze a web of twinkling lights beckoned us to a door. Inside, tables, counters, and sidebars were crowded with the fruits of Shirley's labor, an astonishing one-woman show. Hors d'oeuvres, salads, entrées, breads, fruits, desserts. Everything tempted. Everything enticed. We enjoyed an evening of laughter and conversation, merriment and fun. This was accompanied by foods to delight every palate.

An activity-packed week at school followed. Just before Thanksgiving the big kids and their teachers had begun preparing for the annual Christmas play. Auditions were scheduled, rehearsals commenced, costumes were organized, and construction of sets began. With the exception of Abbey, who had thirty-one lines to memorize, and Jonathan, who emitted a few barks as Jack Frost's dog, the little kids didn't have speaking parts. But they were thrilled about donning their costumes with bells on their green twinkle-toes and appearing on stage as Santa's elves.

Melissa and Peggy, the big kids' teachers, threw themselves into this production with an intensity that spared no effort, took no quarter. Each teacher supervised half a dozen jobs. Among other responsibilities, Melissa was drama coach, Peggy directed music.

All the big kids had lines, all the little kids had stage appearances. And everyone got to cut out paper snowflakes, and more paper snowflakes. We taped snowflakes to the gym walls until we were encircled by a blizzard.

On the last Thursday morning of the fall semester, the last rehearsal of the play was staged. Then thespians, faculty, and staff worked together setting up folding chairs in the gym. The school Christmas play was a community event, and *everyone* was expected.

That evening the children delivered a lively performance. The nine elves hit their marks, Jonathan barked authentically, and Abbey delivered her lines flawlessly and with feeling. The applause was deafening. The encores many. Afterward came the cast party at the opposite end of the gym, and the audience was invited.

Spread on three long tables was a build-your-own-sandwich buffet with all the trimmings. And fruits. And salads. And desserts. Shirley had struck a second time. Soon we were eating, laughing, and visiting. Again.

The next day featured the children's gift exchange and a luncheon honoring the sponsor group and the classroom volunteers. School was dismissed at noon; the students went home; the teachers and staff wiped down the tables and swept up the floor. Then I walked across the playground, up the hill, home. It had been a tough first semester, but it had ended well. I felt successful, and I was incredibly happy.

Truth be told, happy is pretty much normal for me. Because of an early literary experience. Because of a book I begged my grandmother to read to me. Over and over. Until I could read it for myself. Over and over. I have the book still. Inscribed to my grandparents. In red ink. Christmas.1916.

This is the book that shaped my character, influenced my world view, predestined the sentiment of my soul. *Pollyanna*. Eleanor H. Porter. A bit embarrassing, isn't it?

But today my happiness is brighter, is radiating farther. I can't put my finger on it. Flicker of a memory. Wisp of a melody. Echo of a distant bell. Deep within, obscured in a soft opaque mist, lies the trace of a fantasy. Whose?

I meant to sort it out, the source of this untold happiness, but I never got to it. The feasting and camaraderie continued. On Christmas Eve we joined two other couples at Peggy's home for a warm, congenial evening. On Christmas Day we attended a holiday pot luck luncheon. The park superintendent and his wife furnished the turkey and dressing, and each guest brought a side dish.

This was December in Big Bend. December as celebrated by our park family.

CHAPTER 4

Encountering *Dicotyles tajacu*, Wall Maps, and TBSI

In field guides they are collared peccaries, but along the Texas-Mexico border they are called by their Spanish name, *javelinas*. This translates as javelin or spear and probably refers to their razor-sharp tusks. Ranging throughout the deserts of Texas, New Mexico, and Arizona, they are the only wild, pig-like animal found in the U.S. Their bristly coats of gray to grizzled black are highlighted with whitish collars that whorl up along their jaws to their shoulders. Succulent desert plants and cacti are their preferred foods, with adults weighing 35-65 pounds and measuring about two feet tall at the shoulder.

Javelinas tend to ignore humans unless they feel threatened, but these Big Bend peccaries can be sassy little creatures. They've been residents of a national park for sixty years, many, many generations, and they know they own the place. Unlike the normally shy, reticent javelinas of my young life on the ranch, these javies are bold. They stand their ground. Their hearing and their sense of smell are much stronger than their eyesight, but that hasn't stopped the teenagers from perfecting the impudent stare.

"Whaaat?"

The javelina herd that visits our area numbers around fifteen, including young ones of various sizes. Their territorial circuit brings them through Panther Junction about once a month and they usually spend several days in the neighborhood before wandering on. Many times when I left school at dusk, the herd would be strung out across the playground blocking my path. With a lot of respect and a little apprehension, I'd skirt around them, always aware that I was a trespasser in their territory and outnumbered.

Once as I returned to school after lunch I encountered a javelina between the two boulders that mark the entrance to the playground. It was kneeling on its front legs to more effectively reach some tender prickly pear pads. I approached within 15 feet and suggested in an assertive voice that it unblock my way. It continued kneeling, but turned its head and glared.

"I'm *eating* here!"

"Well, *excuuuuuse, me!*"

I stepped off the trail, treaded through high weeds, stumbled over rocks, and arrived on the playground with minor abrasions. Evidently my assertive voice isn't all that assertive. Anyway, yielding to wildlife is a national park rule.

National parks have other rules. Don't remove artifacts. Don't drive off-road. And, of course, don't plant non-native herbs. But what joy it would be to share my butterfly obsession with the children. Black swallowtail butterflies. Yes. I placed a call to the park Science and Resource Management office.

"No, you won't need a permit, but keep it in pots and keep it on campus." Yahoo! I added gallon pots, potting soil, and parsley seeds to John P. Seawell's January shopping list. (Yes, that's what I really call him. To clarify. Because four friends were John. Because when I told my family I would marry John, my mom asked which one. I've made it clear ever since, and four decades of students have liked the novelty of it. They insert "Mr." and they're good to go.)

Personalizing garden pots, measuring soil, counting seeds, writing ID tags. The growing of parsley requires many educational steps, and, like all gleeful scientists, we kept meticulous watering, sprouting, and growth records. Fortunately, 98% of our seeds germinated. We had six pots of parsley, three dark moss curly, three Italian flat leaf. Determining butterfly taste preferences was part of our experiment.

Rather than troop my little ones out to the greenhouse every day, I chose to keep this gardening project inside the classroom. This way we could observe and document its every scientific development. But there came a beautiful, warm day when it seemed cruel not to treat our young plants to some sunshine.

This excellent idea had one major flaw. It arrived in the form of a herd of hungry javelinas. Unaccustomed as we were to taking pots of parsley outside during the morning, we were even less accustomed to bringing them back into our classroom in the afternoon. Sometime between the hours of seven p.m. and seven a.m. the javelinas visited our parsley garden and devoured our six pots of crisp, fresh greens. Mid-winter bonanza for them, scientific catastrophe for us.

When children feel acute disappointment, they produce tears. But we were, after all, scientists still. We recorded our observations, formed new hypotheses, counted more parsley seeds, and reassembled our scientific apparatus. Next time, when we give our plants access to sunshine, it will be from the picnic tables inside our screen-enclosed shade ramada.

A convenient thing about butterflies is that most species are plant specific. Most species have only one plant or group of plants upon which the females will lay eggs. When the eggs hatch, the larva immediately begin feeding on the plant the female selected. Unlike *The Very Hungry Caterpillar* who gobbles its way through an amazing variety of fruits and human groceries, real caterpillars stick to the basics. They trust their mom's judgment. They eat only the food their mom has chosen for them.

The children interpreted this plant-specific characteristic as a sign of good and careful parenting. They chatted among themselves about conscientious butterfly mothers searching for nutritious fare and choosing only the best for their babies. The idea worked for them. It works for me.

I knew we had black swallowtail butterflies in the park because I'd seen them. And I knew black swallowtail females would lay eggs on parsley. Plant it and they will come. We planted it. Again. Now we'd have to wait. Again. It's hard work being a scientist.

While we were waiting for our second parsley garden to sprout, the concession hired a Filipino man to manage the kitchen at the Basin restaurant. With him came his two young daughters. The older child was five so she joined Lauren and Erik in our kindergarten class.

John was alarmed when he discovered the little Filipina appeared to speak no English, but I wasn't concerned. I know how easily young children acquire language. In addition to several experiences with Spanish-speaking children learning English, I had taught an unusual kindergarten class the year we lived in Korea. This class was attended by twenty-six children of the diplomatic community. I had Asians, Africans, Europeans, and South Americans, one five-year-old from each country represented. Few of these children understood me or one another. Yet within days the children had acquired enough common language to play exuberant, raucous games together at recess, and within weeks they were conversing with me and with each other in the classroom.

I urged John to relax and proceed with Story Writing 101 as usual. Our English immersion program was already up, running, and successful. It was being conducted by the ten young native English speakers in our class, and Edgar was proof of their program's effectiveness. At this point he could communicate as easily in his second language as he could in his first.

All the little kids delighted in welcoming our new student. She was a cheerful little nymph who settled quickly into the school routine. Since her father was occupied with his responsibilities at the restaurant, it was her nanny who supervised her interactions with the school.

And it was the nanny who, within days of her arrival, became a person of mystery. She gave intriguing accounts of her background, describing herself as a microbiologist on sabbatical from her teaching post at a university on the west coast. She was a friend of the family, helping out at a difficult time.

She was also heiress to a vast fortune which she was attempting to disseminate. She had an inoperable brain tumor. She had only seven months to live. To her new friends in the park, she was magnanimous. Over the next weeks she offered her ranch in Montana to one, her home in Santa Fe (including her O'Keeffe painting, a gift personally chosen for her by the artist) to another. She would pay for the Daisy troop's rafting trip and their adventure to Disneyland. She had also decided to allocate 1.6 million dollars for the construction of a gym at Big Bend High School.

On the afternoon of the meeting to finalize the transfer of funds for the gym, the nanny met with the school administrators. Her attorneys were to have been present but they had missed a connecting flight because of bad weather on the east coast. After the meeting she became ill. She refused Kathy's offer to call the park EMS, but allowed me to drive her to the hospital in Alpine.

We spent several hours at the emergency room while she underwent tests. It was late evening when she was released and well after dark by the time we got back to the park. She was quiet during the one-and-three-quarter hour trip home. She seemed tired. Although I didn't ask, she volunteered that she could not discuss the results of any of the tests she had been given.

The nanny had thought her attorneys could send the paperwork for the transfer of funds allocated for the gym, but she learned that was not possible. The attorneys insisted on being present for the transaction. Legally it was complicated. She asked to schedule another meeting so they could attend.

The last time any of us saw the nanny, her vehicle had been pulled over in PJ by a park law enforcement officer. She had been handcuffed and was being led away. We knew not why then and we don't still, but several days later my little Filipina student reported that she had visited the nanny in Alpine. At the jail.

Oh, do not ask, "What is it?" Let us go and make our visit.

Not so long after that, the Filipino man and his children left the park. The nanny had been hinting of their eminent departure for weeks. She told us she was getting her friend a better, much more lucrative position elsewhere. She said his talents deserved a broader venue.

All of us missed the little Filipina student. And, yes, all of us missed the nanny.

A few days after the nanny's departure, I sat with all the little kids on the floor in front of our Texas wall map. We were helping Scott, one of our second graders, plot his journey. He traced the highways with his finger and read aloud the names of the towns and cities through which he would pass. He would travel east to get there, west to get back home. On the mileage grid the rectangle where Big Bend and Galveston converge reads 651 miles. Texas can change a great deal in 651 miles. Scott would go from the desert to the beach, from an elevation of 3,750 feet at Panther Junction to an elevation of 0 at the

Gulf of Mexico. We noted that our river, the Rio Grande, empties into the Gulf of Mexico. The first graders located Galveston on our U.S. map, the second graders found it on our world map, and we all helped the kindergartners point out Galveston on our globe.

Maps and globes. Children can glean a wealth of information from maps and globes. Twenty-five years ago I read a study about geographic illiteracy, about how American children are the most geographically illiterate children in the western world. Embarrassing? No, scandalous.

I thought about my own geographic illiteracy and examined my life as a student. I remembered the globes of my elementary classrooms. They sat serenely on the tops of high cabinets, too precious to be touched by small hands. As for wall maps, there weren't any. However, my high school classrooms had wall maps, banks of expensive, retractable ones. Once or twice each semester a teacher would select a map and cautiously roll it down. I knew to ogle quickly. Its appearance would be fleeting.

The sad, unpleasant realization that I had been geographically deprived throughout my school years was upsetting. I put down the disturbing report I'd been reading and grabbed my car keys. Never again would I contribute to the geographic illiteracy of an American child. Never again would I teach in a classroom without wall maps.

For the price of a caramel macchiato I purchased two, big, colorful wall maps at my local discount store. One of the U.S., the other of the world. From the Texas Department of Transportation I acquired an attractive, up-to-date, state map for free. Three new wall maps and a roll of tape transformed an empty wall into a permanent learning space. From this day forth, every reference to county, country, continent, state, or nation will become a geographic moment. I do solemnly swear. Guerilla geography. Flash learning. The ten-second pause.

Through the years, as I moved from school to school, my wall maps sometimes created confusion. The occasional high school student hesitated to walk into my classroom on that first day of school. No way this could be an English class, not with those three, big, scary maps on the wall. And once a school board member got a surprise in my pre-k room.

"Why do you have all these maps on the wall?"

"Aldo, please show Mrs. Harrod where your Uncle Tomas is."

"Right here. Saudi Arabia, see?"

"Can I show Georgia?"

"Go ahead, Ana. I'm sure Mrs. Harrod would like to see where your Aunt Gloria lives."

Suddenly all the four-year-olds wanted in on the action. Everybody wanted to be a part of the show. Little hands flew up, and Mrs. Harrod and I were treated to a full-blown world geography extravaganza. Wow. I was stunned. When did they learn all this stuff? Let's hear it for the ten-second geographical pause.

"You know Bill and Pete? Best friends on the Nile? See this blue line? That's where they live. The Nile. Egypt's close to Saudi Arabia. See?"

Yup, I *do* believe in wall maps. Scott was the one going to Galveston, but in our imaginations we could all travel along. During the two weeks he was absent, children often sat on the floor in front of the wall maps when they had a minute. They traced Scott's route from Panther Junction to Galveston and from Galveston back home. They traced the Rio Grande from the park to the Gulf of Mexico. Then, depending on the child, he or she found Massachusetts or Arizona, California or North Carolina, Wisconsin or Colorado. Grandparent states hold special meaning for a child.

Although our school is tiny, with only 22 students this year, many of society's challenges are represented in these few children. Scott is hearing impaired. Yet with the help of monthly visits from a speech pathologist and powerful hearing aids, his speech sounds like that of any other seven-year-old, and he hears most anything he chooses to hear. But Scott was born without open ear canals and without external ears. Last summer he began a series of surgeries to construct ears. Cartilage removed from his ribs is being used to build his ears and the process will take several years. He is scheduled to have his second surgery soon.

Scott's parents are hard working people. His father is a handyman for the concession and his mother works as a waitress at the Lodge Restaurant. The children's hospital in Galveston where the surgery is being done does not charge for its services, but when the family travels there, they provide their own transportation and living expenses. And when they prepare to go, the park family helps with costs. This time three co-workers organized an enchilada dinner and everyone from the park superintendent on down attended. The donation was supposed to be $5 a person, but I expect everyone gave more. The longer we stay out here, the more we grow to love this close-knit community.

A total of twenty-two Shriner's Hospitals for Children are located in the U.S., Canada, and Mexico. They provide specialized care for orthopedic conditions, burn injuries, and spinal cord injuries. They also provide reconstructions for cleft lip and palate. The Galveston hospital specializes in burn injuries, a specialty which includes reconstructive surgery. Scott's first new ear is complete and is healing into a work of art. He is proud of it, and so are we.

My admiration for those men and women who devote themselves to helping children in need is beyond description, and I am in awe of this brave little boy who is already looking forward to beginning the construction of another new ear.

After we bid Scott and his family a safe and successful trip, and the children had organized a letter-writing campaign to cheer him on and keep him informed about school happenings, I took a few minutes one afternoon to organize my professional file.

In addition to teaching, I was learning. By mid-February I had accrued several training certificates: Gifted Education Foundation Series; Language Proficiency Assessment Committee; Instructional Models & Strategies for Differentiation; Writing to Accommodate Gifted Learners; and the infamous PDAS. I'd completed three of these training sessions on campus through our distance learning capability. The other two entailed overnights in Presidio and Odessa. I'd also had five technology training days on campus and driven to Sul Ross State University where I took and aced the Generic Special Education ExCET. (Courtesy of my husband and his skillful highlighting of the prep materials!)

I had also participated in the Labor Day trip to the Ft. Davis Nature Preserve to scout out learning opportunities for our students. The bonding weekend. We four teachers laughed and hiked, planned school activities with the Preserve education coordinator, and counted the stars. Meanwhile, Shirley prepared hearty, mouth-watering meals for us. This trip was a happy experience that will live on in cheerful detail in my memory, but it took three much-needed days from my classroom.

Although the training I was getting was worthwhile, much of it was occurring while school was in session. Preparing lesson plans for a substitute took hours, and usually turned into a half-nighter. Being away from an elementary classroom isn't easy.

"Pat, you and Melissa need your TBSI. It's being given at Sul Ross next week."

Shirley was at my door again. Was she talking about a medical exam? A drug test? A criminal clearance?

"TBSI?"

"Texas Behavior Support Initiative. Training for severe behavior – how to handle out-of-control children without hurting them."

"But Shirley, my children aren't out of control."

"Not an option. It's a new requirement. Get with Melissa and plan your trip. Kathy will give you the truck keys and the credit card."

Oh, great. Mumble, mumble, mumble. More lesson plans for a sub. I hardly know Melissa. She teaches the big kids. What'll we talk about cooped up in the truck for three-and-one-half hours? Mumble, mumble.

Melissa had always been friendly to me, but we were both busy. We rarely saw each other and hadn't really become acquainted. I was in awe of her and, bizarrely, a wee bit jealous. She was heroic, larger-than-life, a superstar. She and her husband had come to the park for a two-year sojourn. Their sojourn had stretched into fourteen years. Big Bend National Park was their true home. They *belonged* here. They had hiked and biked hundreds of miles in this wilderness. While I had been drifting about in my San Antonio butterfly garden Melissa had been living my dream. For fourteen years!

In spite of my misgivings, the TBSI training turned out to be fun. It was basic karate. During the eight years prior to this teaching assignment, I'd taken taekwondo classes. Now I was teaching this Korean martial art to my little kid PE class. As for hardly knowing Melissa, after spending a whole day learning to control each other's out-of-control behavior we knew each other quite well.

For Melissa, a day without a serious run or bike ride is a day without orange juice. She participates in marathons and bike races and rallies. She and her husband have biked thousands of miles across the U.S., Canada, and Mexico. Every summer she joins a group of bicyclers for several weeks. This group has done many tours including the Sound to Sea from Seattle down the coast to Eugene, and the Continental Divide. For the past two summers they have been traveling the Lewis and Clark Trail.

I've never been a bicyclist and I'd stopped running long ago, but I share Melissa's enthusiasm for physical exercise and staying healthy. She suggested we begin working out together in the park weight room.

A brilliant idea. The weight room is the front half of the park residents' small, weathered, honor-system library. It is enclosed on two sides by walls, the other two sides by screen wire. Had this building been on a farm rather than in a national park, I would have guessed it to be a chicken coop. Though short on fitness-center ambiance, it is well-equipped, rarely used, and only thirty yards from my classroom. Our twice weekly work-outs gave us time to visit, laugh, and plan activities while striving to become younger and stronger. It was in the weight room that the Lewis and Clark project was hatched, the Cottonwood project materialized, and the Slime Mold project got organized. We also used weight room occasions to discuss our classroom challenges and work out solutions, solve most of life's mysteries, help each other plan retirement homes, and become forever friends.

And what about the TBSI training? Since none of our students exhibited behavior that was out-of-control, Melissa and I practiced on the burly, young man who works for park maintenance and moonlights as our school custodian.

"Wow! You can control Romaldo? Did you actually take him down?"

"No, but I took him to the office!"

Training and technique. It's all about training and technique.

In addition to the weight room workouts, the two-mile stroll John and I took before school every morning, my weekend walks with Mandy, and the bit of exercise I got teaching the little kids PE four days a week, I was enjoying some excellent stretching and strength-building warm-up sessions with Janelle.

Twice a week Janelle comes up from Terlingua to teach our students gymnastics and dance. A professional dancer by training, she settled with her husband in this out-of-the-way corner some twenty years ago, raised a family, and brought dance to the desert.

On carports, in garages, on basketball slabs, and in parking lots Janelle taught dance. Some of her students had been able to pay for the lessons, some had not. Now she was teaching at our school and the Terlingua school. She also had a studio for private lessons.

That she takes dance seriously is evident in her students' achievements. In 1998 she created the Paisano Folklorico Dancers at Big Bend High School. These students entertain throughout the region and have won many awards at the Viva Aztlan Festival in Lubbock. Somehow this small, cheerful woman persuades big, macho, teenage boys to dress up in ethnic costumes and perform for the public. Somehow she persuades them to devote hours to dance practice each week. She tells me they only come to flirt with the girls. Perhaps that's what brings them, but I'm not convinced that's what makes them stay.

On her two visits per week, Janelle leads the PE warm-up sessions, and on the other three days I try to emulate her routine. Once a week my little kids take their turn dancing or tumbling under her expert guidance; once a week she works with the big kids. All of our students look forward to this break in their regular PE class and work to perfect their techniques. I am amazed at the physical feats they accomplish. Gymnastics and dance in the desert. Who would have guessed?

CHAPTER 5

Experiencing Creatures, Large and Small

March began with a burst of wildflowers and yucca bloom, followed by a magnificent array of cacti blossoms. The days were sunny and mild. The skies a revelry in blue. Spring in the desert is too beautiful to miss. How can I get myself and my kiddoes outside to absorb this splendor?

Birds. Maybe we should focus on birds. Over 450 species have been identified in Big Bend National Park. It's the most bird-intensive site in the national park system, a birdwatcher's paradise. The Colima warbler comes from Mexico to summer here. This is the only place in the U.S. where nesting pairs can be seen. The peregrine falcon, capable of the fastest flight of any bird in North America and not long off the federal endangered species list, nests here. About a dozen pairs maintain aeries on high cliffs in remote areas. Scores of other intriguing facts must surely be lurking beneath feathers. Yes, we should focus on birds.

While all the little kids appreciate birds and most of them collect Audubon bird stuffies (each with its own authentic call), Jonathan is the recognized authority. He has the most knowledge. He has the most stuffies.

"There it goes again. It looks like a female cardinal."

"Oh, that's a pyrrhuloxia, Dr. Seawell."

"Okay, I'm writing that down. I wonder how to spell pyrrhuloxia."

I whipped out my pack of 3x5 cards. I never leave the classroom without it.

"Mmmm, I'm not sure. I should know that."

"Well, Jonathan, I don't think it's on the first-grade spelling list, but I suppose you should learn it since you're going to be an ornithologist."

"Yes, Jonathan, that's definitely something an ornithologist should know how to spell."

"I might be an ornithologist, also, Dr. Seawell. Like Jonathan."

"Good, Edgar. Then you should probably learn to spell it, too. I'll be happy if I can remember how to pronounce it."

"Just say it over and over ten times, Dr. Seawell. Then you'll remember it."

"Thank you, Jessica. I'll try that strategy. Okay, I'm going to spell it the best I can. We'll check the spelling when we get back to the room. Kiddoes, say it for me again, please. Slowly. Just say one syllable at a time so I can write it."

"P-y-r ... did you sweeties know the prefixes 'p-y-r' and 'p-y-r-o' refer to fire. 'Pyr' means fire. In the Greek language, I think. I wonder why a bird would have a reference to fire in its name."

"Well, it's got that little bit of red on it."

"And the rest of the feathers are gray, Dr. Seawell, like ashes. That's why the red shows so nicely."

"Dr. Seawell, can I see the card? Look how long it is! Pyraluxia has nine letters."

"Yeah, and ...five syllables."

"That's a bunch."

"I'm not sure if I spelled it right. We'll check when we get back to the room."

We checked. Pyrrhuloxia has eleven letters. "Pyr" has an extensive derivational background, but we stuck with the Greek and located Greece on our globe and wall maps. I taped the corrected 3x5 card to the front of my file cabinet so Jonathan and Edgar could learn to spell it and I could learn to pronounce it. The bird project was off to a good start. All of us had learned something.

We investigated birds by writing field reports, drawing pictures, making sighting lists, researching our favorites, examining feathers under microscopes, studying and constructing nests, creating a bird museum with Audubon stuffies and information cards, watching birds along the Lost Mine Trail in the Chisos Mountains, and having Abbey's dad come in with his visuals and recordings to give his ranger talk. When we passed the quiz at the end of his presentation he issued certificates to each of us proclaiming us Official Bird Brains.

Learning about birds is easy when you live among 450 species in a vast, secluded place. A place protected. A place on a major bird flyway.

Despite its popularity among birders, with only 400,000 visitors a year Big Bend National Park is one of the most underused parks in the system. Not just because it's remote. Not just because Texas summers are hot. Big Bend National Park is a love-it or leave-it sort of place. People either like this untamed, rugged part of the world or they don't. Thumbs up. Thumbs down. Black or white. There's rarely any gray.

But those who love Big Bend, love it with a passion. Almost half of this park's visitors have been here before. They return to camp, hike, experience the wilderness. And with such a substantial wilderness available, they can spend their average stay of four days without seeing another human soul if they so choose.

This sense of wilderness has a curious and subtle affect on those of us who live here. Most of the year the park is a big, quiet, empty place. Our very own big, quiet, empty place. But March through April brings bright red bushy tips to the ocotillo, four-foot creamy-white blossoms to the yucca, spring breaks to the schools throughout the nation, and an influx of visitors to the park.

We residents are startled when we see more than four cars in the Visitor Center parking lot; we're shocked when we notice three people in line at the post office; and we're downright exasperated when we have to wait while two tourists check out ahead of us at the convenience store. In our minds, a group of more than five people constitutes a crowd and six vehicles in the parking lot spells traffic jam.

Park residents react to the busy season by bunkering up. We wait until after the post office window closes before we venture down to pick up mail; we stay off the hiking trails; and, we don't even think about having dinner at any of the area restaurants. But these adjustments aren't too inconvenient, and it seems only fair to accommodate the visitors for their limited stays. They deserve to enjoy the park for two months of the year; we have it for the other ten.

Spring break season affects the park rangers, the concessions staff, and everyone else who supports the functioning of the park. These people do not take vacations during March and April, and, sometimes, even retirements are delayed until after this time.

To add an extra bit of excitement to this year's spring break season, a large mountain lion was sighted walking through our housing area a few evenings ago. John thinks it was just trying to get away from all the visitors, but the residents seem to be taking its presence seriously, to the point of over-reacting. Mothers now put their children into the family SUV and drive them the two or three blocks to and from school, and after-school bike riding has come to a temporary halt. Shirley even asked one of the rangers to come by and give the children a review on how to behave if confronted by a big cat. The main teaching point: never run! Running encourages the predatory instinct. We were also told to remain on alert for the next few days until the lion moves on.

Even Mandy is on high screech. She rarely raises her voice, but last night she wanted to go out and bark at midnight. John said he would rather have the lion than the tourists, but I feel city dwellers deserve their sojourn in the wilderness. Still, I admit that John and I have both grown rather selfish and possessive of this exceptional place we now call home.

Our own spring holiday is next week, so we had an Easter egg hunt for the little kids before the break. Lauren's mother organized the egg hunt and some of the other mothers helped her with all the work. The eggs, both the boiled variety and the plastic kind with treats inside, were hidden among the structures on the school playground. No grass tuffs or bushes amid all these rocks!

It was a joy to watch the children's excitement as they found their eggs and candy, then sat on the ground in the bright, 90 degree heat, sharing their loot, and cracking and eating hard boiled eggs. I sat on the ground with them, showing them how to shell eggs and helping them with the project. Although my husband and I are much taller than these children, we had every bit as much fun at the egg hunt as they did.

On Easter morning John and I awoke to a surprise. In our back yard, drinking from Mandy's water dish and munching in a clump of grass was a bunny. True, there are many rabbits in the housing area; in fact, we are over-run with rabbits, both black-tailed jackrabbits and cottontails. But Mandy's presence and/or smell has always kept them from venturing through the hole in the fence and coming into our yard. Except on Easter Sunday. The little cottontail partook of our back yard's bounty for most of the morning. A coin-cidence, of course, but we will always remember it as the Easter Bunny.

When school reconvened after our break, and the mountain lion incident had begun slipping into memory, another lion event occurred. As Abbey's dad arrived and opened the Basin Ranger Station just before eight in the morning, a bleeding tourist appeared in the doorway. The tourist had been hiking about a mile from the Basin Station when a lion stepped onto the trail 50 yards in front of him. The man photographed the lion. Then as he began backing away the cat rushed him. The man did all the things people are told to do in such cases – stand tall, wave arms, speak firmly and loudly – but the lion didn't respond normally. Instead of backing off, it stopped and stood its ground. The tourist kept yelling and waving his arms. He picked up rocks and threw them at the lion. The cat backed off, but as the man began a slow retreat, the cat fol-lowed him on a ridge above the trail.

The lion persisted in this stalking behavior as the tourist continued back-ing slowly down the trail. During the next half hour, the cat charged the man several times but was successfully deterred. The tourist had almost reached the safety of the Basin cabin area when the lion attacked again. This time it grabbed him by the leg and pulled him to the ground. The man hit the lion on the head with a rock he had in his hand. It may have been the rock that saved his life. He was able to beat off the lion, but he ended up with some serious wounds.

Needless to say, all the Basin trails were immediately closed and all the visitors were cleared from the backpacker campsites. Trained tracking dogs were brought in and the lion was eventually treed. After a failed attempt to dart it with a tranquilizer, it was shot and killed.

This was a sad day in the park. Mountain lions (also known as panthers, cougars, catamounts, and pumas) are beautiful creatures but since they require so much space, they aren't that abundant. The home ranges of males normally encompass 80 to 200 square miles and the females need 20 to 100 square miles. Approximately twenty-four mountain lions are believed to range in the park.

A couple of weeks ago John and I were amused by the extreme precautions parents were taking with their children after a mountain lion was sighted in the housing area. Now we know they were right to be concerned. Although researchers have learned a great deal about normal mountain lion behavior, there are always exceptions to the rule.

Over the next few weeks, the body of the lion was studied extensively. The cat was an old, emaciated female. Both of her canine teeth were broken. By analyzing the blood under her claws, the Department of Public Safety forensics lab in El Paso determined this was the same cat that had attacked the tourist. The necropsy performed by the Texas Veterinary Medical Diagnostics Lab at Texas A&M University showed nothing but a few skunk hairs in her intestinal tract. A lab in Montana specializing in cementum annuli analysis (determining age by tooth rings) concluded that the cat was eleven years old. Eleven years is quite old for a cat living in the wild. She may have lost her ability to provide food for herself, and her attack on the tourist might have been an act of desperation. Life's end can be heartbreaking.

As the days continued unfolding in our classroom, the children were having fun and great success with a reading project Mr. John P. Seawell had been helping them with. Lists of words for students to learn abound. Many word lists are divided into sections correlated to grade levels, and students are expected to master the list that corresponds to their grade. Although I'd never embraced activities that suggest "skill and drill" because they tend to "kill" construction and creativity, Shirley had handed me a copy of the Fry Instant Words during one of my frantic, hand-wringing moments early in the year. I had decided to use words from this list as an addition to the weekly spelling words and I had asked John to spend the first five minutes of his sessions playing a quick Instant Words game with the children.

Before I introduced the Instant Words, I explained their significance to the class in elaborate detail. I explained that these words are ranked in frequency, beginning with "the," the one word used most often in the English language. I told the children the Instant Words are usually little short words that look easy, but often aren't because they don't make sense in isolation and don't always follow pronunciation or spelling rules. I emphasized the importance of these words, explaining that about half of all written material is made up of the first 100 words on the list. If they could learn to recognize *instantly* these 100 words, they would be able to read about half the words on every page of almost every book.

I delivered this information with enthusiasm, and the children responded with enthusiasm. They were excited. They were motivated. They couldn't wait to get started. They were about to learn to read the 100 most important words in the English language!

Within days all the children in one of John's groups had mastered the first 100 words. They knew the list backwards, they knew it forward, they knew the words presented in isolation and at random. We couldn't trip them up. They recognized these words *instantly*. Now they could read about half the words on every page of almost every book. What a powerful accomplishment for a beginning reader. This was cause for cheering. This was cause for celebration.

"We should have a party!"

"A 100 Word Party!"

The children planned their party, enlisted help with refreshments from their mothers, and invited the rest of the class to share in the joy of their achievement. On the designated party day our normal snack time was given over to cup cakes and party hats. Hooray for us all.

So, what do children who have mastered the first 100 most important words in the English language do next? They clamor, whine, and beg to begin learning the second 100 most important words in the English language. Of course.

A few days later John's second group began planning their 100 Word Party. A trend was emerging. Maybe it was time to initiate a class discussion about healthful party treats.

Sometimes, but never often enough, I thanked my husband for his help. The time he spent with the children was quality time. He was supervising activities I was not able to get to. He was filling in some of the gaps I was leaving. I have standards. I have principles. Maintaining my standards and principles was a daily struggle, an uphill scuffle, a battle I did not always win. As important as were his contributions to the children, the unforeseen contribution he was making to my peace of mind was immeasurable. Having Mr. John P. Seawell in the classroom gave me hope. Perhaps we were hitting *most* of the high points. Perhaps the children were learning *most* of what they should be learning. Clearly John was doing his part to make it happen.

The children were increasing their reading power with the word lists, but John was even prouder of the writing skills his little journalists had developed since the beginning of the year. Erik, one of our kindergarteners who just turned six, is one of his most advanced students. Erik is Russian-born. He was adopted when he was just a few months old by American parents who give him lots of attention and intellectual stimulation. From an early age Erik was fascinated with the alphabet and the sounds the individual letters symbolize. When the year began he was already reading as well as a second grader, and now he has added story writing to his literary repertoire.

I am pleased with the confidence the children have as they approach their writing assignments. They begin most of their projects with a brainstorming session. Then they write their topic in the middle of a blank sheet of paper, circle it, and draw six spokes out from it – a spoke for each of the five W's and "how." They invent their own spelling or ask for spelling help as they answer the six questions about their topic. Finally they write their stories on a second sheet of paper and dictate them to John so he can key and print them. Their writing will become more sophisticated with experience, but the framework John has taught them is serving them well for now. I give the children varied writing activities throughout the day, but I know much of the writing progress they have made this year is due to their participation in the Story Writing 101 class every morning. Cheers for you, Mr. John P. Seawell! Many, many cheers for you!

Through the spring other on-going projects continued. Since January we had been practicing taekwondo once a week during PE. Now Janelle had given us a thrill and an incentive by inviting us to give a demonstration at the Spring Fiesta in Terlingua. She plans and coordinates this event annually. It gives the students from our two schools opportunities to perform for the public some of the dances and gymnastic routines they have learned during the year. The fiesta also includes music by the high school and middle school bands, songs by various classes and choirs, and an exhibition of student art and writing projects.

I scrambled around searching the Internet for uniforms for the children's demonstration, but it was my former taekwondo instructor in San Antonio who came to our rescue. He sent me fourteen white uniforms, sizes 00 – 2, for my small martial artists. During the next few weeks we added belt tying to our regular class of kicking, punching, and KEE-OPP's! We were white belts all, and proud to be.

Taekwondo in Terlingua

By April the parsley we had replanted in January had filled the pots, thick, green, and ten inches high. We borrowed a picnic table from the ramada, set it outside near our classroom window, and placed our pots of parsley on it. Swallowtail moms were invited. Javelina herds were not.

Three weeks later, on a warm, still day, a swallowtail mom arrived. The children stood at the window holding their breaths. She hovered, fluttered away, returned to investigate, hovered, fluttered away.

"She's back! She's smelling it! She's smelling with her feet!"

"Please, pleeeeeease, like it!"

"She's on it! She likes it!"

A gleeful chant of "She likes it! She likes it!" rocked the room. Oh, happy day!

"High five, low five, and pat yourselves on your backs. She likes your parsley. She's laying eggs."

Black swallowtail butterfly eggs are pin-head small, pale yellow, and round. At recess we counted five eggs. They were attached to leaves of both the dark moss curly and the Italian flat leaf. By the end of the day, the egg count had reached fourteen. Enough. With utmost care, the children moved the pots back into the screened ramada where the eggs would be safe.

Four days later the first caterpillars munched themselves out of their egg shells and began chowing down on the parsley. But we scientists were in for a surprise, an unanticipated outcome. Within five more days we had a total of twenty-seven caterpillars. Somehow we had miscalculated. Somehow we had missed a few. The discrepancy between the fourteen eggs we had counted and the twenty-seven caterpillars now devouring the parsley was enough to make any scientist blush.

"We should of been more careful."

"We should of used our magnifying glasses."

"Good idea. Next year we'll use the magnifying glasses."

Our embarrassment was tempered by the fact that we now had twenty-seven cute little caterpillars to observe. At first they were tiny and dark brown with white saddles. They outgrew their brown exoskeletons and dropped them to the picnic table several times before emerging encircled with bands of black, white, and gold. Their coats of many colors. They outgrew and shed these colorful coats a few times.

"All they do is eat, poop, and sleep. Eat, poop, and sleep."

"And get too big for their britches. Look, here's another exoskeleton somebody outgrew."

Twenty-seven caterpillars. Six pots of parsley. In a week the largest caterpillars were the size of a five-year-old's pinky finger, and all twenty-seven were growing bigger every day.

"Hello, Shirley? Sorry to bother you with this, but we've got a little problem here. It's about the caterpillars. We need more parsley. Could you stop by an H.E.B. on your way home and pick some up?"

"Parsley? You mean from the produce isle? How much do you need?"

"Yes, the produce isle. Two or three bunches, please."

As the butterfly project continued, interest grew. The children's enthusiasm spread to their parents. Within days of the first hatchings, the ramada became a popular after-school destination. As I worked in my classroom I would glance out and see ever-changing circles of children and adults crowding around the parsley plants. The caterpillars were attracting many fans. Half the population of PJ seemed to be hooked on watching them graze.

The potted parsley was but a memory and the three bunches Shirley brought from the supermarket were disappearing fast. I made a "protective custody cage" and placed it over the gluttonous caterpillars and their jars of parsley. The cage was cylindrical, three feet in diameter, three feet high, of 3"x 4" wire with fine nylon net stretch around the perimeter and across the top. We could still watch the caterpillars through the net and when they were finally satiated I knew they would climb onto the inside of the cage and make their chrysalises. But not a caterpillar took the hint. Not a caterpillar stopped gobbling parsley. By this time some of the caterpillars had reached thumb-size, their white bands had turned light green, and their black bands had narrowed and were decorated with gold dots.

"Okay, Junior Lepidopterists, we've got a crisis here. The caterpillars are eating us out of house and home. I'm declaring an official parsley emergency. What comments and suggestions do you have?"

"We could plant some more parsley ... but it probably wouldn't grow fast enough."

"We could ask Ms. Coleman to go back to the H.E.B. and buy some more."

"I'll check with her, but I don't think she has any meetings in Midland this week."

"What about Mr. John P. Seawell? He could go to Alpine."

"Yeah! Mr. John P. Seawell could go to Alpine!"

It was settled then. Mr. John P. Seawell did go to Alpine. The dear man made two parsley emergency runs before the twenty-seventh caterpillar finally stopped gorging, wandered onto the cage frame, and entered into the third phase of its metamorphosis.

After coping with the parsley crisis and the endless activity provided by twenty-seven caterpillars, we were somewhat exhausted and glad to relax for a few days. Mysterious and amazing changes were occurring inside the chrysalises, but these changes didn't require any action from us. The junior lepidopterists took a breather from caterpillars to cast their eyes upward into the night sky. It was time to learn some of the spring constellations.

One great benefit associated with teaching in a national park is having dozens of rangers available, each with several areas of expertise. Shamelessly, I had called on these knowledgeable and accommodating men and women throughout the year to provide activities for the children. This time I called the astronomy expert and scheduled a Star Party. Then I began preparing the children for a celestial experience.

We read stories about how the stars were interpreted in past ages and about their importance as navigational tools. We used star maps to select the constellations we would locate, practiced outlining them, and learned their relationship to each other in the sky. Finally we covered the glass in our flashlights with red cellophane so we could consult our star maps without compromising our night vision. Big Bend National Park is located in the darkest part of the contiguous United States. Twinkle on, little star. We are all set.

On Star Party eve moms, dads, and siblings accompanied my students to the school tennis court. Like a small tribe of nomads we stretched out on sleeping bags and blankets and focused on the sky. The ranger gave her lively and informative presentation, the children located their constellations, and we all took turns gazing at planets through the two telescopes that were available. At party's end we sealed our new knowledge with Starbursts and Milky Ways. Astral evenings in Big Bend are always sweet.

CHAPTER 6

Breaking a Leg Followed by Summer

Life never slows down when youngsters are involved. Appearing in the Christmas play had given the little kids a nibble of stardom and they savored the taste. By the middle of April the occasional suggestion that we have "our own play, with *lines*" grew in frequency and volume. Plays require scripts. And rehearsals. Costumes. And sets. My plate was full. I didn't have time for a play. I couldn't follow the lead of the child. Not this time.

"La-la-la-la-la. Speak to my hand. I'm not hearing this."

But when the rumble finally became a roar, I began searching for a project. A quick and easy project. We're running out of time here. Then the little kids' math teacher agreed to help with the venture, and I took heart. We would do this! The little kids would have their own play. With *lines*.

Long ago I saw a clever production of *Night Noises*, a book by Mem Fox, at an International Reading Association conference in Canberra, Australia. Delightful story. Lots of speaking parts. Not too complicated. Not too difficult to reproduce. But how would it play in PJ?

During the year we had read several of Mem Fox's books. My autographed copy of *Koala Lou* was especially well liked, and enacting this story using my Australian animal puppets was a popular free-choice activity.

I found a copy of *Night Noises* in our school library, and although its characters were humans rather than the Aussie animals my students so admired, the children liked the story and recognized its potential for becoming "our own play, with *lines*."

Parts were cast. Rehearsals began. Costumes were collected. Sets were organized. And *everyone* had *lines*.

Night Noises does feature one animal, a sweet, aged dog, Butch Aggie. Butch Aggie's lines consisted of barks and growls. Abbey, maybe because she adores dogs, begged for the part. Abbey, maybe because she had been the only little kid with lines in the Christmas play, left the speaking parts to her classmates.

The plan was for the children to simply retell the story, acting it out in the retelling. Their *lines* would be sentences memorized directly from the book. But the story has a large cast, and we were only twelve. The plot revolves around Lily Laceby on her 90th birthday. As she sits dozing and dreaming by her fire, Butch Aggie at her feet, a series of strange noises erupts from outside. The noises are created by her five children, her 14 grandchildren, her 35 great-grandchildren, her great-great-granddaughter, and her 47 friends arriving with a birthday cake.

"Dr. Seawell, where will we get all the extra people?"

"I know! We could get the big kids to help us!"

"That's only eight kids. We need ... like ... about a hundred!"

"Okay, I'm declaring an official people crisis. Put on your thinking caps. Let's hear some comments and suggestions."

As with many crises, this one was solved in the weight room. In addition to being the big kids' teacher, Melissa is the art teacher for all the students. She promised if we would get several big sheets of cardboard from the recycle center, her art classes would take care of the rest.

Rehearsing for our play created immense fervor and excitement among the children. My greatest directing challenges were persuading them to be quiet when they were off stage and audible when they were on. During the first few rehearsals I was so preoccupied with ten of the children, that I ignored the other two. And it was the other two, Andrea and Gabriel, whose parts were the most complicated. Gabriel had three costume changes, Andrea had six.

Apryl played the 90-year-old Lily who sat dreaming and flashing back to events that had happened in her life. Andrea played Lily in the flashbacks and Gabriel played her husband. Andrea and Gabriel enacted the dreamy flashbacks in an archway we set up stage right and covered with translucent fabric. The spotlight would come up, focus on them, then fade to black. By the time I was able to help them, these two first graders had worked matters out for themselves. They had learned to assemble their costumes so that, with only seconds between appearances, Gabriel drifted from old age to young adulthood and Andrea floated from old age back to childhood. They were managing without a flaw and their performance was awesome.

We were well into production when two new students arrived. They were brothers, a sixth grader and a third grader. We had no other third graders that year, and since we were so near the end of the school year and Quincy had completed his academic requirements in Arizona prior to his arrival, it was decided by Shirley, Quincy, and his mom, that he would fit most comfortably grouped with the little kids.

As always, my children were thrilled to have a new student. Quincy, older and wiser, was impressive. He helped the second graders with their math. He did all his writing in cursive. He awed us with explanations of how things were done in big schools. And, he could draw *anything*. Quincy became our star, our class hero. But even though all of us invited and begged, we could not persuade him to take part in our play. The little kids, group oriented and inclusive, found this troubling.

Then the spotlight caught Quincy's eye, and he found his true calling. He became our chief lighting technician. Stretched out on a mat behind a bank of plants, he controlled the dimmer switch for the dream sequences. Now we had our "light man," the whole group was participating in the production, and everyone was happy.

The play was performed without a hitch. We had a cast of 102 characters, ninety-one of whom had been created from cardboard. The audience chuckled as each child appeared carrying the additional people needed to tell the story. It took two children to carry the panel of friends. After all, forty-five people are heavy, even though they may be made of cardboard.

Night Noises

Although most of the audience seemed pleased with the play, one criticism rang out as the cast took their final bow. "That play was *too* short!" No one could mistake little four-year-old Anna's deep voice.

Because Anna was right about the play being too short, we had a surprise bonus for our audience. While Erik entertained them with our State song, "Texas, Our Texas," the other children were changing from their *Night Noises* costumes into their taekwondo uniforms. Since some of the parents had been unable to attend the Spring Fiesta, the children used this occasion to repeat their martial arts demonstration. We concluded the evening by relocating to the ramada for punch, cookies, autograph signing, and chrysalis viewing as the sun set on another fine day in the park.

The following morning, the actors and actresses assumed new roles. Mr. John P. Seawell's little journalists became entertainment reviewers for mythical newspapers throughout the world and their rave reviews were made available for immediate release to all national and international news media. Evidence of both their journalism instruction and their theatrical training was evident in their reviews. Judging by the number of references to projection and staying quiet backstage, those must have been my focal points. But then, no need to stage a play if no one can hear the actors, right? Happily, the reviewers reported that everyone had been successful on all counts.

As with several of our writing assignments, I collected the children's reviews and published them together in spiral-bound project books. Then each child was given a project book to keep as a souvenir. Two excerpts from the Rave Reviews book are included for your reading pleasure. The first is an individual effort which included the full routine of brainstorming, completing a graphic organizer, writing a first draft, and reading the draft aloud for keying. The second is a collaborative effort that went directly from brainstorming to dictating for keying.

Night Noises
By Andrea, 1st Grade

There was a play on Monday, May 19, 2003. The time was 6:00 p.m. It was called *Night Noises*, by Mem Fox. The play was at the San Vicente School gym in Big Bend National Park, Texas.

There were twelve children in the play. There were two old ladies called Lily Laceby. The second Lily was the dream lady. Apryl was the main Lily Laceby and Andrea was the dream Lily Laceby. Gabe was Andrea's husband in the dream.

Abbey was main Lily Laceby's dog called Butch Aggie. Francella was the cake lady. Quincy was the light man. Destiny was the three daughters. Edgar was the 14 grandchildren. Lauren was Emily, age $4\frac{1}{2}$, and Jessica was Lauren's mother in the play. Scott was the two sons. Andrea and Gabe were two of Lily's 47 friends.

The set looked good. They had a table, a lamp, a chair, a teapot, and a cup.

They're sorry if you did not come. They did very good, Guys. I could hear them. I liked their play.

Night Noises
By Erik, Francella, Lauren, Apryl, and Destiny
K & 1st Grade

The play called *Night Noises* was presented by the K-3rd grade children at the San Vicente Elementary School gym in Big Bend National Park, Texas. It was on May 19, 2003.

The play was good. The children were very good in the play. The children's voices were loud, but they were not yelling or screaming. The children were quiet backstage. They were not talking or squeaking their chairs.

The characters were fine. Lily Laceby was played by Apryl. She was sitting quietly. Butch Aggie was played by Abbey. She was sleeping. Emily, age 4½, was cute and was played by Lauren. Jessica played Emily's mom. Francella was the cake bringer. Erik played one of the thirty-five great-grandchildren. Destiny played one of the three daughters. Scotty played one of the two sons. Gabriel played one of the forty-seven friends. Andrea played Gabriel's wife. Edgar played one of the fourteen grandchildren.

Quincy was the light man. He did a very good job on the lights.

Nobody saw the children until the end because they were saying their lines from backstage.

The set was beautiful because the fireplace was right by Lily Laceby. The light was beautiful because it was shining right on Lily Laceby. The walls were all brown and they had pictures of flowers on them. There were beautiful plants on the floor.

The play was fun for the children and fun for the people to watch. The children loved the play so much. It was good and we wish they would do it again. Anna (Lauren's 4½-year-old sister in real life) said, "That play was too short!"

With the *Night Noises* production over, time was short. The school year was nearing an end, and I needed to evaluate the children's scholastic growth. One of the tests we used for this required that the children be assessed individually. Because chance and good fortune had provided me with an always available, always eager-to-assist, enthusiastic, and experienced classroom volunteer, I decided I would complete all the assessments in one day.

After congratulating myself on the brilliance of this plan, setting up a schedule, and briefing the children, I asked John to take over the regular classroom duties for a day, and, one by one, the children met with me in the library for their evaluations.

My day went smoothly and I completed the testing in one glorious burst. Success! One big project finished! I was delighted with this coup, this triumph, this efficient use of time and resources. Coming back into my classroom that afternoon after John had walked the children to music class, I couldn't stop patting myself on the back.

"Hat's off to you! Hat's off to all teachers!"

It was my classroom volunteer. He was slouching in a chair at my computer desk. His tongue was hanging out.

"Well, thanks, Sweetheart. What brought this on?"

"Believe me, I have new-found respect for you – for all teachers. When I was a military service school instructor I thought a four-hour block of teaching was a killer! And that was without having energetic little kids to deal with! And I was 30 years younger!"

"Weren't the children cooperative? Didn't they behave?"

"They were fine. They were great. But I'm exhausted! I love the kids and the instructional process, but I could never do this full time! Take me home. Please! I'm going right to bed."

I began the individual testing for the Presidential Physical Fitness Challenge the following day, but my classroom volunteer didn't assist me. He was absent. He was still in bed recuperating.

Then, as suddenly as it began, the school year ended. On the last Thursday of May we attended graduation festivities for San Vicente's two eighth graders. Along with the other older PJ students they'll be commuting to Big Bend High School in the fall.

The next day, our last day, featured a buffet luncheon and the coincidental launch of five more of the butterflies we had raised. For days we had been watching butterflies crawl out of their chrysalises and unfurl their crumpled wings. The children had been taking turns releasing them. Even this farewell event is a fascinating thing to see.

First, I carry the cage outside the ramada, set it on the ground, then tilt it so the open bottom is exposed. Next, one of the children reaches in and puts a hand right in front of the butterfly. For some mysterious reason, the butterfly usually climbs onto the extended hand. The child stands up with a bright, beautiful butterfly perched on his or her hand.

After a few seconds, the butterfly flutters its wings and floats away. I've been helping children launch black swallowtails for several years, and I've launched well over 100 of them myself, but this ritual never fails to hold me spellbound.

Many of the children will be scattering for trips to the beach and visits to far-away grandparents, but my vacation hasn't really started yet. I'll leave at six in the morning to make my eight o'clock bus driver training class in Alpine. It's a three-day course so I'll spend the next couple of nights in a hotel.

Since our school is so small, Shirley requires that her teachers and staff all become State certified to drive our school bus. We only use it for field trips, and although it's boxy and yellow, it's really just an oversized, 15-passenger van. But in order to get certified, I will have to learn to drive and parallel park the monster buses that large school districts use. Never in my wildest, most imaginative flights of fancy did I ever envision becoming a Texas school bus driver.

I'm not too worried about this training though. I've always liked driving; it gives me something to do with my hands and feet when I'm confined in a vehicle. Besides, I've had decades of experience behind the wheel. My brother taught me to drive the summer I was ten. Curiously, the summer I was ten, my brother was six. Our driving lessons were casual; parents were neither consulted, nor involved. One of our favorite forms of entertainment that summer was practicing backing the ranch cattle truck up to the loading chute. Unforgettable are the joys of childhood and the splendor of those carefree stick-shift days.

The bus driver training began with classroom sessions devoted to traffic rules, safety issues, and pre-trip inspection routines. Part two of the training involved sitting in the driver's seat of a 48-passenger school bus chugging through the streets of Alpine. There were about a dozen of us in the class so the people who were not driving rode along as "the kids." We practiced letting each other off and on at bus stops; practiced doing train checks at railroad crossings; practiced disciplining "the kids" when they became rowdy. We even practiced an emergency evacuation in which we were to keep the kids in a group, off the highway, and away from the disabled bus. This was to be done while setting out the emergency triangles at exactly the right distance behind the bus and making a 911 call for help.

A friendly thing about West Texas drivers is that they wave to each other when they meet and pass on rural highways. Surprise! They also wave at bus drivers when they meet and pass a school bus in town. Naturally, when I was in the driver's seat I responded to their gracious behavior. However, I wondered if the citizens of Alpine would have been so cheerful had they known the danger they were in each time I lifted my hand from the steering wheel to return their waves.

Toward the end of the class, rumors began circulating about the very gracious, friendly, grandmotherly woman who administers the road test for school bus drivers at the Texas Department of Public Safety in Alpine. It was said that this lady is the strictest, most fearsome tester in the State. The tales about repeated failures were alarming. By the end of the class I was terrified. I wondered how many times I was destined to fail the driving test.

But I passed on the very first try. I only had to parallel park that big long bus once, and I did it perfectly. I'll never, ever, even try to do it again. And I had no trouble, whatsoever, with that gracious, friendly, grandmotherly woman who administers the road test for school bus drivers in Alpine. I took my road test from that gracious, friendly, grandmotherly woman who administers the road test for school bus drivers in Ft. Stockton.

I became bus driver certified just after the men who had been driving for the Diablos transferred unexpectedly to other parks and Big Bend was left without certified drivers. The summer fire season was just beginning, and the Fire Management Officer was anxious.

The Diablos are a firefighting crew of Mexican nationals who live in the three villages just across the river from the park. Trained by park personnel to fight fires in remote areas, these men work here and in other places including national parks and forests throughout the western states when the need arises. The Diablos are driven to these fires in two 48-passenger converted school buses.

"Hey, Pat, drivers are paid big bucks. Are you interested?"

While I'm conversant and comfortable in Spanish, and was thrilled with the idea of barreling down Interstate 10 in a big white bus decorated with dazzling orange and yellow flames, pitchforks, and spicier-than-PG-rated statements about fires (in *español*, of course), my life was somewhat complicated at the time.

John and one of our kitties had just returned from a ten-day stay in College Station, home of the Texas A&M University vet school hospital. The kitty had undergone middle ear surgery. She was home now and doing well, but she had to have medication twice a day and it took John and me, working as a determined, well-organized, intrepid team, to administer this medication. Then there was Mandy, our18-month-old, rambunctious, 95-pound puppy.

"I *am* interested! I'd *love* it! But I'll have to take John, Lisa the kitty, and Mandy the puppy, along."

"A dog and a cat?"

"And a husband. We're a package deal."

"Oh. Well. Thanks, Pat. I'll … let you know."

Since my Diablo driving career seemed doubtful, I went on with my plans to attend a workshop for teachers at McDonald Observatory.

Located on Mt. Locke, sixteen miles northwest of Ft. Davis, McDonald Observatory is one of my favorite spots on the planet. During this three-day workshop, I would be enriching my science-teaching skills, rubbing elbows with astronomers, visiting with enthusiastic grad students, and living in the astronomer's dorm. The stars at night are big and bright deep in the heart of West Texas, and I was thrilled to have this unique opportunity to study them.

McDonald Observatory is named for William Johnson McDonald, an unmarried, well-educated, prosperous, Northeast Texas banker. When he died in 1926, he left over a million dollars to the regents of The University of Texas to be used "for the purpose of aiding in erecting and equipping an astronomical observatory to be kept and used with and as a part of the University for the study and promotion of astronomical science."

The only people more dumbfounded about this bequeath than his heirs were the regents of The University. While the distraught heirs protested that their relative could not have been of sound mind, the stunned regents scrambled about attempting to establish an astronomy department.

After years of debate and legal proceedings, The University of Texas ended up with $800,000 and a thirty-year agreement with The University of Chicago. Texas had money, but needed astronomers. Chicago had astronomers, but needed an observatory. Necessity had created an unlikely alliance.

While collaboration among universities is widespread and common today, it was a rare and daring concept in 1932 and both universities entered into the partnership a bit warily. But the venture proved to be beneficial to both schools and to astronomy in general. McDonald Observatory has grown into one of the major astronomical research facilities in the world. It addition to its research mission, it provides award-winning educational programs for children and adults, and it is the only major observatory where time is reserved for public access to the research telescopes.

After three days of exploring our solar system under the guidance of the skillful staff at the Observatory education center, I could hardly wait to begin preparing my students for a visit. Hands-on, minds on. Three cheers for astronomy.

But wait, there's more! After the bus driving school and the McDonald workshop, I participated in a week of technology training in Dallas. With the exception of Melissa, who was bicycling along the Lewis and Clark Trail, our whole staff attended this training. For reasons already explained in detail, John and Lisa the kitty accompanied me. While I pondered the mysteries of PDA's and DANA's, they were enjoying room service breakfasts, browsing in bookstores, and ambushing pigeons on our sixteenth-story window sill. (Mandy, meanwhile, was safely ensconced in a pet resort in San Antonio, complete with daily play sessions and her own private wading pool.)

After a week of technology in Big D, we returned home to some sad news. A member of the park family had died. One of the first things we saw from a distance during our first week in Panther Junction was a black flag suspended on a high flagpole in front of one of the houses in the residential area. From a distance it looked like a pirate flag, but then we recognized it as a POW-MIA flag. We soon learned that its owner was a three-year Army veteran who had served in Vietnam, and was quite a luminary in the park.

Tony was a Mexican American who had worked in the park maintenance department for many years. Although he had no family living with him, his seniority allowed him to live in one of the largest houses in the park, and, without doubt, the one with the tallest flagpole.

In addition to the POW-MIA issue his other passion was riding motorcycles. He spent much of his free time zooming around on these mountain roads. But one night he missed a curve, and he will ride no more.

The black flag is gone now, but in the Texas-Mexico border culture tradition, his family and friends have set up a little roadside shrine at the site of his crash, a *descanso*. It is decorated with artificial flowers, a few pieces of motorcycle memorabilia, a cross, and three small flags: U.S., Mexico, and a black POW-MIA flag.

Other changes were occurring in the park. When John was a young Army second lieutenant his first commanding officer advised him to "get on the summer cycle as soon as possible and stay there." He had to betray his ignorance by asking what his boss was talking about. The commander explained that officers and NCO's did their utmost to get transferred during the summer months so that their children's school year would not be interrupted. Consequently, most command and key staff positions opened up during the summer months. Not moving during the summer cycle could mean a less desirable job at one's new post.

Now we find that the summer cycle is alive and well in the National Park Service. New people are moving into the park and we are losing a few, including some of our students. Two families are going to different parks in Alaska, one is going to Indiana Dunes in the Chicago area, and another is transferring to Cape Hatteras. If we stay here long enough we may end up having friends in all of America's most beautiful sites.

School begins in three weeks with the promise of a reduced teaching load. Our 19 students have been reshuffled among the four of us and I have been relieved of second grade. Since the bulk of my students were last year's first graders I will begin the year with only two students in my reading, math, and science classes, a kindergartener, and a first grader. In my social studies, Spanish, and PE classes, I will have all eleven of the little kids (K–3rd). This year's one pre-kindergartener will come two mornings a week, as usual.

Had I, before my second school year in the park began, glanced back at the serenity I had abandoned in my San Antonio butterfly garden, I might have shaken my head in disbelief. The reality of this adventure didn't match the images of my daydreams. It didn't come close. Peace, quiet, and long periods of contemplation were not materializing. Solitary desert hikes and sweet hours of sunsets were not happening. If spiritual growth had been offered, I had been too overwhelmed to notice. If life lessons had been presented, they had been lost in the frenzy of my hectic days. I hadn't even had time to wonder about that distressing incident that had happened on the day of my original visit to the school. That distressing incident that had rocked my boat and made me gloomy and weepy-eyed. (I knew it was important to analyze that incident because actions speak louder than words; however, I was secure in the knowledge that everything comes to she who waits.)

Even my summer had been crowded with school-related activities. In some vague, hazy, unfocused way, I knew I was on the road less traveled and was now bouncing cross country in a huge, unwieldy vehicle I didn't exactly know how to drive. Yet, I was relishing this unforeseen journey. I was fearless. I was smiling. My road was bumpy, but I was hanging on tight.

CHAPTER 7

A Second Beginning

Texas teachers begin school a week before their students. Most of the week is devoted to meetings: staff organizational meetings, safety review meetings, child neglect and abuse meetings, motivational speaker meetings, technology update meetings, legislative update meeting, textbook checkout meetings. These meetings are not optional.

My threshold of pain for attending meetings is low, so when I first began teaching I would be exhausted and a little depressed by the end of the week. Exhausted and depressed. What a way to begin a new school year.

Attending these meetings was stressful when work, tons of it, was waiting in my classroom. As I sat at the meetings, these classroom tasks would swirl and tumble through my head, begging, begging, begging to be done. I'd work in my classroom before and after the meetings, but there was never enough time. By the middle of the week I'd be fighting panic and gloom.

The solution to this nightmare was easy. I began starting school *two* weeks before the students arrived. The first week I organized my classroom and prepared my lessons. I did everything I could to get ready for the main event: my students on their first day of school. Once I had that important aspect of teaching organized, I could deal with the meetings. Bring 'em!

Shirley always did what she could to make the first week bearable. She sent the schedule to us early so we'd know what to expect, she prepared elaborate snacks so we'd have tasty things to munch, she squeezed out as much classroom "work-time" for us as she could, and at the end of the week she drove us up to the Lodge Restaurant for lunch. Still, that first week tends to be tedious.

At one of our meetings this year an expert on the teaching of reading and writing presented his workshop for us. His ideas were sound and he delivered them in an energetic and entertaining way. However, one of his ideas was that we could increase our students' vocabularies by introducing two new words to them each week and devising ways for them to use these words.

Yeah, well, okay. I'd heard this idea before. I wasn't too impressed. I wasn't convinced introducing random words would work. But Shirley wanted to try it. She suggested we focus on the vocabulary words every morning after flag ceremony. We'd call them the "bonus words" and get them from the vocabulary list of last year's SAT college entrance exam. We'd give each student 15 seconds to create sentences, and write the student's name on the back of a ticket each time he or she used a bonus word correctly. We'd drop the tickets into a big plastic jar and draw two tickets from the jar each Friday. The two lucky students would receive a little prize. At the end of each six weeks, we'd total each student's tickets and award a larger prize to the big kid and the little kid who had accumulated the most tickets. Little prizes for luck, big prizes for merit. Every student could be a winner.

Throughout the day we teachers were to encourage the use of the new vocabulary words by awarding another ticket each time a student used a bonus word. Shirley would explain the plan to the students at flag ceremony on the first day of school.

Flag Ceremony is how we begin each day. At 7:55 the students and teachers assemble in front of the school, two of the big kids unfold and raise the U.S. and the Texas flags, then Shirley leads us in the Pledge of Allegiance. Next we say the pledge to the Texas flag and Peggy, music teacher for all the students, calls on someone to choose a patriotic song which we sing together.

In front of us tower Pummel, Wright, and Panther Peak in all the shades of burgundy and rose the morning sun can invent. Cool breezes carry perfumes in from the desert. Beside me and all around me are children I love. Often Anna, my tiny kindergartner, stands on my left side with her arm wrapped around my leg. Lauren, my first grader, stands on my right side with her arm wrapped around my other leg. Two little sisters and their tall teacher. It matters not that Shirley occasionally rolls her eyes at our behavior. We stand firm. Safe, secure, and confident. We are happy and all is right with our world.

"Emotive" and "jocular" were our bonus words for the first week of school. We posted them on Shirley's office window so we could see them after flag ceremony. We posted them in the gym so we could see them while we did our warm-ups. We posted them in the four classrooms so we could see them while we studied. And Anna's phrase, "Uh-oh! Ticket!" became the expression heard often throughout the day as students worked these words into their conversations. All students are emotive and jocular when there's a contest afoot.

The first day of school has never stopped being an exciting event for me, but this year was unique. Unlike teaching in a school where all my students would be new to me, I already knew all but one of my students and all but one of my students already knew me. There would be little of that first day apprehension or awkwardness that sometimes worries children. We could begin right where we had left off two months earlier.

Andrea and Erik had moved on to other parks with their families during the summer. They would be missed, but we had a new second grader to welcome. Alex was new only to me because he had attended pre-kindergarten at

San Vicente Elementary before spending his kindergarten and first grade years in Alaska. I had often heard the little kids speak of Alex. Alex, the Boy. Always he was Alex, the Boy. This was because Alix, the Girl, had also been in their pre-kindergarten class. It was awhile before the little kids were able to call Alex's name without adding "the Boy." For a time I feared Alex Just Alex would become his new moniker as they corrected and retrained themselves, but by mid-September the name question was settled and Alex was settled back among his young friends.

To take advantage of the cool desert mornings, PE is the first class of the day for all our students. After leading the students in our warm-up stretching routine, I would release the big kids to their PE teacher and keep the little kids with me. I had never taught PE for kindergarten through third grade before I came to this school, so I didn't know how much fun I'd been missing. From the planning to the playing, PE with these little kids was a delight.

In addition to learning skills and games, we spent some time each week training for the Presidential Physical Fitness Challenge. Although the children set individual goals and I posted their accomplishments on their personal charts, we worked together as a team at this Presidential Challenge. We cheered each other on, worked as each other's personal trainers, and celebrated each other's accomplishments. The standards for the Presidential Challenge are rigorous, but most of the children understood that building strength and endurance takes time, so they worked with diligence and determination toward their distant goals.

After PE, the second and third graders were dismissed to their homeroom teacher and Anna, Lauren, and I began our academic day. For the next three hours I followed the lead of my two students through language arts and math.

Since both children had been read to, probably by both parents, probably every day of their lives, teaching them to read for themselves was effortless. In the simple act of reading to them, their parents had already done all the hard work. These girls were a reading specialist's dream.

After we'd played our way through the prescribed reading skills of the day, read the assigned stories, enacted favorite scenes, written and illustrated summaries or critiques, and discussed the author and his or her use of language, we'd assemble ourselves on our floor pillows and I'd read a book the girls had chosen from our well-stocked classroom library.

The read-aloud always began with the girls sitting on each side of me on their floor pillows, but somewhere in the course of the story they would duck their heads under my arms and wriggle closer. By the end of the story the three of us would be huddled together in what can best be described as a group hug. At first I wondered if this home behavior should be allowed at school, but then I looked at the big picture. These little sisters would have many opportunities to be in more traditional reading classes, but they might never again be in a class so small it could be completely absorbed by a hug. Unique situations invite unique responses.

Though they adored language arts and reading, the girls were not as enamored with math. Lauren had not yet decided to become an astronomer, thus recognizing the importance math would play in her future. As for Anna, her world spins in a more generous orbit than most, so the concept of a problem with only one right answer simply did not fit her definition of reasonable.

Therefore, I coaxed. I cajoled. If I couldn't inspire, at least let me do no harm. The games we played were elaborate and rich in detail, but many of them skirted along on the far edge of math and some of them seemed to miss the mark completely. I was torn between my determination to make math exciting and my fear that we weren't covering all the bases. The lessons in our math program were entertaining enough, but the follow-up practice sheets the girls were required to complete were not thrilling. Even though both girls looked forward to choosing and playing the lively computer math games with which our class ended, getting them to the last problem on their practice sheets sometimes required serious prodding.

However, despite games that wandered off course and foot-dragging through practice sheets, the girls consistently scored well on their evaluations, so Anna was allowed to continue turning her math facts into "movies" which she produced with colored pens on acetate sheets and presented on our overhead projector, and Lauren was allowed to continue brewing and sipping imaginary pots of tea as she worked her way through her problems. Thus with Mozart's Greatest Hits floating through the background we floated through our math class, playing all along the way. It is through play that humans learn most effectively, right?

Our two-morning per week pre-k program isn't mandated or funded; it is simply made available as a community service to give the four-year-olds a preview of the school routine. This year Don was our only pre-kindergartner. On the mornings he joined us, John would take him through some of the traditional pre-k songs, games, and crafts, I would help him with a few pre-reading or math activities, and finally he would select a book or two for John to read to him.

Don was eager, polite, and lovable. I looked forward to the mornings when he came to school and I treasured his hugs and his compliments. ("Dr. Seawell, you're a gu-wait teacher!")

This was the year Lauren and Anna's mom began volunteering once a week in our classroom. And along with Lisa came Allison, the youngest sister. Our classroom was livelier than ever during this weekly hour and a half. Anna and Lauren idolized their three-year-old sister and enjoyed introducing her to school activities. Usually they also had new projects and accomplishments they had prepared to present for their mom. The mornings Lisa volunteered produced show-and-tell at its finest, and all of us had a good time.

In the afternoons, the second and third graders joined us for social studies and Spanish. Afterward Lauren, Anna, and I experimented our way through science class before I walked them down the breezeway to Peggy or Melissa's room for music or art.

Year Two was easier. My long hours were paying off. I was almost keeping up. But this was still the hardest job I'd ever had.

September 4, 2003
Dear Parents,
    In social studies we have been reading about, discussing, comparing, and contrasting urban, suburban, and rural neighborhoods. As one of our activities, the children have planned a Different Neighborhoods Parade. Each child has created a headband depicting the neighborhood of his or her choice and is now preparing cards with a brief written description of the neighborhood of choice to pass out along the parade route. Since we didn't have time last year to hold our pet parade, we're including pets in our Different Neighborhoods Parade, thus making this The Different Neighborhoods Pet Parade.
    The parade will be on Friday, September 12, at 1:00 p.m. The entrance to Escuela Vista Street will be our staging area. From there we will high-step our way onto Javelina Drive, turn left onto Bobcat Loop, and circle back to the school.
    The rules concerning the pets are as follows:
    Dogs: only one dog per person (with extra dog wrangling parents and/or strong friends allowed and encouraged)
    Cats, Hamsters, Guinea Pigs, Fish, Birds, Hermit Crabs, etc.: all felines and small critters must be secured in cages or tanks (the cages or tanks may be pulled in wagons with towels beneath the cages or tanks to minimize the bumps)
    You are cordially invited to participate in the parade or watch as it winds through your neighborhood. All adult participants and watchers will receive artistic, informative, student-created hand-outs.
                                                                Thank you.
                                                                Pat

With our boom box playing a tape of marches Peggy had selected for us, we high-stepped our way along the parade route. There were only four or five viewers to receive our carefully researched and crafted handouts, but we were not disappointed. Our precious pets were on parade, and since we had learned the characteristics of rural neighborhoods, we were not expecting great throngs of people along our route.

The pet parade was a little kid event, but our next social studies venture involved the whole school. To celebrate the bicentennial of the Lewis and Clark Expedition which will occur between now and 2006, Melissa and I planned a school-wide project. To recreate some of the drama and excitement of the expedition we attempted to engage everyone in an ongoing, reenactment. With Melissa as Clark, Shirley as President Jefferson, and me as Lewis we introduced the project by putting on a skit in which Jefferson charged us with specific tasks to be preformed. We, in turn, solicited help from the students in preparing for the trip by letting them choose individual Corps of Discovery jobs – botanist, cook, soldier – nineteen different jobs in all.

The students bought into this fantasy with their usual zeal. They choose their jobs, and name tags with job titles were soon forthcoming. This was the year we would prepare for our journey, so we helped everyone organize a plan for learning how to perform their chosen duties.

Although we have not yet told the children, we will begin our journey on the fourteenth of May, the 200th anniversary of the date the real expedition set out on the Missouri River near St. Louis. The Rio Grande will be our substitute for the Missouri. We will travel downriver for a few miles, and when we stop for lunch, the students will carry out their assigned tasks and record their impressions in their journals.

The Lewis and Clark Expedition included a dog, a male Newfoundland named Seaman. He turned out to be extremely useful to the expedition, scaring off Indians attempting to steal horses, protecting the men from bears, rescuing those who fell overboard, and even bringing in food. He survived the entire expedition, although he almost died at one point from a bear attack.

Our Newfy, Mandy, is playing the role of Seaman. Yesterday we presented a skit right after flag ceremony. As Lewis and Clark, Melissa and I reported to President Jefferson on the progress of our preparations for the journey. Melissa reported on supplies purchased (sugar, flour, firearms) while I reported that I had purchased a dog for $20. The president questioned this purchase since $20 in those days could have bought many supplies.

I outlined the qualities a Newfoundland has that would aid the expedition. They included strength, loyalty, and swimming ability. Then I asked the president if I could present the dog to him. That was John's cue to bring Mandy onto the scene. (They had been hiding in the gym).

I had been training Mandy at the flagpole for several days, but without children present. Mandy is so exuberant and so loves all these kids we weren't sure if she could focus on her tricks with all of them present.

However, she exhibited exemplary behavior, showing her ability to shake hands (useful when encountering friendly strangers), lie down (so as not to tip over the pirogue when she was a passenger), and "whisper," giving a barely audible bark (useful for alerting the men without giving away their position when unknowns were approaching).

Later in the afternoon all the students met in the gym to munch popcorn and watch a National Geographic video about the expedition. The video included a large, black Newfoundland. When they saw the dog, the little kids shouted, "Look! It's Mandy!"

The Lewis and Clark Project was off to a great start when I received an email from a first grade teacher I met at the technology workshop I had attended during the summer. She teaches in the Allen school district near Dallas. Wanting to use our newly acquired skills, she suggested we stage a video conference between our schools' first grade social studies classes. Since her school has 80 first graders and the park school has only one, I invited my entire K–3rd grade social studies class of eleven students to participate in the event.

The topic of the video conference was "Our Community" so our children prepared some information about this community to present and thought of some questions about their community to ask the children from the Dallas suburb. We rehearsed sitting still with our hands in our laps, remaining quiet and still, and above all, refraining from nose picking.

Our conference began with my students standing up in turn and introducing themselves. Little Anna stood up and said, "My name is Anna. I am the kindergarten class." Then her sister Lauren reported that she was the first grade class. The seven second graders stood up together and their spokesperson said, "We are the second grade class. We have the biggest class in our school." Finally, the two third graders stood and introduced themselves.

Our children presented themselves well, just as rehearsed, and they couldn't help but smile as they saw some of the other children talking, wiggling, and yes, nose picking.

Each of our students had a chance to ask questions on camera and respond to those from the Allen children. Some of our questions betrayed an ignorance of city life, for example,

"What kind of snakes do you have where you live?"

The most amusing moment came when Anna responded to a question from one of the city children about what insects we have in the park. She named a few and then said, "We also have crotch roaches. Everyone in our family *hates* crotch roaches!" Of course this flew right over the heads of the 80 first graders, but we adults had to chuckle.

John says watching our children's lives is almost like entering a time warp. In many respects they linger in the more secure and certain days of the 1940's and '50's. Most of the children live with both parents; many of them go home to a hot lunch; and, except when we have a mountain lion alert, the kids walk or ride their bikes to and from school unescorted and unafraid. There is a true feeling of community in our tiny neighborhood. Life is good for little kids in the park – and for big kids like John and me as well.

This school year my faithful classroom volunteer is working four mornings a week. Like he did before, he guides the children through Story Writing 101 and plays Instant Words games with them in preparation for the next 100-word party. But with only Anna and Lauren in the room on the days Don isn't at school, he often has time to add some art or keyboarding to his sessions.

One morning recently he was helping Anna with art. After setting out the water, brushes, paper, and paints, and helping her into her painting smock, he sat down to see what she would create. She was using reds, blues, and yellows in such vivid, dramatic swirls that he was reminded of Georgia O'Keeffe's evening star paintings.

After watching her for awhile he said, "Anna, you really have a talent for this. You might grow up to be a famous artist."

Anna always becomes completely absorbed in her art work, but his remark made her look up, and her eyes showed a mixture of shock and surprise.

"I'm *already* a famous artist!" she announced, and then, having dismissed him and his ridiculous comment, this little five-year-old returned with total concentration to her creation.

We hung Anna's evening star paintings on the cabinet doors to be admired by the visitors we had this week. Twenty-five eighth graders from London ISD are here for their annual camping trip. When they came by so our big kids could give them a school tour, Anna and Lauren were delighted to show them around their classroom as well as have an audience for their explanations about our preparations for the Lewis and Clark Expedition. The visitors told the girls a bit about their school and located Corpus Christi for them on our wall map. I am always happy to have classroom visitors. I view each of them as a learning resource and a way for my somewhat insular students to broaden their horizons.

Next Tuesday will be the last day at school for Abbey. She and her family will be leaving for Alaska on Wednesday so I invited her to the Lodge Restaurant for a farewell girls night out this week.

Last year John and I met a young woman who was waiting tables at the Lodge Restaurant so she could "get out of Ohio." We were amused by her reason for being here, but we admired her courage and independence.

Carly stayed at the Basin for a full year, something of a record for waitpersons there. Many of them stay only a month or two, sometimes moving on to other parks, taking other jobs, or going back to school. Last April Carly left the park. We missed her and we didn't hear where she had gone.

Yesterday when Abbey and I arrived at the restaurant, we were surprised to see Carly. She had stopped by the restaurant to say hello, but they were shorthanded so she was helping out for a few days. I was surprised to learn that she was just returning from a five month backpacking trip through South America. This young lady is definitely achieving her goal of getting out of Ohio! In a place where faces change as quickly as the West Texas wind, it was nice to see Carly's familiar face.

One face that has been familiar in the park for many years will be leaving in a few months. It is that of Captain John Davies, U.S. Border Patrol. Over the weekend John and I were privileged to attend a retirement party in his honor. The celebration was held in the old enlisted barracks in Castolon. The barracks, as well as houses for both the NCO's and the officers, were built in 1919 when the U.S. Army established a presence in the area and stationed a cavalry troop in Castolon to combat the decades-old Mexican bandit problem. This historic area is the park's most remote settlement. It is on the Rio Grande some 35 miles southwest of PJ.

A Texas swing band played songs from our childhood and youth – Hank Williams, Bobby Bare, Ray Price. People danced in the dirt outside the barracks, visited around picnic tables in the shadow of Santa Elena Canyon, ate copious amounts of good food, and took turns kidding John.

John has 33 years of Border Patrol service, and for the past 17 years he has been chief of Border Patrol operations in Big Bend. This is one of the places where the Border Patrol still uses horses to get around in the rough terrain, and John's horse, Río with him for all but the first six months of his time in the park, will be retiring also. The Border Patrol agreed to sell Río to John for a dollar so his friends chipped in and bought the horse for him. The inscription on the farewell cake read, "Happy Trails, John and Río."

As a nineteen-year-old, John shipped to Vietnam where he became a radio operator, a favorite target of snipers. But he survived his years in combat, and has a continuing interest in the military, particularly military history. He and John P. Seawell have spent many hours discussing this mutual interest.

John is a modern legend in Big Bend National Park. Conscientious and dedicated to duty, he has also been ever helpful to and supportive of his community. Our country is lucky to have men like him, and my husband and I are proud to call him a friend.

The end of October brought another exciting Halloween to the park children, and a special treat to John and me. In an isolated area such as ours where contact with the outside world is limited, the kids seem to get more excited about all holidays, and only Christmas is bigger than Halloween.

The Halloween parade of trick-or-treaters and their parents usually starts at the highest point in Panther Junction and winds down through the residential streets like a giant caterpillar negotiating the veins of a leaf. The parents have as much fun as the children, and no one *ever* misses Halloween.

This year, however, one of my second graders developed a case of croup that impaired his breathing so much he ended up spending three days in the Alpine hospital. Gabriel was due to be released on Halloween afternoon, but we didn't expect him to trick-or-treat so I set aside a bag of goodies to give him after he returned to school.

Trick-or-treat came and went. It was all over shortly after 8 p.m. The goblins and ghosts returned home to devour their candy and chicken soup with rice while the javelinas ventured out of the bush to see if anyone had been foolhardy enough to leave a real pumpkin jack-o-lantern on a porch.

John and I were entertaining old friends dating all the way back to Ethiopia days when the phone rang around 9 p.m. It was Gabriel's mother asking if we were still up. She and Gabe had just returned from the hospital, and he had a request.

"I want to go show Dr. Seawell and Mr. John P. my Halloween costume."

He only asked to go to one house, ours. So a few minutes later, coughing, and still a bit weak, Gabriel appeared in his skeleton outfit, and we and our visitors got to admire it.

The life of a public school teacher has its obstacles, frustrations, and exhaustion, but its rewards are many. This extra special trick-or-treater filled John and me with renewed energy and dedication.

John & Río, Happy Trails

CHAPTER 8

Confronting Government, Dinosaurs, and *The Velveteen Rabbit*

A few days later Gabriel was feeling fine. He was back at school, and all of us were ready for something new. After our units on neighborhoods and communities, local government was the next thing we explored in social studies. I scheduled a field trip to Alpine so we could see local government in action. As always, there are at least five hundred things K–3rd graders can do to prepare for a field trip and we did about a hundred of them.

This trip was to include lunch at McDonald's. Would placing their own orders be a good learning experience for the children? Of course. Fast food. Part of the American dream. Each child decided what he or she wanted to eat (plus a second choice, just in case!), and we practiced lining up and giving our orders. I played the McDonald's gal, punching away at my imaginary keypad and doing my best to prepare the children for unexpected developments.

"And to drink?"

"No apple juice. Sorry."

"Size?"

"You want fries with that?"

"Here or to go?"

Our practice sessions also included manners. Please. Thank you. And a smile.

The second and third graders' homeroom teacher, who was kindly helping with this trip, volunteered to drive the bus to Alpine, so I accepted Edgar's invitation to sit with him for the first leg of the journey.

Each child had prepared a local government packet which included road maps and maps of the tri-counties, Brewster, Presidio, and Jeff Davis. The maps had been annotated, footnoted, color-coded, and otherwise carefully studied. I kept the packets in an accordion folder and passed them to the children each time they requested them. Thus we bounced along with packets traveling up and down the aisle in a frenzy of final inquiry and review.

Edgar and I chatted as we rode along and I was touched when I noticed he had looped his arm in mine, an amiable and culturally appropriate gesture for an eight-year-old Mexican American child on a trip with his teacher.

"Cheeseburger, please. No mustard, please. No pickles, please. Pickles. Piiiiickles."

This would be Edgar's first visit to McDonald's so he was rehearsing.

"Dr. Seawell, will you write it for me so I can practice?"

He stuck the 3"x5" card in the window next to him.

"No piiickles. Please."

After we passed the 26-mile marker but before we reached the north gate of the park, I saw a gold SUV a quarter of a mile behind us. Yes!

I had been surprised at the intensity of my relief last year when Jonathan's parents told me they would follow our bus on our first field trip. Had I really been that anxious? Evidently so. Any number of obstacles could impede our progress, all sorts of mishaps could halt our advance. I would be traveling through the back of beyond with a dozen children under the age of eight. After exiting the park there are still 40 miles to go before reaching the first village. What could I have been thinking? Now having Jonathan's parents following the bus had almost become routine, a routine I sincerely appreciated.

Yes, we had the school satellite phone and all the emergency numbers. But we would be out of satellite phone range much of the way. Yes, we had done the pre-trip bus check, examined the tires, and filled the diesel tank. But the mouse that had chewed bus wires last month could have returned to re-chew this morning. Yes, we were all happy and healthy. But children get homesick and adults get heart attacks. I had driven this 70-mile stretch from the park headquarters to Marathon several times without seeing another vehicle. But today we were not alone. Today Jonathan's parents were following us.

Of all my children, Jonathan's roots ran deepest into this remote part of Texas. Before the park was a park, his family ranched here. Before his father was born, his family ranched here. Jonathan's grandparents, his great-grand-parents, and one of his great-great-grandparents were *born* here. His great-grandparents and his great-great-grandparents are *buried* here. Here! In what became a national park.

When the park was established the family moved to Marathon. Jonathan's dad completed twelve years of school there, graduating from Marathon High School. Through Margarito's eyes Brewster County is not a harsh, austere, unforgiving place. Through his eyes Brewster County is *home*. Easy to navigate. Simple to traverse. When he is following us I relax. He will solve any problem that arises. He will get us out of any scrape.

On this trip there were no scrapes. We arrived in Alpine on time and on schedule.

We visited the tax assessor/collector's office where, in addition to learning the duties of this public servant, the children were given packets that included pencils and Uncle Sam masks, then treated to red, white, and blue cupcakes. (The tax assessor/collector's mom owns a bakery.) Next we walked across the street to the 1887 red brick Second Empire-style courthouse, checked out the county judge's office, peeked into the records department, and did some role-playing in the empty courtroom. Then we walked next door to the sheriff's office.

When I visited the sheriff during my pre-trip reconnaissance, he asked if I wanted to include the jail as part of our visit. I had seen the barred windows on the top floor of the red brick building that housed his office. They looked much like the barred windows on the top floor of the courthouse in the county where my brother was sheriff for twelve years. Other than providing a Saturday night's lodging for fellows who sometimes drank too many Lone Star beers, my brother's little jail wasn't full very often. This familial connection made me something of an authority on the county jails of Texas. I knew all about them.

"Sure, great idea. Thank you. My social studies class would love to take a look at the jail. Just another part of local government."

"I'll need a signed permission from each of their parents."

"Not a problem."

An additional permission. Strange. Maybe the stairs up to the little jail are rickety. The county probably needs the permissions for insurance purposes.

On field trip day we trooped into the sheriff's office only to learn that the sheriff was out on an emergency call. But a deputy could show us the jail. That's when I should have tucked the signed permissions back into my accordion folder. But when the deputy held out his hand, I passed them over.

"Follow me, kids."

Out the back door. Across the street. Down the block. Over a bridge. Where are we going? Where is this man taking my children? And what is that building over there?

Surprise! Texas counties raise revenue by making jail cells available to the federal government. For *federal* prisoners. As we stood in the lobby of the *real* Brewster County Jail I saw a chart on the wall that listed *48* federal prisoners. *That's* when I should have thanked the deputy and backed the children out of the building.

Instead we followed the officer through a series of doors that opened with keypad codes and clanged shut behind us. We were shown an enclosed basketball court and an area where visiting is done by phone through glass partitions. Then we were escorted down a narrow hall with cells all along the side. Forty-eight federal prisoners in orange jumpsuits were staring at my children. Unbelievable! Apryl and Destiny were clinging to me, my other children were clinging to each other.

Our parade halted at the end of the hall.

I have seen the moment of my greatness flicker,
And I have seen the eternal Footman hold my coat, and snicker,
And in short, I was afraid.

"Do you kids have any questions?"

The other teacher and I exchanged a horrified glance and said in unison, "Let's do that in the lobby!"

The children may have asked questions when we got back to the lobby. I don't remember. I know they asked for the 3"x5" cards on which they had written their questions. I know I fished the cards out of my accordion folder. But whole parts of the local government field trip have escaped me. I'm told memory loss often follows traumatic experiences. I do remember that I had scheduled one more local government office visit before lunch. Cancel!

"Everyone, into the bus! Everyone! Lunch time! McDonald's!"

Apryl and Destiny hadn't stopped clinging. There were creases in my slacks where they were hanging on. Hurrying to the bus with little girls dangling from my legs wasn't easy.

"I don't want to go to jail, Dr. Seawell."

"I don't even want to go to court!"

"Good decisions, Girls. Into the bus!"

I was still hyperventilating when we lined up inside McDonald's, but the children had already forgotten the 48 federal prisoners. They were hungry and well rehearsed. They did a first-rate job ordering their meals, although Edgar almost got cold feet.

"Dr. Seawell, maybe you should say it for me."

"You can do it! You know what to say!"

The big smile on Edgar's face told me his ordering experience had been successful.

"And, Dr. Seawell, I remembered 'thank you.'"

A visit to the Presidio County Courthouse was next. My turn to drive. Barring an emergency, no one may speak to the bus driver, the bus driver may speak to no one. Ensconced in my cocoon of silence, I steered the bus along U.S. 90 through the caldera of the Paisano Volcano toward Marfa, twenty-six miles away. Lava dikes, rhyolite zones, collapse breccia, and an expansive alluvial plain soothed me and helped put the shock of the morning into perspective. By the time the beautiful Second-Empire stone-and-brick 1886 courthouse came into view my heart was thumping at its normal pace and I was no longer gasping.

After the children heard a brief history of the courthouse and an overview of its restoration, they asked a few of the same questions they had asked at the Brewster County courthouse. Comparisons. Contrasts. Then we were left on our own to explore the magnificent old building. This investigation culminated with an exhilarating climb into the third floor cupola. *Giant* country. Beyond the town was forever, was the golden horizon, was the earth's curve.

"Hello, Shirley. We're back in Alpine, ready to head home."

"Have you had a good trip?"

"Well, something ... something ... pretty awful ... happened. I didn't know they were going to march us right by the cells of the 48 federal prisoners in the Brewster County Jail. It was horrible. I don't know what the parents are going to think! I'm really, *really* sorry."

"Were the kids scared straight?"

"*I* was scared straight!"

"Good! That should keep you out of trouble! Now, before you leave town swing by the pharmacy and pick up a prescription for Allison's earache. It should be ready. Lisa called it in around noon. Have a safe trip home. See you in a couple of hours."

After visiting with the little kids the next morning Shirley wrote an account of our local government field trip for the parent letter that went out that afternoon. She reported that the students had learned a great deal about the courthouses, the tax assessor/collector's duties, and the Brewster County Jail. She noted that what seemed to have made the biggest impression on the children was the height of the courthouse in Marfa and the steepness of the stairs coming down from the cupola.

Learning that the little kids' memories were filled with their joyous descent on those dark, narrow, one hundred seventeen-year-old stairs gave me hope. Perhaps not all was lost. Perhaps our local government field trip hadn't scarred my children for life. A flicker of optimism surged through me. Maybe I could banish the jail visit to the closet where I hide all my other skeletons. Maybe. Someday.

I was still recovering from our local government field trip when an opportunity for a science outing arose. Dr. Tom Lehman is a paleontologist from Texas Tech University who has been conducting research in Big Bend for many years. He was to give a presentation designed to update the park's rangers on his team's findings, but Gabriel's dad, Chief of Science and Resource Management, invited the school students to attend, as well.

After convincing myself that investigating science would be less taxing than investigating social studies, I drove my two-child science class down to park headquarters for the professor's lecture. As it turned out, Lauren and Anna were the only two students present.

My little girls and I arrived at the community room a few minutes early and the paleontologist seemed somewhat surprised to see Lauren, the first grader, prepared to take notes with her school-provided DANA (a compact, wireless computer), and Anna, the kindergartener, asking permission to take his photo using the camera function of the PDA she had brought along. Maybe he thought we would be in the backwoods of technology just because we're in the backwoods of Texas. Or maybe it was the size of the students who came to listen that gave him pause.

Anna recently told John that she is *already* a famous artist, and yesterday she told me her art *talks* to her. John is saving all the watercolors she gives him; he thinks "early Anna's" will be worth a fortune some day. However, where anything other than art is concerned, Anna has the attention span of a normal five-year-old. So, even though the girls were thrilled when I told them they were mature enough to attend a lecture for grown-ups, we had planned a graceful way to leave early should the lecture become too long.

Fortunately, interspersed among his slides of charts and graphs, Dr. Lehman had lots of dinosaur pictures, and both Anna and Lauren gave his hour-plus presentation their full attention; Lauren pecking away on her DANA, Anna sketching dinosaurs on her clipboard.

When the lecture was over and the presenter asked for questions, I turned to Lauren to help her finish her notes. That's when I heard Anna's deep voice.

"Dr. Lehman, why did the T-Rexes disappear?"

Dr. Lehman seemed delighted with the question and spent about ten minutes answering it in detail.

My little scholars were something of a revelation to the 30 or so park personnel in attendance, including their father, the Chief Ranger, who later admitted he had held his breath when he saw Anna's hand go up. The park people knew the girls only as cute little kids running and playing. They did not realize what budding intellectuals these young students are.

Few things make one *sound* like a budding intellectual as convincingly as does having a good vocabulary. Maybe that is why Shirley has been relentless in her Bonus Words campaign. In addition to casting these words in the lime-light at school, she is including them in the weekly parent letters; she is solic-iting the use of these words at home. What began as a way to build student vocabulary is evolving into a community project, and we adults are being forced to learn something new.

Mostly because Shirley was so determined that our students expand their vocabularies, but also because I needed a focusing activity for my social studies class after lunch recess, I presented each child with a spiral Bonus Word Journal at the beginning of the school year. The children's routine was to walk into the classroom, wash hands, hydrate (extremely important practice in the desert), and then begin writing in their journal using as many bonus words as they could incorporate into their creative essays or stories.

Bonus words that had been introduced were printed in letters two inches high and displayed on the wall. A list of the words with their definitions and sample sentences hung on the file cabinet. The children could copy the spelling from the words on the wall and check the definitions from the list on the file cabinet.

Once a week the students edited their writing and underlined their bonus words. I collected the journals, wrote some cheerful comments in them about their work, counted the underlined words, and added everyone's additional tickets to the bonus word jar.

Four days a week I gave each child ten seconds by my stopwatch to use as many bonus words orally in context as he or she could. Sometimes I'd take a minute to encourage the use of a word that was getting neglected. Sometimes I'd correct a student's use of a word. Sometime I'd read aloud from the definition list because my students and I were still learning a new word or had forgotten an old one.

This whole focusing activity took less than ten minutes, got the children settled and in classroom mode, and – dare I admit it? – actually increased their vocabularies. Spotting a bonus words in the course of their reading gave them a thrill and incidents of this increased as the weeks passed and we accumulated additional bonus words. I treated the whole project as a game and the children responded by attempting to regale their classmates with their cleverness.

"In the nether part of an immense, gargantuan, hinterland, a quaternary of emotive and jocular javelinas were hobnobbing with an impudent skunk while they scrutinized a thaumaturgic sunset. This is a fictive story."

"Thank you! Twelve tickets in ten seconds! Superb!"

With local government field trips and dinosaur lectures behind us, and vocabulary building becoming a way of life, the children began looking ahead to our next holiday.

A Thanksgiving tradition at our little school is a trip to the Terlingua campus for a student-prepared feast. The day before the trip our older students meet at Melissa's home to bake the three or four different kinds of breads they have chosen to take for their contribution and the younger students meet with me in the classroom to prepare our famous Pilgrim & Indian Trail Mix.

The ingredients for this trail mix vary from year to year, depending on the number of little kids involved. Days before we prepare our delectable contribution we read about Henry Ford and his assembly line idea, and on project day we set up our own assembly line. As the big bowls are passed along the line of desks, each worker is responsible for adding his or her contribution, be it a cup of pretzels, a quarter-cup of pecans, a tablespoon of M&M's, or whatever else we have imagined and purchased that should go into a Pilgrim and Indian Trail Mix. When we have assembled several gallons of this mixture and secured it in big plastic bags, we use our leftovers to make one last bowlful for ourselves. After long minutes on an assembly line, we workers are hungry and deserve a sample of our product.

The next morning we climb into the bus, the truck, and the school car, and point our caravan toward Terlingua. The Big Bend High School students have prepared the turkey, the stuffing, and all the other dishes with which we traditionally celebrate Thanksgiving. When we arrive we add our contributions and take our places in the serving line. Then, outside under a shade ramada, surrounded by buttes, mountains, and mesas, all the students from our two school districts sit down together and the feasting begins.

By the day of the Thanksgiving feast Melissa, Peggy, and all our students are always well into the production of the Christmas play, and just before the end of the fall semester, it is staged for all to see.

Presenting a Christmas play has been a decades-long tradition for our school, but even the old timers out here say there has never been one as dynamic as this year's. All nineteen San Vicente students had speaking roles, the costumes were elaborate and well designed, and the hand-painted backdrop was beautiful. But the thing that really blew the audience away was the energy and vitality that was put into the show.

The play was a musical adaptation of the children's classic *The Velveteen Rabbit* and I think even Bob Fosse would have been impressed as the children sang, danced, kicked, and cartwheeled across the stage. The gymnastics they've learned from Janelle was showcased, and Janelle also lent her professional expertise in choreographing the production.

Perhaps a few of the solos were a little off key, but nobody minded. I agree with John when he says the important thing was that they *did* it. He says he couldn't see himself in elementary school (or now!) having the courage to stand up before an audience and belt out a number while dressed like a rabbit, a teddy bear, or a toy soldier.

The little kids were mostly floppy-eared bunnies and some of them were so enamored with their costumes they asked to wear them home after the show and keep them over the Christmas holidays. They were thrilled when Melissa allowed them to do so.

The parents were delighted with the presentation, although most of the fathers had to wait until they got home to actually see the play since they spent the entire time standing in strategic locations off stage videoing the performance. The whole community was present for this lively, exuberant show, and the student's rendition of *The Velveteen Rabbit* truly added an extra sparkle to this year's holiday season. Thus ended our fall semester, framed with flair and with fun.

CHAPTER 9

Visiting and Visitors

In early January I began making plans to take our K–3rd grade classes to McDonald Observatory. This was a science field trip and all four grades were officially preparing for the trip during science class, but we had our logistical discussions during social studies class since that was the time of day when all the little kids were in my room at once.

In a young child's life few events are as magical (thaumaturgic!) as a birthday, and in our school most of the children can remember each other's birth dates as easily as their own. Our field trip was scheduled for February 27. Apryl's birthday. Everyone knew it. On the rare occasion of her absence from school, Scott suggested we incorporate a surprise birthday party for her into our field trip. My sugar-crazed children recognized the brilliance of this idea in a nanosecond.

"Yes, Dr. Seawell, you should order a birthday cake to go with our lunch!"

"For our dessert!"

"Girls and Boys, we read the whole menu when we were making our lunch order. They don't serve cake at the Star-Date Café."

"We'll sing "Happy Birthday" and "Las Mañanitas" just like we do at flag."

"Yes, Dr. Seawell, we'll be leaving before flag. We'll have to sing to her up there. Then we'll eat the cake!"

"Girls and Boys! Hellooooo! The Star-Date Café is just a tiny restaurant. They don't *have* cake."

"Get chocolate, Dr. Seawell. That's Apryl's favorite!"

"Students, *please*. We're going to an astronomical observatory, not a bakery!"

"Just ask them, Dr. Seawell, okay? Just email them again. Please!"

"Yes, please, pleeease, Dr. Seawell. Just ask them to make a chocolate cake for us. For Apryl!"

"Yes, for Apryl!"

January 17, 2004
Dear Frank Smith,
    Young children have taken over my classroom and are making all the cru-
cial decisions. Short people are running the tall person's show. I realize I have created this dilemma myself through my conscientious and overzealous attempts
to follow the lead of the child; however, I am now being accosted by a dozen
small bullies. Today it's chocolate birthday cake, who knows what it might be
tomorrow. Please advise.

Signed,
Paranoid in PJ

We were still making our plans for the observatory visit when our international visitors began arriving. Our first guest was a five-year-old boy named
Arlo. His father is English, his mother is American, and he lives in France.

His mother was a college roommate of the wife of one of our rangers,
and the little family was visiting the park. We invited Arlo to spend a day at
school, and it turned out to be a memorable day for all of us.

Arlo, an outgoing and precocious little boy, fit right in. All the little kids
were fascinated with his British accent and his vocabulary. They just couldn't
understand why he called a cookie a biscuit.

During the morning library visit Lauren picked out a children's book
about France, and after lunch when our social studies group convened, we
read and discussed it, Arlo volunteering supplementary information about
school and games in France.

Later, by sheer coincidence, our school was holding its local round of the
National Geographic Geography Bee. It was held in the gym with the whole
school in attendance, although only the big kids were participating in the bee.

My little kids are becoming increasingly map literate, and they have
learned quite a bit about the world, so I told them when they knew the answers
to any of the questions, they were not to blurt them out; rather, they were to
wink at each other instead.

One of the questions turned out to be, "What is the new monetary unit
that many nations in Europe have adopted?"

None of the participants knew the answer, but we had discussed the Euro
just a few minutes earlier and there was enough winking going on among the
little kids and their European visitor to distress an ophthalmologist.

The international flavor continued with the arrival of our next visitors.
They were two Fulbright scholars from Korea spending a year at Sul Ross
State University studying rural education. Since there aren't many schools
more rural than ours, they asked to come down for a visit.

I had taught conversational English to similar grad students at Seoul
National University in 1965-66 while John was stationed in the Korean demilitarized zone. (I know what you're thinking, "If it was demilitarized, what was
the U.S. Army doing there?" Don't ask.) Knowing the visitors were coming, I

told the little kids a few facts about Korea and the Korean culture before they arrived.

The guests came at a time when my whole, eleven-student social studies class was present. The scholars were surprised when the children stood up, bowed, and greeted them with "How do you do?" in Korean as they came through the door.

Anna, the famous artist, exhibited her latest art project and cautioned that working with oil pastels was very messy and required extensive hand washing afterwards. Lauren, the elder sister, showed off her DANA and PDA, as well as the three new desktop computers in our classroom. The visitors were quite taken with the use of technology in such a small school.

I had told my students that the Korean alphabet was different from our own, so they asked to see samples of Korean writing. The visitors gave us a short phonics lesson as they wrote their names on the board. Then they delighted each child with a Korean postcard on which they wrote the Korean equivalent of the child's name.

Once again, parts of the larger world discovered Big Bend, and, once again, our visitors became learning resources for our students. (And did we locate France and the Korean Peninsula on our maps and globe? You betcha!)

A few days after hosting our international visitors, the eleven little kids assembled in the school parking lot just before sunrise for the 2½ hour ride to McDonald Observatory. The focus of this field trip was our solar system, so our bus boarding passwords that morning were "My very enthusiastic mother just sent us nine pizzas," the mnemonic they had learned to help them remember the planetary order.

Anna and Lauren had done extensive preparation for the trip. They conducted Internet searches, read many astronomy books from the school library, and used the pre-visit materials sent to us by the Observatory.

One of the projects the girls completed was an enormous yellow paper "sun," across the middle of which they glued 109 blue "earths" they made with a hole punch. This was to show the relative size of our planet compared to our nearest star. They decorated their sun with sunspots, flares, and prominences, used it as a visual aid in their pre-trip presentation to the second and third graders, then brought it along to give to the education director at the Observatory.

As an additional gift (and because art is her life), Anna created a colorful spectrograph with white paper and colored felt-tip markers. This was the perfect thing for a five-year-old to do during a long bus ride to an observatory.

I have only praise for the educational programs the personnel at McDonald Observatory have developed for student groups. The activities are varied and age appropriate; the instructors are knowledgeable and enthusiastic; and, the pre- and post-visit materials provided to the schools are innovative and beneficial.

Our children were scheduled to visit the 107-inch telescope and the real-time sun viewing theater, but the education coordinator was so impressed with their knowledge and interest that he took them to see a recently completed telescope as well. This new telescope consists of 91 hexagonal mirrors, each about a meter in diameter, and is one of the largest telescopes in the world.

Next on the agenda were activities in the Observatory classroom. The children had thought of questions they wanted to ask prior to our trip and had written them on cards. But before the Q&A time came, Jessica, one of our second graders, had a chance to demonstrate her grasp of earth science. The instructor was using a toy dinosaur and a spotlight to teach the children about the earth's rotation. Then he mentioned that many experts believe a giant meteor had caused the extinction of the dinosaurs, and asked if anyone knew why that might have happened. Jessica's hand went up immediately.

"The meteor caused a cloud of dust that blocked out the sun, so that killed all the plants. That caused all the herbivores to die because they didn't have any plants to eat, and that caused all the carnivores to die because they didn't have any herbivores to eat."

The instructor leaned over to me and whispered, "Wow, that wasn't the answer I was expecting!"

After learning about our solar system through several hands-on activities and purchasing matching McDonald Observatory T-shirts at the gift shop, we climbed back onto the bus for the trip home. Along the way, we stopped in Alpine so the children could do a timed run on the Sul Ross State University track. Our school track is fine, but it's not exactly flat. Anyway, after being cooped up most of the day I knew the students could use a little exercise. I convinced them that training for their Presidential Fitness run on a "professional" track would be exciting, and with their usual fervor, they bought into my scheme and a good run was enjoyed by all.

Through this study of the solar system, combined with our Star Party knowledge from last year, we have learned quite a bit about our universe. Happily, exposure to all this celestial phenomenon has inspired Lauren, our first grader. She has made the decision to become an astronomer.

In the tiny town of Ft. Davis, the ladies who serve up the Foccacia bread sandwiches and three-bean salads at the Star-Date Café located a chocolate birthday cake. They're that kind of ladies. White frosting, yellow roses. Apryl's favorite. Amused strangers joined us in singing the English birthday song, but my children belted out the Spanish version all alone. This was Apryl's special tribute, made possible through the optimism and persistence of her caring classmates. What's not to love about these children?

By the end of February the park exploded in bluebonnets, the official State flower. The bluebonnets are especially dense near the school because children have planted seeds there over the years.

The little kids are fiercely protective of these flowers. Last year there were even a few altercations with the big kids because of careless feet around the playground. Stepping on a flower is a serious crime in their young minds.

Although this year's bluebonnet crop around the school is exceptionally dramatic, something disturbing has been happening. Whole sections of the playground have been stripped of flowers. The children have been genuinely upset. They have suspected some malicious big kid of committing the unspeakable, and have suggested that the law enforcement rangers initiate a 24-hour stakeout, catch the offender, and make him pay for his transgressions. However, that will no longer be necessary because today the crime was solved.

Returning to our classroom after a trek to the restroom, my two little girls and I counted eleven javelinas as, one-by-one, they ambled up out of a draw near the far end of the school track. As we watched, this little herd began a slow-motion meander across the playground toward us. And as the javelinas meandered, they munched – bluebonnets!

In full view and without a trace of fear the javelinas drifted from flower to flower completely oblivious to the turmoil their epicurean practice has been creating.

In the afternoon when the rest of the little kids were in the room for social studies, and Anna and Lauren were revealing how they had solved the mystery of the vanishing bluebonnets, the javelinas materialized again for another round of early spring treats.

As the children stood at the windows watching, they were faced with a grave choice – their precious flora versus their precious fauna. Should they go out and drive the javelina herd off the playground or should the javelinas be allowed this once-a-year feast?

A long debate ensued. In the end, like all ecologists respectful of life's eternal web, they agreed that nature must take its course. So the bluebonnet vandalism case has been solved, but the culprits will go unpunished.

A few days later, came a St. Patrick's Day morning too gorgeous to miss. I needed some pretext for getting my children and myself back outside after PE. Actually, there had already been broad hints from the two little sisters with Boston in their background that something special should occur on St. Patrick's Day. During free-choice time the day before they had constructed little pointed paper hats and painted shamrocks on them. Anna announced they were for the St. Patrick's Day party. News to me. Other than furnishing both the big and little kids with green necklaces left over from a Mardi Gras celebration, my only planned activity was to allow the children to put a few drops of green food coloring in their water sippers.

However, the lovely spring morning and the student expectation conspired to produce the first annual St. Patrick's Day Parade in the park. There were five participants: Anna, Lauren, Don (our pre-k student), Kathy (our school secretary), and me.

Lauren carried the classroom American flag, Anna the Texas flag, and Don proudly hoisted a Chinese silk kite shaped like a bird. There is no significance to the latter; I just didn't want Don to be left out and we only have two flags. Everyone wore a paper hat decorated with shamrocks.

With excited dignity the little parade did a turn around the one-fifth-mile track that surrounds the playground. Since all the other students were in class, the only audience was the bluebonnets yet to be eaten by the javelinas, but that did not dampen our enthusiasm.

When the parade reached a mobile home adjacent to a portion of the track, two concession employees came out on their porch and applauded.

"I never expected to see a St. Patrick's Day Parade today!" one of the young men called out.

After a circuit of the track, we returned to the classroom for green water and morning snacks.

It was impromptu, tiny, and brief, but our St. Patrick's Day Parade may well become one of those crystalline memory capsules that lives on in our hearts.

As the spring continued we expanded our study of butterflies. Having learned a valuable lesson about the eating habits of Black Swallowtail caterpillars last year, we have an eighteen-pot parsley garden this year. We will put only one pot outside to collect a few eggs and use the other pots for caterpillar food. We're hoping that Mr. John P. Seawell won't have to make parsley emergency runs to Alpine this year.

We also collected a few caterpillars from the hundreds we observed on the silverleaf around the school. Providing them with jars of fresh silverleaf, we raised them in the classroom, and released them when they completed their metamorphoses. Gabriel's mom helped us identify these small colorful butterflies as Theona Checkerspots.

In the midst of butterfly season we had to say goodbye to Destiny when she moved with her family to Marathon. She has been with most of these children since pre-k, and we will all miss her.

Throughout the year, interspersed among the video conferences, the field trips, the international visitors, the butterflies, and the 100 Word Parties, we prepared for our journey to the Pacific with Lewis, Clark, and the famous Newfoundland dog, Seaman.

During the summer I had read Patti Eubank's beautiful picture book, *Seaman's Journal On the Trail With Lewis and Clark*. Her information is accurate and is written from Seaman's point of view. I wrote and thanked her for a job well done and told her how helpful her book would be for our Lewis and Clark Project. In response, she sent us an autographed copy of the book, inscribed to the children, Mandy, and me. *Seaman's Journal* was read and re-read by the children and they studied Ms. Eubank's magnificent watercolors for style and technique.

Curators at the Jefferson National Expansion Memorial sent us their Patrick Gass "traveling trunk" filled with materials and artifacts that intrigued us and helped us understand some of the things the Corps of Discovery participants saw and did.

We conducted Internet searches and wrote letters to national and state parks along the Lewis and Clark Trail requesting materials. Each child was to choose two parks and write two letters, but once the packets containing brochures, maps, postcards, booklets, pens, and other exciting items began arriving, most of the children decided to cast a wider net. By the time Abbey left for Alaska, she had received materials from seventeen different parks.

Glennallen, Alaska

March 4, 2007

Dear Dr. Seawell,

We were making a Lewis and Clark newspaper as a project while reading the book *Seaman*. We were researching on the computer for information and I brought all the big packets of brochures and stuff I had gotten in 2nd grade. The kids in my group all stared happily and exclaimed, "Where did you find that?!" I proudly announced, "My awesome teacher in Big Bend taught us about Lewis and Clark and we all got info like this!" All of it really helped out. During the project I just couldn't stop thinking of you and our fun times in Big Bend. I am still sorry I missed out on the fun rafting trip the school did. I still remember I was the blacksmith.

Love,

Abbey

We ordered several books about the Lewis and Clark Expedition to augment our library collection. These books included a cookbook with recipes of some of the foods members of the party might have cooked and eaten on their journey, and field guides to the flora and fauna they observed along the Trail.

I found a book which included twenty-one hands-on Lewis and Clark activities for children, and we began working our way through them, recording the experiences in our Lewis and Clark journals. Among other things we made apple fruit leather (which we shared with the big kids) and cold cream/red food coloring face paint (which we saved to present to the Native Americans we might encounter, right after trying it on our own faces and showing ourselves off to the big kids).

And we learned how to study flowers.

"Each of you may choose three different samples – for example, you might choose one bluebonnet, one verbena, and one desert marigold."

"Dr. Seawell, are you *positive* it's all right for us to pick wildflowers in a national park?"

"Yes, for this project it's fine. We have special permission."

"Who gave us permission?"

"Mmmm, well, Ms. Coleman gave us permission."

"But ...who gave her permission?"

"You know, I'm not sure, Alex, but the school has been given special permission to conduct science projects."

"But this is a social studies project, Dr. Seawell."

"Mmmm, well, you're right, Scott. But remember that one of the things President Jefferson wanted the Corpsmen to do was collect samples of the flora they found along the Trail. That was science. The President wanted everyone to learn about all the new plants."

"So is this a *scientific* social studies project?"

"Exactly! This is a *scientific* social studies project! You each have special permission to pick three flowers to preserve so you'll know just how the Corpsmen did it. We'll walk completely around the track and we won't take more than one flower from any one plant. Now, what other questions and comments do you have?"

"All set, then? Newspaper, spray bottles, bags, scissors?"

"Check! Check! Check! Check!"

"Corps Botanist, are you ready to lead us?"

"Check!"

"Okay, Corpsmen, let's do it! Follow the Corps Botanist, stay together, stay on the track, and watch out for rattlesnakes."

We picked and pressed our flowers. We used field guides to identify the ones we didn't know and wrote detailed scientific information about each one on separate note cards, just as Anna and Lauren's mom, the plant ecologist, had instructed us. After a few weeks we encased the dried flowers in plastic and mounted them in our Lewis and Clark journals along with the identification cards we had made. Big Bend National Park sacrificed bluebonnets, vervain, desert marigold, verbena, woolly paper-flower, globe mallow, and purple groundcherry that day. Thirty wildflowers in all. May the knowledge gained from this scientific social studies project live on in our minds forever.

In April some dear friends came to the park for a visit. When Pete offered to bring along his iceman materials and perform for our students, I was delighted. I didn't realize that these materials would fill the back of his pick-up! Pete, who teaches science through art, has done extensive research on Otzi, the 5,300-year-old Alpine Neolithic man whose well-preserved body was found in Italy in 1991. One of this creative man's hobbies is giving presentations in which he pretends to be Otzi. He appears in costume, complete with an arrow protruding from his back, and tells his story using authentic reproductions of the tools and other artifacts associated with his life and times. Just as Otzi had done eons ago, Pete fashioned his hat and the soles of his shoes from bear skin – after making a four-hour drive in the heat of a New Mexico summer to collect the "ripening" 250-pound carcass, then skinning it in his barn. (But that's another, somewhat *stinky*, story!)

The whole school turned out for the iceman presentation and afterward everyone examined all the artifacts in detail and to their heart's content. Pete, ever lively and knowledgeable, charmed the students by remaining in character while answering their questions. All of us appreciated the time and effort he spent making our morning educational and entertaining.

After the presentation, we moved to the playground for the annual Easter egg hunt followed by the Newfy Parade. Our visitors are the people from whom we got Mandy, and they brought Mandy's mother and father along on the trip.

Anticipating the appearance of two additional Newfies in the park, Anna and Lauren were inspired to plan a Newfoundland Parade. So right after the Easter egg hunt, the girls assembled Mandy, her parents, and all the students on the school track. Then, with three or four children hanging onto each dog's leash, these patient, gentle Newfies made a slow lap around the playground.

Before the parade, however, an emergency operation occurred. While all the humans were attending the iceman's presentation, Mandy's father, the massive 150-pound visitor, decided to step over our back fence and explore the neighborhood.

When a ranger spotted him, he thought a black bear was roaming through the housing area and prepared to persuade it to move on. As he closed in, he realized the big, black animal was only a curious Newfoundland. Assuming it was Mandy he took it in tow and headed for our back yard. Imagine his astonishment when he opened our gate to put the wanderer back inside and two more big, black, bear-sized animals bounded over to greet him. Nothing like a trio of Newfies to spark up an Easter break.

But Mandy's dad wasn't the only unauthorized domestic animal prowling through the housing area this spring. With the grasses and flowers so lush and inviting, the park service mules decided to investigate. These six or eight animals are kept in a large enclosure just behind a low hill about a half mile from the PJ housing area. The rangers use them to pack out injured tourists and to haul supplies up to the line cabin in the Chisos Mountains where young Student Conservation Association volunteers live while doing maintenance on the trails.

The sights and smells of the season apparently became too much for the mules. They found a weak spot in their fence, squeezed through it, and scattered out into the housing area. There they grazed in front yards, wandered along streets, and generally made themselves at home.

The alarm was not sounded until Kathy, relaxing in her back yard after dinner, was startled to see a mule staring at her over her back fence. Then the great roundup began, and it wasn't over until well after dark.

The next creature affected by the joys of spring was a reptile. On our first day back at school after Easter the children found a 12-inch Black Tail Rattlesnake on the playground. Small snakes always alert extra caution since a juvenile could be one member of a larger family. However, additional snakes were not spotted, and a ranger came by and removed the snake for relocation.

With all these exiting spring events going on outside our classroom, it became more important than ever to create some excitement inside. Taking advantage, once again, of the park's many experts in the natural sciences, we asked the park's education coordinator, Dr. Rob Dean, to come in and give the little kids a lesson in geology.

Rocks have always been of particular interest to our students. A look around their landscape explains why; rocks are everywhere. The little kids pick them up, scrutinize and discuss them, check out books about them, and although Gabriel is the only one who has selected geology as his life's work, rocks seem to fascinate all the children.

In preparation for Dr. Dean's presentation, Gabriel brought in one of his geology books to share with the class. It covered the history of a boulder over many millions of years as it broke off a mountain ledge and slowly worked its way to the sea, being ground down smaller and smaller until it finally became a grain of sand, and then became sedimentary rock. Anna listened as I read the book to the class, then she gave an accurate synopsis.

"That book is about the life cycle of a rock."

For his presentation Dr. Dean brought along an amazing variety of rock samples for the children to examine and he talked with them about the volcanic origins of many of the rocks in the park. During this discussion he asked if anyone knew what magma was. Anna was the first to raise her hand.

"Rock juice."

Dr. Dean admitted that he had never before heard magma called rock juice, but agreed that it was an apt description.

Rocks with life cycles. Magma as rock juice. These ideas have cast a subtle new light on geology and intensified my interest in the subject. Anna's world spins in a wider orbit than that of most five-year-olds, and it's always enlightening to get a glimpse of things from her broader view.

CHAPTER 10

Year Two: Going, Going ...

Scott, Don, and their mom had been telling me for weeks that a new student would be joining us soon. One afternoon I even got a peek at her and a brief introduction as she sat with the two little boys in the back seat of their parents' truck.

Finally, with only six weeks of school to go, Tanya, her mom, dad, and baby brother moved from Terlingua to PJ. Her father had taken the kitchen manager position at the Lodge Restaurant.

As always, the arrival of a new student caused quite a bit of excitement. Anna and Lauren set about making this little five-year-old feel welcome and Mr. John P. Seawell made it his job to begin teaching her to read the100 most important words in the English language.

Tanya was bright, upbeat, and bilingual. She had had an excellent educational experience in Terlingua, was well-versed and grounded in the basics, and had gorgeous handwriting. I amended my answer to Anna's occasional "Am I your favorite kindergartener in the whole world?" to "You're my favorite blond, blue-eyed, kindergartener and Tanya is my favorite brunette, brown-eyed, kindergartener."

"In the whole world?"

"Yup, the whole world."

That satisfied, reassured, and was true. The two five-year-olds would look at each other and giggle, then go on with their work. Since Lauren already knew she was my favorite brunette, blue-eyed, first grader in the whole world, she rarely asked.

With the arrival of May came the annual Terlingua Spring Fiesta. Janelle and Peggy had prepared our students well. The little kids performed two folk dances and played a few tunes on their recorders; the big kids presented a choreographed basketball routine.

After the open-air dances and musical presentations in the morning, the little kids had lunch followed by a long recess with the Terlingua elementary children in the afternoon.

Earlier in the school year we had done a research project involving wind and kites. Among other things the children learned some history of kites and their relationship to Benjamin Franklin and the Wright brothers. We had completed our study by building kites and spending an afternoon flying them. I had ten kites left over from this project and, without much thought or any real plan, I grabbed them as we left the classroom and took them along to the Fiesta.

When we got to the playground for the afternoon recess, I opened my pack of kites. Few of the Terlingua youngsters had flown a kite, but most were eager to try. I paired my students with Terlingua students and organized the pairs so everyone would get a turn.

An abundance of wind is usually a given in West Texas and that afternoon was no exception. The Terlingua children enjoyed learning a new skill and the park children enjoyed helping them.

One Terlingua child's inexperience caused a kite to escape, and in minutes it had gained so much altitude that it could scarcely be seen. The little boy who had lost the kite was upset and close to tears when he came to apologize for the mix-up. I assured him that it was all right and that, in fact, it would be a wonderful surprise for some little boy in Mexico when he retrieved the kite that the winds had blown south.

This afterthought, this simple kite-flying pleasure, made for a memorable day for both the park students and the Terlingua children. Skills had been shared, friendships had been formed, and no one wanted to leave when it was time to reel in our kites and gather up our water bottles.

Ah, yes. Water. It is always the first item on the field trip checklist. Dehydration can be deadly and can come quickly in our desert. My children and I understand this and take proper precautions. In the classroom we sip throughout the day from the water bottles we keep on our desks. We empty our bottles, refill them, and continue to sip.

"Hydrate, Dr. Seawell. Don't forget!"

"Thanks for reminding me, Don. Happy hydrating to you, too!"

On field trips, in bottles or backpacks, everyone takes water. No one climbs onto the bus without it. We carry along a five-gallon container for refills. We value water. We are somewhat obsessed by it, and the magic of water sets the rhythm for our field trips.

"Okay, everyone to the restroom before we get on the bus."

No one needs to go. Everyone already went. I know to wait.

Jonathan understands my dilemma. He is a peacekeeper and a diplomat. He is also a leader.

"Well, we could go and just *try*."

All the children trot off to the restrooms.

I am grateful for Jonathan's power. His is stronger than mine. Because the children respond to his suggestion, I have forty-five minutes before I have to activate the emergency blinker and pull the bus to a stop. On the side of the road. In the middle of nowhere. My children scramble out. All of them have been successful in avoiding dehydration.

"Girls, take the pink bushes on the east side of the road. Boys, take the blue bushes on the west side. Everybody watch for rattlesnakes."

My little boys have the advantage. Squatting is a skill. It requires practice. Decisions must be made about maneuvering clothing, placing feet, selecting cactus-free areas, balancing on inclines.

I am summoned to a pink bush.

"Dr. Seawell, I need something to hang on to!"

"Here, try holding onto my arm."

"Perfect!"

We climb back onto the bus. We remind each other to hydrate.

"Seat belts, Everyone!"

"Yes, Miss Frizzle."

I check the rear-view mirror. Not a vehicle in sight. I pull back onto the highway, and we're off to the next clump of pink and blue bushes. I know I'll find them in approximately forty-five minutes. The predictability of their spacing is reassuring, and the synergy between these color-coded bushes and the hydrating proficiency of my children is remarkable. Our stars are aligned and there is balance in our universe.

Although the Spring Fiesta prevented a commemoration of the Lewis and Clark Expedition on May 14, 2004, the 200th anniversary of the date the Expedition set out up the Missouri River from St. Louis, we carried out our reenactment the following week.

We had been learning about the Expedition and participating in various activities connected with it all year. Each student had taken on a special Corps of Discovery duty and had learned a bit about the specifics and the skills associated with his or her job.

This San Vicente Corps of Discovery river trip was Melissa's idea, and she organized and coordinated the adventure. At 8:00 o'clock on the morning of May 19th our little caravan headed east from the school to a point on the Rio Grande about four miles upstream from Rio Grande Village, the eastern settlement in the park.

The launching was quite an operation: 16 students, three teachers, and three park rangers set out in three park-owned rubber rafts, plus one kayak and one inflatable canoe that were the personal boats of two of the older boys.

In addition to the people, the rafts were packed with the food and water that such an expedition requires, plus waterproof bags filled with the equipment the students would need to perform their assigned tasks. Moms served as transportation coordinators driving the bus and the trucks from the drop-off to the pick-up point after the explorers had embarked.

The children, especially the younger ones, were quite serious about their Expedition jobs. They brought along their journals, clipboards with pencils attached, pens, markers, paper for sketching and drawing, watercolors, field guides, and the tools of their trade. Anna, the tailor, had her sewing kit which included a bone needle her father had made for her; Tanya, the blacksmith, had read about shoeing horses and repairing metal cookware, and was prepared to identify equine tracks; Lauren, the botanist, had her sketch book and field guide; Alex, the cartographer, had his compass and map-making supplies; Gabriel, the geologist, had his rock hammer; Jonathan, the meteorologist, had his anemometer; Apryl, the ornithologist, had her watercolors; Edgar, the biologist, had his animal track chart; and Scott, the musician, had his harmonica.

Just as the expedition had done 200 years ago, this little group set out early "… under a jentle brease." I traveled in the raft with Anna, Lauren, Tanya, Gabriel, Jonathan, and "Captain Mike." The kindergarten girls were apprehensive at first, but their fears soon melted with the excitement of setting off down the river. Captain Mike was patient with all the help he got from the young oarsmen and women. He appreciated that they were rowing with all their might, even if a few of their strokes were misplaced.

The rangers got into the spirit of the expedition, calling out for the meteorologist to identify a cloud or the ornithologist to identify a bird. The geologist was pleased to be able to point out igneous rock overlaying sedimentary rock on the face of a cliff we paddled passed. A mid-morning stop was made so the children could have a snack and investigate plants and animal tracks along the river bank.

As the day progressed, the students developed new "sub-specialties." Scott decided he would try to reproduce bird calls on his harmonica. Alex became fascinated with the red-spotted toads he encountered and announced he would also become the expedition's herpetologist.

One of the highlights of the day was the ambush of the raft that had been dawdling behind. Just around a bend in the river, those of us in the other four boats lay in wait behind some boulders and pounced on the laggard when it showed up. Squeals and laughter erupted through the canyon as the slow boat was halted, encircled, and splattered from all sides.

The lunch stop included a tasty dish prepared by one of the older girls who had chosen the job as corps cook. Afterward the students took time to record observations, create watercolors, and do some exploring. Finally the flotilla loaded up again and proceeded on down the river to Rio Grande Village.

In spite of the hot weather the explorers did not suffer any casualties to sunburn or heat stress. The water felt chilly even after the air temperature climbed to above 100 degrees, so the children splashed themselves and each other to stay cool.

The trip took only six hours, but the memories will last much longer. To top off such an exciting day, when we disembarked at Rio Grande Village the little kids and I were rewarded with the sight of a bobcat in the campground as we trudged up from the river bank to the bus.

The next day the little kids collated their field notes and drawings to produce a report of their trip for "the President" and copies of their reports were displayed on one of the breezeway bulletin boards for everyone to read.

Tanya summed up our perfect day in a drawing she made of the rafts setting off. In a speech bubble above one of the children in a raft, she wrote, "What a great field trip!"

The next Friday was the last day of school, and it was unlike any last day I remember from my own school years. I looked forward to summer vacation with anticipatory joy. On the last day my classmates and I were always in a state of controlled hysteria, hardly able to wait for the final bell to ring.

But my little scholars reacted differently. On the last day they seemed glum and agitated. Tanya's usually cheerful little face was solemn. Anna's mother reported that Anna had had several crying fits at home during the last week, and Anna told me she wished she could go to school "every day of my life."

During PE Lauren took her volleyball and sat down in a corner of the court, removed from all the other children.

"Lauren, I've noticed that you aren't playing with the others."

"I'm too sad to play."

"I'm so sorry. Do you know what has made you sad?"

"Yes. This is the last day of school. That really makes me sad."

Lauren, Anna, and their mother made a beautiful end-of-school gift for me, a quilted wall hanging. The butterfly and heart designs on it are made from the children's hand prints, little angel hands. The signature block includes Lauren and Anna's first day of school photographs and a lovely inscription. Needless to say, this is already one of our family treasures.

Teaching is hard work and I have always looked forward to summer vacation. But with a year like this one, the last day had me as teary-eyed as my girls, and just like Anna, wishing I could go to school every day of my life.

CHAPTER 11

How I Spent My Summer Vacation

O ur second summer in the park began, and we were staying home. There was no other place we wanted to be. We would have time for early morning hikes, for entertaining family and friends, and for reading in the shade of our backyard ramada with Mandy snoozing between us.

The Big Bend Natural History Association, headquartered in PJ, champions "the mission of the National Park Service in facilitating popular interpretation of the scenic, scientific, and historic values of Big Bend and encourages research related to those values." Among other things BBNHA conducts seminars, publishes books, maps, and guides, and supports the park's volunteer, Junior Ranger, and educational outreach programs.

To keep our gifted and talented certifications current, Texas teachers are required to take pertinent workshops every year. Since I had completed the G/T workshops being offered through the region educational center only months earlier, I checked the BBNHA's website for some other learning opportunities.

Many attractive seminars were offered, but I chose "Butterflies in Big Bend" and "Geology Jeep Tour." Fun for me. Information I could pass on to my students.

The butterfly seminar was conducted by a former Big Bend National Park Chief Naturalist, now retired. In addition to learning some butterfly basics, we spent three days in the field visiting different eco-spheres and elevations, hiking desert, river valley, mountains, and canyons. By seminar's end we identified 58 different butterflies, and I added two additional ones to my list later in the summer.

The geology tour was led by the park's resident geologist. After an orientation at the large topographical map in the visitor center, we climbed into Jeeps and spent the day examining limestone in canyons, sandstone on hills, and immersing ourselves in many other geological wonders. An earlier decision to become a geologist in my next life was strengthened and reinforced. Geology rocks!

As the long, lazy days continued, I found additional amusements including making a new friend. Shelley lives next door with Melissa and her husband. She had been adopted during the previous fall, inherited from their teenage nephew. When her new guardians began planning a backpacking trip, I volunteered to look after her.

Although she had a box of commercial food and she relished kernels of corn, every kid in PJ knew fresh, live grasshopper was her favorite cuisine. I began brushing up on a childhood skill.

Cats, dogs, horses, camels. Just above and between their eyes is the spot they most like petted and scratched. I wondered about Australian Bearded Dragons. I hadn't had much experience with reptile pets.

"Shelley, do you like being petted?"

She stopped smacking her lips and gave me a lengthy stare.

And I have known the eyes already, known them all –
The eyes that fix you in a formulated phrase...

"You know, Shelley, petted. Do you like being petted?"

When she cocked her little dragon head to one side, I reached over and rubbed that spot. The one just above and between her eyes.

"John, guess what? You'll never guess!"

"She bit you."

"No, she let me pet her on the head. She *closed her eyes* while I petted her!"

"Oh, please. Don't say it. Don't say she started purring."

Communicating with Shelley gave me an odd, unexpected delight. I began fancying myself a lizard whisperer. I'd walk through the front door calling her name. If she wasn't already waiting near her feeding mat, she'd come sashaying from under the couch to greet me. I'd feed her grasshoppers, one by one, and after the feasting and the smacking, she'd listen to my soliloquies, cocking her little head at appropriate junctures. Finally I would pet her and she would close her eyes.

Shelley *does* purr. It's just that humans can't hear sound at lizard frequency. Pity.

Developing a friendship with a lizard was something new, but I also made time for something old. Growing tomatoes and peppers is a well-loved, life-long hobby, and I had spent many weekend hours during the winter and spring preparing a garden plot. My Big Bend garden consisted of a dozen holes, twenty inches wide and deep, which I wrestled from the alluvial composite in our back yard. This composite consists of rocks ranging in size from peas to bread loaves that have washed down from the mountains and packed together. Excavating twelve holes was a challenge in which a hammer and chisel were my most useful tools. For every pound of rock I removed from the holes, I gleaned a tablespoon of soil. But once sculpted into the ground, I filled these spaces with wonderful organic things – rotted hay and manure from the mule barn, fruit and vegetable scraps from the kitchen, native grasses from weed-whacking ventures in the front yard, and the few tablespoons of soil that I had originally removed.

I recessed these materials about three inches below the natural ground level, thus creating basins so water poured into the depressions would descend directly to the root zones. This is a desert, after all. Water is precious and not to be wasted.

And I wasted not. The water I collected while waiting for shower and dishwashing water to get hot was enough to keep my twelve holes hydrated. To help keep the soil temperature constant and conserve moisture I covered the whole garden area with mulch four inches deep. Finally I outlined my garden with the rocks I had wedged from the twelve holes. Beautiful.

Nestled in the desert floor my tomato and pepper plants produced from mid-June until the first freeze in November. Many rewarding horticultural events are sprinkled through my life, but the pleasure of creating this garden, tending it, and harvesting its gifts is the happiest of my gardening experiences. Desert fruits are the most precious.

During these lazy days I finally had time to organize my classroom. It was crowded and cluttered with materials that had been accumulating for years, materials whose time had passed, materials I was not using. I emptied every cabinet, cupboard, shelf, and drawer. I cleaned, sorted, inventoried, and tossed. I hauled furniture and boxes to the storage building and garbage bags to the dumpster. Using the name of our imaginary playmate, Ted, I played on one of the classroom computers until I mastered all the new learning games. And when I peeled the 72 bonus words off the wall, I stuck them to the ceiling.

Of course my Friday evening dinner dates with John P. Seawell continued. With more time and less exhaustion we branched out, and by the end of the summer we had visited most of the restaurants within a 100-mile radius. Among our favorites are the Starlight Theater and the Phat Café in Terlingua, and in Lajitas, the Candelia Restaurant and the Thirsty Goat Saloon.

The Starlight Theater exists because of geology, because cinnabar was beneath the ground, because cinnabar ore yields mercury. In the 1930's the Chisos Mining Company built a movie theater near their company store to provide entertainment for the miners. The mine closed in the '40's, and the miners' village became a ghost town. At some point the theater roof was dismantled and sold for scrap. In the '70's the free spirits who moved into the area began using the theater as a gathering place. Dances, jam sessions, even live productions awakened this old structure without a roof – this abandoned adobe building that welcomed starlight.

In the '90's the roof was replaced, the interior was refurbished, and the building emerged as the Starlight Theater. In addition to being a gathering place and a venue for live music and theater, it is now also a restaurant and bar. It's a friendly, family place where Chad and Summer serve up the supper and make their guests feel at home.

Evenings, on the long porch that connects the theater to the company store, tourists mingle with locals for the two sunsets. The first, to the east, reflects the burgundy and rose hues that dwell among the Chisos Mountains, thirty miles away. The second, to the west, showcases the golden farewell of the fiery, desert sun. Pageant precedes night in Terlingua.

The Phat Café is hidden off the beaten trail in an adobe house nestled against a pale limestone bluff. Prayer flags and candles greet you in the courtyard; Nathan greets you at the door. The restaurant is small, dinner reservations are required, and fresh veggies come from the garden in the side yard.

Nathan trained in San Antonio at one of our favorite restaurants. After spending seven years polishing his culinary talents while leading treks in Nepal, he settled in Terlingua to bring Asian fusion to south county.

The year the Phat opened, we dined there almost every week. Besides enjoying the menu which revolves from Japanese, to Indian, to Chinese, to Thai, John P. Seawell was determined to help insure the success of this impressive restaurant, this amazing surprise in the desert.

Nathan rewards John's support by preparing alternate dishes when the menu features foods he is not allowed. John has never requested these substitutes. Nathan attends and anticipates, and we take great pleasure in the informal charm and culinary delights he creates.

In Lajitas we eat at the Candelia, but the real attraction is Cowboy Doug. He performs just across the breezeway at the Thirsty Goat. Doug sings and strums whatever we want to hear. This talented musician has an encyclopedic knowledge of singers and song. Between requests he and John discuss music and musicians. In detail. Into the night. Pull your chair closer, let's hum another round.

And it was during this second summer that I finally had time for those walks. Those solitary, contemplative walks I had imagined myself taking before I started teaching at San Vicente. I was fond of the mountain trails, but the desert was my darling. Open spaces. Sweeping vistas. Uncluttered. Clean.

Unlike the vast sand dune expanses and emptiness the word "desert" invokes, this part of the Chihuahuan Desert contains a respectable amount of vegetation. Amid the rock outcrops and the alluvial composites, a great variety of grasses, cacti, agaves, yuccas and scrub brush compete for space. Along areas where the sparse rainfall drains, golden-ball lead trees, Texas persimmons, mesquites, desert willows, buckeyes, several varieties of oaks, and a few cottonwoods can be found.

Throughout the summer I meandered up silent draws and down hushed dry washes. I used field guides to identify trees and grasses, and long quiet moments to identify mysteries in my heart.

Wind and water waltz with the earth and change it, yet the waltz can be measured, deliberate, slow. And it was this unhurried waltz that invited, that drew me in. In its gentle rhythm I loitered, I lingered. I was being nurtured by the desert, and I became ever more receptive to its offerings, greedy for its gifts.

Suddenly summer was over. Year Three began.

CHAPTER 12

Back to Business

Yesterday was the first day of school, and its onset brings changes to the life and rhythms of the park. Lights go on earlier in the housing area, and John and I have to use flashlights for our morning walk. During the day Panther Junction is quiet – except at recess and lunch time – and children no longer play catch in the streets or gather at odd hours on the school playground.

But mid-August also brings a more profound change in life rhythms, one that has nothing to do with our arbitrary school calendar. Summer comes early to Big Bend – May is usually our hottest month – but summer also releases its grip earlier than in the rest of Texas. Temperatures moderate and the rains we receive in June and July bring flowers and greenery to the mountains and desert. Life awakens from its summer torpor.

This time of the year, mid-August to mid-October, is known locally as the fifth season. It's a secret interlude, and a great time to be in the park.

On the school front, San Vicente ISD welcomed three new students this year. Jessie and Alicia are in the third grade and Don, who attended pre-k two mornings a week last year, is in kindergarten.

Other school news involves Janelle, our dance and gymnastics teacher. During the summer she was selected K–12 Educator of the Year by the Texas Association for Health, Physical Education, Recreation and Dance. She will be honored at their annual conference this fall, and we are all delighted that she has been recognized. She knocks herself out for the children of south county and she clearly deserves this tribute.

I resumed teaching the weekly after-school taekwondo classes I began last year. This Korean martial art, which emphasizes kicking, punching, flexibility, and balance, is great exercise for children and adults. The classes are free, everyone is invited, and teaching them compels me to keep up my own training.

The Lewis and Clark Corps of Discovery members are back on their journey. Yesterday during flag ceremony Lauren presented information about Sergeant Charles Floyd and shared some postcards she received from the Sergeant Floyd National Historic Landmark near Sioux City, Iowa. Sergeant Floyd died 200 years ago yesterday and was the only member of the expedition who died during the trip.

Anna and Tanya are my first graders this year. Born four days apart, wonderfully alike, wonderfully different. Tanya of the real world, Anna of the many worlds of her own creation. Tanya practical, patient, prudent, precise. Anna inventive, imaginative, innovative, inspired. Black to white. Ying to yang. Two strong personalities that challenge each other, complement each other, and combine to create an amazing learning environment. These young six-year-olds love school and love learning. They view weekends as unfortunate intrusions into their intellectual quests. (Occasionally there are actual tears on Fridays. "Can't we have school tomorrow? Please, Dr. Seawell, pleeese?")

Don is my kindergartener. Eager, enthusiastic, engaging. In addition to spending part of his day learning with the first graders, his schedule includes one-on-one time with John, with me, and with Peggy. He works hard, does his best, and never fails to return my smile. There is one other thing about Don. His parents leave for work at the Lodge long before school begins so he finishes his night's sleep, has breakfast, and dresses at the baby sitter's. Then he is the first to arrive in the classroom every morning. That gives us time to visit, to update, to switch cowboy boots to the correct feet, to re-button shirts, and to wash cocoa puffs off faces. Don and I are student and teacher, but at the beginning of the school day we are also grandmother and child.

Alicia, our business manager's daughter, was one of the two new little kids that I hadn't taught before. Beth commutes from Terlingua and Alicia had completed kindergarten, first, and second grades at the Terlingua school. For third grade Beth transferred her to San Vicente.

Throughout Alicia's school career, Beth had told us about her daughter's stubbornness, her willfulness, her hard-headedness. She had talked about the struggles the two of them had over homework. It created whining, complaining, and tears. At one point she announced that Alicia was "absolutely refusing" to learn to read, and she spoke of how vehemently her daughter hated school. In short, Alicia had received some rather bad press.

Given this background, I was somewhat hesitant to call on Alicia that afternoon when she came to my room for the first time, sat down at her desk, and raised her hand. She had come with the second grader and the six other third graders for social studies and Spanish. Her hand was still up. In a class of eleven children, I couldn't pretend I didn't see it. I smiled and took a deep breath.

"Alicia's hand is up. Let's all listen to Alicia."

"Dr. Seawell?"

"Yes?"

"You know that letter?"

"Yes?"

"That letter you sent?
"Yes?"
"Down there in Terlingua?"
"Yes?"
"That letter you sent me?"
"Yes?"
"I liked it."
"Oh. Good! I'm glad you liked it, Alicia."

Any apprehension I had harbored disappeared. I knew I would have no problems with this sweet child. She *liked* my letter. The first day of school is usually a bit stressful for students be they four-year-olds or high school seniors. A welcoming letter can set the scene and let them know their teacher is prepared for them, is expecting them, is looking forward to meeting them. New situations are always less daunting when we know what to expect. Besides, it's always fun to get a letter. Down there in Terlingua or any place else.

Since *scientific* social studies projects had become something of a specialty with us, I began the year by propelling my eleven students into a multi-level, multi-discipline study of manatees. Manatees in the desert? But, of course! The project was initiated by a cousin of mine who lives and teaches in Crystal River, Florida. During the summer when she saw a manatee mom and baby splashing in the canal that borders her back yard, she thought of our land-locked children and wished she could share the sight with them.

Her wish became her inspiration. Before school began she sent me two big boxes of manatee materials: books, brochures, maps, bookmarks, pens, pencils, jewelry, stickers, magnets, and T-shirts. She even included a toy manatee – a stuffy that squeaks when one of its flippers is pressed. (And which, for some inexplicable reason, the children named Baby Erica.)

It was easy to slip the study of manatees into our social studies class because Citizen Heroes are periodically featured in the K–3rd grade social studies textbooks. Citizen Heroes are ordinary people who do extraordinary things to make the world a better place.

Perfect. This year we would have our very own Citizen Hero, Ms. Ilaine Palmer. The extraordinary thing she does is teach children about the big, gray, whimsical-looking animals she sometimes sees frolicking in the canal behind her Florida home. These animals are on the endangered species list. These animals are manatees.

I took all the manatee materials to school and the fun began. In addition to devouring the information Ilaine sent and reading several books about manatees from the school library, the children developed a list of additional questions they had about these gentle giants, these sea cows, these mermaid prototypes. Then they began searching the Internet for answers.

By the time some of the children had branched out to dugongs and were mapping areas of the world where these manatee relatives can be found, we realized we were accumulating too much exciting data to keep to ourselves.

Therefore, we learned the proper procedure for approaching our student government and wrote a proposal requesting a designated Manatee Day on which to share our new knowledge with the community. The student council accepted our proposal, and after due course and proper deliberation, granted our request. In fact, since all the big kids were on the student council, they respectfully submitted an offer to help us with the project.

We grouped the little kids and assigned a big kid or two to mentor each group. A flurry of brainstorming ensued as each group considered ways to communicate the plight of the manatee. The children wrote scripts, worked up a power point presentation, created set designs, and generally stirred up dust with a storm of creative activity.

We had hoped to have a video conference with our Citizen Hero, but due to the hurricanes that kept sweeping across Florida in August and September, Ilaine's school was not in session or online consistently. We will try a video conference later, after the weather settles.

By the second week of September the manatee research was complete and the presentations were polished. Manatee Day arrived. The little kids donned their matching manatee T-shirts, and the big kids set up their video equipment. Then, with parents and community members in attendance, the show began.

One group did a mock television news program, reporting on the most recent hurricane in Florida and how it affected the manatees. They had created weather maps to use as visual aids and they also used photos taken from the Internet of a real life manatee rescue.

Three children conducted a television talk show, "You Have To Ask To Know," in which the hostess interviewed a manatee couple and their Baby Erica, asking them about their lives and problems.

One child and his older helper, using a clear, water-filled tank, a remote controlled model powerboat, and a plastic manatee, gave a demonstration to show how boats can injure the animals.

The grand finale was led by Anna and Tanya. These two first graders read their scripts in loud voices, with lots of emotion. In their presentation they discussed how worried they were about the plight of the manatees and wondered what they could do to help. They came up with the idea of making signs drawing attention to the problem and parading them through their town. Then all the children picked up the placards they had prepared ahead of time and paraded around the gym, singing a song composed for the occasion. After the parade they presented manatee bookmarks they had decorated to everyone in the audience.

Ours was a small splash in a small school, but the children were totally engrossed and our Citizen Hero had made the world a better place for manatees. The citizens of our desert community had learned more than they had ever imagined knowing about manatees, our students' parents were delighted, and the young scholars could tuck another successful scientific social studies project under their belts.

Shortly after Manatee Day, Scott, Don, and their parents made another trip to the Schriner Children's Hospital in Galveston for Scott's next ear surgery. We will keep in touch, send him cards and letters, and look forward to his return in two weeks. Bit by bit, centimeter by centimeter, his new ear is taking shape.

While Don was with his family in Galveston, Anna and Tanya moved full speed ahead and completed their first reading book. In addition to reading their assigned readers, they are both reading library books. These two youngsters are enthusiastic and excellent beginning readers and both are reading above the level expected at this time of year.

While Mr. John P. Seawell and I were cheering for the first graders' accomplishments in reading, I got an email from my friend, the camel man.

All right. I confess. I admit it. I *love* camels. *Lawrence of Arabia*, maybe. The long eyelashes, maybe. It matters not why, the point is, I *love* 'em! I rode them in Egypt, I rode them in Australia, but best of all, I rode them in Texas.

When I read *Texas Camel Tales* by Chris Emmet thirty years ago I yearned, *yearned*, for someone to reawaken this obscure chapter of history, revive this amazing saga, retell this incredible story. Doug Baum read *Texas Camel Tales* twenty-five years later and seized my wish from the ether. He reawakened, revived, and retells. I love him for it. I love his camels.

As the owner and operator of the Texas Camel Corps, Doug turned his fascination with Texas history and his admiration for these stately ships of the desert into a business. While we lived in San Antonio I had joined him and his other guests on two treks at Big Bend Ranch State Park, located about an hour upriver from Big Bend National Park. Now this young man was bringing his camels to West Texas again. Marvelous.

Large mammals with desert adaptations. Huge arid regions of the world. Astonishing experiment of a young nation. Hurricane-plagued, forgotten port on the Texas coast. I could feel a new scientific social studies project rolling in. Hands on, minds on. The camels are coming.

We began the project with some preliminary study, then journeyed to Dog Canyon in the northern part of the park about 25 miles from Panther Junction. Dog Canyon is so named because in pioneer days an ox hitched to a wagon was found there with a dog guarding it. No sign of a human was ever discovered.

Chewbacca, Up Close and Friendly

The educational tie-in, besides the geological and biological observations along the way, was the U.S. Army's camel experiment of the 1850's. Inspired by then Secretary of War Jefferson Davis, the Army imported camels from the Middle East, off-loaded them in Indianola, Texas, and conducted extensive testing with them to determine whether they would make better mounts under desert conditions than horses.

Although they eventually trekked all the way across the U.S. to California, and were well thought of by outside observers, opposition from cavalrymen and the onset of the Civil War killed the project. However, in 1859 Lieutenants William Echols and Edward Hartz entered this part of West Texas through a pass in the mountains now known as Dog Canyon. They lead a reconnaissance party which included 23 camels carrying rations for 33 days, baggage for 50 men, and 400 gallons of water. Their mission was to look for alternate supply routes for Army posts in the area; explore the Great Comanche War Trail where it neared the Rio Grande; find suitable sites for Army posts; and continue testing the practicality of using camels in the American Southwest.

We have been in our fall monsoon season, with almost daily showers, and I had feared the field trip might be washed out, but the Friday we had designated for the event was clear and mild, a beautiful day for a hike.

From the park road it is a two-mile hike to Dog Canyon and another half mile to the far side of the pass. Even though most of the children are accustomed to hiking, and I lead them through daily cardiovascular activities in PE, a hike of that distance ensured they would all be tired by the end of the day.

On the trek out, my little scholars were all business. They were identifying animal tracks, scat, birds, butterflies, reptiles, and insects; writing field notes; making sketches; taking photos. Dr. Dean was helping us again, keeping the children on their toes with, "Let's take a look at this. What do you think it could be?" at each new sighting.

Although the other adult on the trip is a law enforcement/EMT ranger, he was accompanying our little expedition in his other, more important, role. He is Jessica's father, and I was grateful to have him along on such an adventure.

The trail was damp, but since the soil in this part of the park is sandy and the terrain is flat, the hike to the canyon was easy. By late morning the outward bound nature walk had been completed.

A lucky occurrence upon entering the canyon was the appearance of two raptors, probably prairie falcons. They came off the cliff with swoops and shrieks then returned to perch high on the canyon wall and glower down at us. Dog Canyon isn't remote, but it's not one of the most popular hikes so birds are not often disturbed there. Our unexpected intrusion gave the falcons every reason to take offense.

When we were well into the canyon, a series of mystery tracks was sighted. The imprints in the sandy soil were two-toed and large, and the children were convinced they had been made by a camel. They *wanted* them to have been made by a camel. Dr. Dean said the tracks were probably made by a desert bighorn sheep, reintroduced in a neighboring State wildlife management area and now regular visitors to that area of the park. The children listened to the reality of the present, but in their heads I knew they were hearing the shuffle of camels' feet from the past.

We hiked through the pass and stopped for lunch at the canyon's mouth. As the children sat on the ground eating, they discovered how much fun it was to play in the damp sand. Soon they were building sand castles just as if they were at the beach. Then they noticed some large boulders along the canyon floor and decided they would make a great fortification. They named the area Fort Camel and began playing a game in which they were members of the Echols Expedition.

From the moment we had climbed onto the bus, Tanya had been thrilled with this outing. This little girl could hardly contain her joy.

"Dr. Seawell, this is the most wonderful day I have ever had!"

The fun continued on the return hike through the canyon as the children suddenly realized that water standing in pockets along the usually dry creek bed could be used for improvised water sports. Everyone's shoes, socks, and jeans soon became sand filled and water-logged as my little scholars spontaneously turned into regular kids on a wading spree.

Finally, during the last mile back to the bus, fatigue overtook the two first graders.

A Dog Canyon Afternoon

"I'm tired! I'm a statue."

With that Anna halted and assumed a pose with a raised arm and feet firmly planted.

"I can't move. I can't walk another step."

Tanya was more direct.

"I'm tired! I wish I had never come on this hike!"

Alas! Her most wonderful day ever had evaporated.

At this point the two men volunteered to carry the first graders backpacks and I pulled my ace in the hole out of my backpack, a large box of graham crackers. The graham crackers revived the first graders and gave the other children an energy boost as well. Eventually everyone made it back to the school bus, wet, tired, sandy, but unscathed.

Back at school I had the children take off their shoes and socks outside, then I hosed down their feet before we went into the classroom. For the rest of the afternoon they remained barefoot while we reviewed the impact camels had had on Big Bend history and wrote reports of our trip. Shamelessly, I left parents to deal with wet, sandy shoes and socks after school. Wading in rain puddles is one of the desert's rarest joys, a joy parents must simply recognize and accept.

Our study of camels in West Texas was to culminate at a celebration in Fort Davis commemorating the 150th anniversary of the founding of the Army post there. When the school calendar was changed, making that particular Saturday fall during our autumn break, half the little kids left the park with their families. But I went ahead with the field trip, and five of the children – coincidentally all girls – participated. Lisa, mother of Lauren and Anna, came along as the accompanying adult and I drove the bus, making the field trip entirely female – a girls' day out.

On the 2½-hour trip to Fort Davis, Lisa entertained the girls with origami lessons. She is their Girl Scout leader, and has a wealth of clever crafting ideas to impart. Creating flocks of colorful penguins and swans kept the girls busy during most of the trip.

Upon arrival at the old fort, we were greeted by Jessica's father. Although he is a law enforcement ranger at Big Bend, he was doing duty at Fort Davis – on horseback. Laura and Anna's father was there as well, with their little sister, Allison.

The exhibit that first attracted us was that of my friend, Doug. He was dressed as a Bedouin, and his companion was in a circa 1850 Army uniform. Doug had brought along three camels, two dromedaries and a Bactrian. (We had learned to distinguish between the two with a simple mnemonic: the D in dromedary has one hump; the B in Bactrian has two humps.) Since we had been learning about the camel experiment for days, the children already knew many things about the beasts and about their association with Fort Davis during the 1850's, but Doug was able to add a few more facts to increase their understanding.

My girls enjoyed petting these gentle animals and feeding them the apples and carrots we had brought along for that purpose. When some of the other visiting children crowded around, my girls shared their treats so they, too, could feed the camels.

Our next visit was to a Buffalo Soldier reenactment troop that had made the trip from Kansas. We listened as they sat around a campfire reminiscing about Army life in the 19th century and then watched spellbound as they did drills on horseback on the parade ground.

Children had not been overlooked in Fort Davis' celebration planning. There were a number of period games that youngsters were invited to participate in including three-legged races, hoop rolling, drop the handkerchief, and races with eggs in spoons. These antiquated games provided my modern girls with many laughs and lots of fun.

We were pleased to see that about a third of the people on the fair grounds were in period costume. On the porches and in the yards of the houses along officers' row various "pioneer" crafts people were making such things as candles, brooms, and horseshoes. In the kitchen behind one of the houses cookies were being baked in a wood-burning oven and small boys carrying basketsful wandered through the crowd passing them out.

Finding a Friend in Ft. Davis

We ate many of the warm cookies as we wandered from porch to porch looking at the craft demonstrations. The Army surgeon re-enactor particularly fascinated Lauren. Last year she had read and re-read a library book entitled *You Wouldn't Want to be Sick in the 16th Century Diseases You'd Rather Not Catch.*

Surprisingly, many of the 19th century medical instruments the Army doctor had were the same as those gruesomely described in the book. The girls were both repelled by and attracted to the live leech display the doctor had, and by that time they were completely into the spirit of living in the past.

At last, it was time to begin heading toward our bus for the long trip home. But a carding, spinning, and weaving demonstration was just too much for the girls to resist. Weaving is a craft Melissa had taught them in art class and they had all completed small projects and had experience weaving on a large loom. After they watched the demonstration, each girl was allowed to card some wool, wash it in homemade soap, and in the one concession to modernity, dye the wool in warm Kool-Aid. I finally managed to tear them away, short circuiting the drying process by putting the girls' damp wool "felts" in plastic bags for drying at home.

On the way to the bus, we made the obligatory stop in the gift shop, and the girls all bought pioneer bonnets. A quick visit to the small post museum was next, with the 2nd and 3rd graders who had participated in the Ft. Davis field trip two years earlier acting as docents for the younger girls. It was gratifying to note how much the older girls still remembered from their previous trip.

When we finally got on the road, it was so late that a dinner stop was inevitable. We dined in Alpine where the five little pioneer girls marched into the Pizza Hut wearing their bonnets. Apryl expressed the hope that the other customers would think they were actresses.

It was after eight when we finally arrived back home in PJ, making the 13-plus-hour trip an endurance record for Lisa and me, but one that I hope will remain a pleasant and lasting memory for the pioneer girls. Camels, new bonnets, and origami lessons all on the same day. Who could ask for anything more?

CHAPTER 13

Acknowledging Compliments, Cottonwoods, and Christmas

The uniqueness of our small school became routine. I took for granted that my two first graders were zipping through their reading books, understanding their math concepts, conducting science experiments, acquiring college-level vocabulary words, expressing their ideas in writing, and mastering the Instant Words. Anna and her father never missed a Wednesday evening NOVA program on PBS television, and I took for granted her Thursday morning reports. After her report we'd all log onto the NOVA website for "reviewing" and "taking notes."

I took for granted the luxury of tailoring a curriculum that supported Don's learning style and buoyed his enthusiasm for school. He was doing fine in math and we were proceeding with reading at his rate. As for science and social studies, Don amazed me with his ability to grasp "the big picture."

And, in addition to studying the material in their textbooks, weren't all the K–3rd grade social studies students in the nation reading daily entries from the Lewis and Clark journals? Hadn't they all learned that the corpsmen had to make moccasins by the dozens because shoes wore out so quickly in the prickly pear country through which they were tramping? Weren't all K–3rd grade students trying their hands at crafting moccasins? And weren't Spanish, music, and art a part of every K–3rd grade child's day?

But this year we had two new 3rd graders, and they were able to offer some perspective. Both had had experience in larger schools where students and teachers didn't have the luxury of small classes. For our new 3rd graders the uniqueness of a small school had not become routine. Their evaluations were candid and positive, and their evaluations made me smile.

First I heard about Jessie's assessment. Shortly before Halloween her father related the following after-school exchange between him and his daughter.

"So, how was school today? Was it an ordinary day?"

"No, Dad! There's no such thing as an *ordinary* day at this school!"

Then Jessie elaborated on the new project that had piqued her interest. This school is so small students' strengths and areas of curiosity can be identified and capitalized on. Few *ordinary* things happen to students whose uniqueness can be celebrated.

Alicia, that sweet child who had suffered such bad press, gave her appraisal at the beginning of a social studies class.

"Alicia's hand is up. Let's all listen to Alicia."

"Dr. Seawell?"

"Yes?"

"You know my other school?"

"Yes?"

"Down there in Terlingua?"

"Yes?"

"My other school down there in Terlingua?"

"Yes?"

"Well, at my other school down there in Terlingua we didn't have field trips, we didn't have journals, and, we *didn't* have desk fairies!"

"Oh. So … are these good things? Do you like having these things?"

"Yeah, they're good. I really like 'em. But we didn't have 'em down there in Terlingua."

The naturalist Edward Abbey wrote that where there is no joy there can be no courage, and without courage all other virtues are useless. San Vicente is just lucky about field trips, not every school has a generous field trip budget. But there are countless ways to create small, unexpected delights that tickle spirits and elicit smiles. A teacher's note in a student's journal. A desk fairy's reward for the neatness of a student's desk. Little gestures are easy to generate, and little gestures can create big joys.

Looking at our little school through the eyes of our two new 3rd graders reminded me of the uniqueness of our situation. True, my afternoon multi-level classes continue to be challenging, but now I know that meeting my students' individual needs is only a scientific social studies project away.

One of the concepts K–3rd grade social studies students are expected to learn is that good citizenship includes caring about and improving one's community. After doing some reading, discussing, and research, my little citizens choose to begin experimenting with tree-growing in an attempt to improve the park environment. If our experiments are successful, if we are able to propagate trees, we will begin a long-term riparian restoration project which involves planting cottonwood and willow trees.

Historically many of these trees grew along the creeks and washes in this area, but most of them were cut down to be used in the mining and ranching industries. The idea of propagating young trees in a greenhouse, then planting them in the park, was new, experimental, something that had not been attempted before. But the children, ever eager and optimistic, wanted to give it a try. Returning trees to the park would be their contribution to Project FLORA, the native grass restoration endeavor the 4th–8th grade students have been involved in for several years.

Shirley helped make arrangements for us to work with National Park Service personnel here in the park and with the Environmental Science Technician at Sul Ross State University in Alpine. After consulting with them we solidified a plan in which we would attempt to root tree cuttings in the greenhouse during the winter and plant them in the park in the spring.

In early November we launched our project. With the help of the park botanist, Dr. Joe Sirotnak, and Gabriel's mom, the students took cuttings from cottonwood and willow trees growing along a creek on the western side of the park. The day was hot so Dr. Sirotnak brought ice chests in which to carry the cuttings, and on our return to school, we transferred the cuttings to a refrigerator to keep them fresh.

Two days later we put our cuttings back into the ice chests and drove to Alpine where we worked with Ms. Patty Manning in one of the Sul Ross greenhouses. Ms. Manning taught the students how to tie cuttings together in 12-stick bundles, then pot the bundles using the six different rooting methods she had designed.

Back in the school greenhouse the children were to monitor the cuttings and fill out propagation records to determine which of the six planting methods was the most successful. When the cuttings rooted, the saplings were to be separated and transplanted into individual pots until it was time to plant them in the park.

Trees
By Tanya, Grade 1

We are planting trees because we want all the animals to come back. We are planting cottonwood trees. We also are planting willow trees. We will plant the baby trees at Croton Spring.

We are rooting our cottonwoods in different ways to see which way works best. The people who helped us cut and root our sticks were Ms. Manning, Mrs. Davila, Dr. Sirotnak, and Mrs. Turner.

We got our sticks on November 10, 2004. We put our sticks in pots on November 12, 2004. We hope our trees grow into gargantuan cottonwood and willow trees.

Making a Tree

By Lauren, Grade 2

We are doing our project. Here's how we are doing it:

1. we got cuttings
2. we went to Sul Ross State University to learn how to plant them
3. we will observe to see the ones that sprout best
4. we will all have our own cottonwoods and willows to plant
5. we will plant them at Croton Spring

We are starting the cuttings in the Sul Ross State University greenhouse. We are starting more in Big Bend National Park. Would you like to help?

Dr. Sirotnak, Mrs. Davila, and Mrs. Turner are helping us. We are very joyful for their help!

We are helping the cottonwoods so more animals will come back to Croton Spring and if all the animals come back, Croton Spring will be complete.

At first, on November 10, 2004, we got cuttings of cottonwood and willow trees. On November 12, 2004, we went to the greenhouse where Ms. Manning was to help us get the trees ready to be planted.

The reason we are doing this is because we are helping Big Bend National Park by planting more cottonwoods and willows at Croton Spring.

The Amazing Cottonwoods and Willows

By Apryl, Grade 3

We are planting cottonwoods and willows to improve the environment and restore the riparian habitat.

We are Citizen Heroes because we are planting more cottonwood and willow trees. Our names are: Apryl, Jonathan, Jessica, Jessie, Anna, Gabriel, Alicia, Tanya, Don, Alex, Lauren, and the teacher is Dr. Seawell.

We are doing this project at San Vicente Elementary School and Croton Spring. Our project started by getting cottonwoods and willows on November 10, 2004. That is when we collected the sticks. We are doing this project by getting cuttings from Alamo Creek. Then we're trying to root them in rooting cubes and soil. When we have sprouts we will plant them at Croton Spring.

The people who are helping us are Mrs. Turner, Dr. Sirotnak, Mrs. Davila, and Ms. Manning.

In addition to launching our tree-propagation project, November brought an activity we observe every year. Veterans Day is always special here, due to the efforts of one man. Travis Simmons is a retired Army NCO, and the only other military retiree in the park besides John. He is proud of his service, and especially proud of being a part of the Corps of Engineers. Now he operates the same construction equipment for park maintenance that he worked with during his Army years.

Twelve years ago Travis began organizing a ceremony to honor park veterans. Since then it has blossomed into a full-blown annual event complete with a guest speaker, participation by our school students and the students in Terlingua, and the individual recognition of each veteran.

This year's speaker was a retired Army colonel, George Sholly. During his service Colonel Sholly became a Middle East specialist, learning three languages and being posted to a number of attaché and intelligence assignments. He also commanded infantry units from company through brigade. His slide presentation revealed an interesting military background.

But there was another reason why Colonel Sholly's life experiences were fascinating to John and me. He is the son of the first Chief Ranger in Big Bend National Park, and he grew up here in the park during the 1940's and '50's. One of his interesting stories was about early schooling in the park. For his first three years there were not enough children to have a school so he and his brother were home schooled via the Calvert School in Baltimore. (I, too, am a former Calvert student. I was home schooled at the ranch in fifth and sixth grades. When John had an assignment in Baltimore he drove me past the Calvert building to show me where I had gone to school.)

When Colonel Sholly was in fourth grade (1948 I believe), there were five or six children in the Basin – enough to start a school. They used a building he describes as a "tar-paper shack," with one teacher in a single room. Since we have less than 20 students today, things really aren't that different, but it was compelling to hear about early school days in the park.

As often seems to happen, the end of the year arrived suddenly, unexpectedly, out of the blue. We began counting down December with the usual park activities. Once again, the school Christmas play was a smashing success. This year, after a fruitless search for an appropriate Lewis and Clark play, Melissa wrote one herself. The play began with the expedition preparing, then setting off from St. Louis, and concluded at Ft. Mandan in North Dakota where the explorers spent their first Christmas.

Since Melissa wrote the play herself, she was able to tailor scripts to fit her actors. And fit those scripts they did! Jessica, one of our most eloquent speakers, appeared in the role of Seaman, narrator of the saga. I don't have any idea how many lines this third grader had to memorize, well over 200, but memorize them she did, and dressed in a big, black, shaggy Newfoundland dog costume, she delivered them in a strong, articulate, expressive voice.

One of the most memorable roles was that of Big White, one of the Native American chiefs who interacted with the explorers. Anna appeared in this role and because she is such a tiny little six-year-old, John P. Seawell and I (along with all the other adults in her circle) had coached and coached that she would have to speak in a *very* loud voice in order to be heard.

When Anna came on stage in the headdress that Jonathan had fashioned we all had to smile. The headdress was almost as tall as she is! She spoke her first line in a somewhat subdued tone, then a light bulb seemed to go on and she boomed out her second line in a voice that rang deep and clear. From that moment on, the audience was hers. This tiny little girl with the rich, powerful voice stole the show.

All the students did a great job. Lauren appeared as Sacagawea with Gabriel as her husband Charbonneau, and Jonathan as her long-lost brother Cameahwait. Most of the other little kids were Native Americans from various tribes. Everybody delivered their lines and songs and dances like the seasoned actors they have become. After spending several years in this little school with its many public performances, these children will probably never fear speaking before crowds.

On the last day of school before Christmas vacation I walked my students to Melissa's room for art, then I continued down the sidewalk to the greenhouse. We hadn't had time to check our cottonwood cuttings for a few days.

Small red buds were present on many of the cuttings. A few tiny green leaves were visible, as well. Every pot had cuttings with red buds and green leaves. All six of our carefully recorded rooting methods appeared to be working.

When the dismissal bell rang I was standing outside Melissa's classroom door when she released the K–3rd grade students. The big sign I held read,

"Your cottonwoods are sprouting!" With excited shrieks, the children bounded to the greenhouse to see this miracle for themselves.

When my mother had asked what I wanted for Christmas, I said one-gallon pots. She gave me 100 of them. She tied them together with a big red bow.

Performing for Lewis & Clark at Ft. Mandan

CHAPTER 14

Hard-working Citizen Heroes

As the second semester began, the K–3rd grade PE students resumed their training for the National and the Presidential Physical Fitness Awards with renewed enthusiasm. They had worked toward these goals a few minutes every morning since school started in August, and by January most of them had passed the requirements at the Presidential level for push-ups and the V-stretch. Four children had passed the requirements at the National level for the mile run and several more were within seconds of achieving this goal. The standards for the National level are high and for the Presidential they are even higher, so students must work hard to meet them.

In January our gymnastics and dance teacher received another tribute. Janelle was named the Southern District K–12 Dance Teacher of the Year by the American Alliance of Health, Physical Education, Recreation and Dance. In March she will be honored during their conference in Little Rock, and the thirteen-state Southern District has submitted her name as their nominee for National Dance Teacher of the Year. (Although Janelle was not chosen for the national award, she was one of the four finalists for the title. It was gratifying that the work of someone from this small, remote community was acknowledged in a national forum.)

The tsunami that occurred in the Indian Ocean during the holidays held my students' attention for several days after we returned to school. We discussed it at length, found the affected areas on our maps, and spent many social studies minutes online learning about it and its aftermath.

With eleven young children using laptops, the classroom always becomes lively. I initiate these sessions by writing a question or two on the board, along with a URL as a starting point, but as soon as the students begin clicking on related links, a competition for the most amazing photos and stories arises.

"Oh! Wow! Look at this! Everybody come look at this!"

Then the two or three students who happen not to be mesmerized by the spot they are visiting rush to look over the shoulder of the student who has found the breathtaking site.

"Oh, cool! How did you get there? Which link did you click?"

I am never sure what my role should be when the children do individual research. I am eight light years behind in the use of technology in the classroom, remember? But this dispersal of information seems to be a good thing. If keeping students engaged is educationally sound, sharing Internet sites is a perfect way to do it. If creating excitement in a classroom is positive pedagogy, sharing Internet sites is hard to beat.

But our classroom does get noisy with all the "Wow's!" And the children do get active with all that hurrying around to peer over each other's shoulders. Semi-controlled chaos. Borderline bedlam. Perhaps I should at least have the decency to close our window blinds when they all have their laptops abuzz. You know, just to prevent passers-by from becoming alarmed because of my obvious lack of classroom management skills.

In addition to the pandemonium created by awesome Internet sites being discovered by eleven young researchers, the potential for simultaneous computer crises is ever present. When they were first assigned their laptops, my students got frantic and I got harried when multiple technical problems arose. Finally, to avoid the possibility of total turmoil in the classroom, we worked out a checklist of crises procedures the children could follow while awaiting my help. The ultimate solution, which is to be invoked only after completing the crises procedures followed by a two-minute wait, is for the student who is stuck somewhere in cyberspace to join a friend who isn't having trouble.

I have my own answer to multiple technical problems. Between troubleshooting events, I maintain my perspective by retreating into the peaceful eye of the storm which Lauren creates at her desk. No matter how many glitches, alarms, and cries for help are swirling around her, this little second grader is the epitome of tranquility. I am calmed and amused when I stand behind her and listen as she coos her way to her goal. Her quiet outpouring of self-guiding talk stops only when she pauses to read something on her screen.

"Oh, this is interesting. Now I'll just click on this link and see what else I find. Oh, I love having my own laptop. This is a great photo. Wait, I better read this story. Oh, this girl saved people's lives. Quite interesting. Now I'll look for some more information. Tsunamis are extremely dangerous. Mmmm, here's another great photo."

Like many people throughout the rest of the world, my students wanted to help the victims of the tsunami disaster. They choose to raise money with a bake sale, and with much help from Alex's mom and Lauren and Anna's mom, they organized the sale and collected $603.53. Next they investigated several aid organizations and sent their contribution to the one that best matched their ideas about assisting disaster victims.

While we worked with the tsunami project, our cottonwood and willow cuttings were thriving and, still tied together in 12-stick bundles, were becoming masses of tangled green foliage. In mid-January Ms. Manning came down from Alpine to show the children how to separate the bundles and transplant each cutting into an individual pot. We were pleased to discover that as the cuttings had been developing leaves, they had been developing roots as well. With care and remarkable patience the children transplanted 46 healthy, vigorous cuttings into individual pots.

Ms. Manning Instructs the Citizen Heroes

A few days later, we assembled in the greenhouse after school. We were taking turns watering the saplings. In addition to the cottonwoods, we also have a dozen hearty willow saplings, but the children are focused on the cottonwoods. I'll follow their lead. A riparian restoration should include both kinds of trees. Maybe we can concentrate on willows next year.

"I just had an idea. Would caring for a sapling on your own be interesting? Would anyone like to take care of a tree at home?"

"Yes!"

Citizen Heroes Transplanting Cottonwoods

"It would be a big responsibility. You'd have to remember to water it and record changes."

"Can we have our own propagation sheets?"

"Sure. Then you can bring your propagation sheet and your little tree back to school when it's time to plant it and we'll compare notes."

"What if something happens? Like our tree dies or something?"

"Well, this is a scientific experiment. We're trying to help the saplings become strong, but we don't know if they'll grow in pots. And even if they do, we don't know if they'll survive when we plant them in the wild. We're experimenting. We don't know what our outcome will be."

"But if it turns out good, we'll be Citizen Heroes!"

"Well, I think you're already Citizen Heroes, whether it turns out well or not. You're trying to restore a riparian habitat, and you've already done a lot of work."

"It'll be better if it turns out good."

"True, but remember what Ms. Forsythe said: even if you end up with only one nice cottonwood at Croton Spring you will have improved the area."

"Jonathan, what were the birds that like cottonwoods?"

"Probably most birds *like* them, but vermillion flycatchers and summer tanagers like to build nests in them."

"Don't forget about the mourning cloak butterfly. The females lay their eggs on cottonwood leaves."

"I really, really like butterflies, Dr. Seawell."

"Me, too, Alicia. If you continue to like them, you might decide to become a lepidopterist when you grow up."

"That's a great idea, Alicia! You could be a lepidopterist!"

"I might."

"I hope our trees grow."

"Fingers crossed, Scientists!"

"I thought this was a social studies project."

"Oh, it is! It's another one of our famous *scientific* social studies projects."

"Oh, yeah."

"You know what I noticed? Every cutting we had in our bundles rooted. How can we use that information?"

"We don't need bundles. Next year we can just give each cutting its own pot from the beginning. One less step."

"Yeah, one less step!"

"And we can use whichever rooting medium we want. They both worked."

"And we don't have to use either one of the rooting hormones. Cottonwoods will root without rooting hormones."

"Well, Kiddoes, we've learned a lot about growing cottonwood trees. Maybe we'll concentrate on willow trees next year. We sort of neglected them this year."

"Let's not get so many cuttings next year. This is a *lot* of work."

"Yeah, being Citizen Heroes is a *lot* of work!"

True, it takes a lot of work to be a Citizen Hero. My own Citizen Hero, Mr. John P. Seawell, is an example of this. Because he does so much work, our first graders celebrated their 200 Word Party the last week in January. Anna and Tanya were feted with a cake baked and decorated by Tanya's mother, and parents and younger siblings of both girls joined us in marking their accomplishment. Besides being able to recognize instantly the 200 most frequently used words in the English language, the girls have begun the fifth book in their reading series and continue to be avid library book readers.

Don was recognized at the Word Party as well. He can already read some of the words on the Instant Word List and he has learned all the letters in the alphabet.

The 200 Word Party

Beginning during the first year we lived in the park, John kept in touch with family and friends through email. He often wrote about the children and the activities that were occurring at school. The following account is a school-related excerpt from one of his emails. His subject line was "My Friend Don."

This year I've volunteered in Pat's classroom four mornings a week, working with her one kindergartner and two first graders. I have become close with all three, but little Don has become a special friend. Don is the younger brother of Scott – the boy who is undergoing surgeries at the Shriner Children's Hospital in Galveston to construct external ears.

I started working with Don two mornings a week last year when he was in pre-k and we hit it off right away. He dubbed me his "fav-wute teacher."

Although he's a bright little boy, his progress in pre-reading goes slowly. Pat tells me he's learning at his own pace, age isn't a perfect indicator of school readiness, and I'm to remain patient and cheerful. It's encouraging that whatever task we tackle, Don does his level best, and we are as proud of each success as we would be of Olympic gold.

Every morning, as I walk the short distance from our house to the school while the children are having their physical education class, he shouts out to me, and Pat allows him to break from the class so he can run to give me a hug. When it's time for me to leave, I get another hug from him and one from Tanya. (Anna, "the famous artist," is far too sophisticated for such vulgar displays of affection.) Don always asks, "Can you come back after lunch?" even though he knows that I will not.

One day he was occupied with one thing, and I was distracted with another. Somehow, I left the classroom without his hug. I was halfway home when Pat shouted out for me to wait, then Don came streaking across the playground to give me my hug. Pat said he burst into tears when he realized I had left, so she sent him out to catch me.

I have had a few successes and kudos in my modest careers as an Army officer and a teacher, but none can top the twice daily hugs I get from my friend, Don. JPS

Our winters in the park are so pleasant and mild that the occasional inclement day shocks and surprises. One dark, stormy morning I got to school early and cranked up the thermostats in my room and in the gym. Don arrived in short sleeves. ("Where's your nice warm jacket?" "I didn't know it was going to be *cold!*") I dug out the "school jacket" for him. Shirley arrived bundled up from head to toe. ("I'm *freezing!*")

Icy winds howled through the breezeway, it began to rain, and we all stepped into my classroom for flag ceremony. The big kids ogled last year's Bonus Words on the ceiling and used some of them to create entertaining soliloquies during their fifteen seconds of vocabulary-building fame.

The guidance counselor we share with Terlingua arrived and was to meet with my students that morning. I needed to return some materials to the library so I headed that way.

Sleet was accumulating along the edge of the porch. I took the shortcut through the teacher work room and saw the homemade cinnamon rolls Shirley had set out by the coffee pot. I popped one in the microwave. The greenhouse is only a few feet from the front door of the library so I dashed over to check the saplings.

Inside the greenhouse it was cozy and snug. Sleet was bouncing off the roof, but I was surrounded by dozens of lush, little cottonwoods, and I was eating a warm cinnamon roll. It occurred to me that I was living my life deliberately. Just like Thoreau. My eyes got misty. Life does not get much better than this.

During the first week in February, the K–8th grade classes began preparing for an extravaganza we called The San Vicente Corps of Discovery II Lewis and Clark Perspectives: Past and Present. This event was to be held during the last week of February, time of our annual Open House. The exhibition would be set up in the gym where the beautiful, hand-painted, wilderness backdrop created by Melissa and several of the other artists in the community had been hanging since the Christmas play.

Melissa's social studies students were working on a timeline to delineate the years of the expedition. Each student was summarizing important events and creating visuals to include on the timeline. The individual components would be ordered and mounted, and the time line would stretch completely around the inside walls of the gym.

Peggy's language arts students were writing Haiku poems about the lives and adventures of Lewis, Clark, Sacagawea, Seaman, and other important figures of the expedition. These would be mounted on freestanding bulletin boards at one end of the gym.

The younger students were preparing individual presentation boards using materials they had collected from state and national parks along the Trail. The presentation boards would be set up back-to-back down the middle of the gym.

In addition to opening our doors to our parents and the park community, we also invited students from Terlingua, Presidio, and Marathon Elementary and Middle Schools to visit our exhibition.

Our plans for this event were elaborate. The students would appear in costume; the Lewis and Clark quilt they had designed would be on view; books and other printed materials they had gathered would be displayed; the keelboat built by one of the older boys and his dad would be exhibited; re-enactments would be staged; all students would deliver oral presentations; and Seaman, aka Mandy, would be present to perform his three famous tricks.

Everyone was invited, everyone was welcome. Light refreshments would be served.

Our classroom came alive with presentation boards, maps, photos, brochures, and pictures as the students sorted through the materials they had received from the many parks they had contacted the previous year. Design and layout decisions were made and executed; captions were planned and created; scissors, tape, and glue were manipulated. Along with these activities, oral presentations were scripted and rehearsed.

When word came that the Marathon kindergarten through fourth grade students would visit our campus on the first day of Open House, and the Terlingua fifth graders would visit on the second day, the little kids became ever more excited. Few things inspire children as much as opportunities to interact with members of their own peer group, and my students were elated over the possibility of having so many visiting youngsters on our campus.

With all these guests coming to call, Mandy, aka Seaman, needed to be in top form physically and mentally. The bath, the trimming of stray hair protruding from between toes, the ear cleaning, and the brush-out went well. She was a glossy, gleaming beauty. Next came a review of her tricks. We practiced in the gym on a weekend.

The keelboat, built onto part of an old canoe, had been housed in the gym ever since the Christmas play. It jumped out at me when I opened the door to the gym.

"Mandy! Let's do your tricks in the keelboat! How dramatic is that?"

San Vicente ISD
Presents

The Corps of Discovery II

An Exhibit of
The Lewis and Clark Expedition

Timeline, artwork, and Exhibits,
including a real Keelboat!
Live performances by Lewis, Clark, the Corpsmen,
The Indians, and Seaman the Dog!!!!

February 28th at San Vicente School
Call for reservations or alternate dates

I rummaged through the yoga mats until I found the oldest, most disreputable one, and laid it on the floor of the keelboat to give my big girl some traction. Then we both hopped into the boat and reviewed her three tricks: shaking hands, lying down, and "whispering." Because it was oral, rather than visual, I always asked Mandy to perform her whispering trick twice, just in case the audience had not heard her the first time. After the second whisper we would hop out of the boat and sashay to the door.

Mandy and I practiced the whole routine a couple of times: walking into the gym, hopping into the keelboat, executing the tricks, hopping out of the boat, and exiting the gym. Enormous fun for both of us.

Open House Week arrived and our visitors appeared. We organized the guests into small groups and each group began a stroll around the gym. The guests paused to examine the exhibits and listen to the presentations as they walked, and all group tours terminated at the refreshment table.

After everyone had partaken of refreshments, the enactments began. In one scene the two older boys who had played Lewis and Clark in the play, discussed their purchase of the Newfoundland dog they had named Seaman. On cue Mandy and I appeared and hopped into the keelboat. I would explain the advantage of a trick to the audience, then Mandy would execute the trick.

Since few of the visitors had ever seen a Newfy, her size alone impressed them, but they were astounded upon discovering that she was also brilliant. Her first two tricks brought hearty rounds of applause. Then it was time for her whisper. And it was the whisper that brought down the house. Gasps of astonishment followed her first whisper. Her second whisper set off peals of laughter and shouts of glee.

Oh, my! This trick is a winner. We'd better do it one more time.

"Mandy, whisper!"

"Are you kidding me, Mom? My contract calls for two whispers and two whispers only. That's what you requested. That's what we practiced. I'm outta here!"

And with that, she hopped out of the keelboat and pranced to the exit, stage right. Performance over! That's all folks! Nothing more to see here!

Mere mortals can neither understand nor alter the enigma that is artistic temperament. Mandy was happy to take it again from the top, but there were to be only two whispers per performance. Period. Dot. I was left to giggle, accept, and, yes, follow the lead of my Newfoundland.

During those moments when they had not been preparing for the Lewis and Clark exhibition, my social studies students had begun learning about our history as a nation of immigrants. To supplement the information in our texts, we were using a series of library books called *Coming to America*. Each book

told the story of a different immigrant group and contained excellent historical photographs. Using these books, each student chose one of the groups to
study more closely.

Mandy in Her Starring Role as Seaman

When Shirley learned that the children were particularly interested in
the ethnic recipes that were in the books, she suggested we add a little flavor
to our study of American immigrants by having the students prepare some of
the recipes. By exploring several grocery stores and supermarkets in Odessa,

and an Asian market in Midland, she was able to find most of the exotic ingredients called for in the recipes. For those ingredients that were not available she purchased substitutes she thought would work almost as well.

I alerted the parents about the project. Then each student took home the book about the group he or she had chosen along with the ingredients for preparing a dish associated with that group. I asked the parents to browse through the book with their child and, at their convenience, supervise the preparation of the special dish. I suggested that samples be brought to school to share with classmates, if possible.

We were sorry to lose Jessie while we were working on this project. She moved with her family to New Mexico. During the two weeks after her departure my students prepared ethnic foods in such generous quantities that we were able to share our bounty with the big kids. Before serving the food they had prepared, the children would tell us a few things they had learned about the immigrants to whom the food was special.

Quite cheerfully we sampled Exploding Chinese Moon Cakes, Russian Honey Cookies, Irish Soda Bread, French Mardi Gras King Cake, Jewish Poppy Seed Cookies, Japanese Kuri Kinton, and Italian Wedding Cookies. In some cases the students had so enjoyed preparing the foods that they made another batch for their families.

With all these desserts being served at school, I thought we might need some intense exercise to balance out the extra calories we were consuming. I poked about in our PE shed and found just the thing.

Spring, baked goods, and jump ropes are made for each other. Although jumping rope is a new challenge for several of the students, two of their classmates answered my call and began giving lessons. Before the end of the week everyone could do several of the basic jumps and many of the students have begun attempting some of the fancier steps. Alicia has been teaching the single bounce step that boxers use for staying in shape, and Apryl has been teaching the crisscross jump that makes the jumper look like a real professional. The jump rope rhyme book Anna brought in from her home library has added much fun and silliness as we work on our coordination and cardiovascular health. Few things are as welcome as a cool spring morning filled with laughter and giggles.

As soon as our Lewis and Clark exhibition came to a close, we focused once more on our tree-growing project. The students returned the cottonwoods they had been caring for at home and compared propagation records. For his home tree Jonathan had chosen a sapling that had developed a few roots but no leaves. He cared for it properly, but it never developed leaves. By the end of February the cutting had become desiccated and Jonathan declared it officially deceased. But all of the other saplings had thrived.

Due to a misunderstanding, or a change of heart, two of the children thought the home trees were to be planted at *home* when the appropriate planting date arrived. The idea of planting their beloved saplings at Croton Spring was causing them anguish and tears. I capitulated.

...I am ...a bit obtuse;
At times, indeed, almost ridiculous –
Almost, at times, the Fool.

Lauren compromised and planted her sapling on the school campus near the tennis court. On May 2, her 8th birthday. The Birthday Tree.

The other home tree was planted at *home*. (Student's name being withheld.) If criminal charges stemming from this "removing flora from the park" incident are brought against me, I will have to insist that the sapling be returned and planted at Croton Spring. Meanwhile, the little cottonwood is alive and well. It is flourishing in the yard of a home on a mesa facing the Chisos Mountains. Down there in Terlingua.

March 4, 2005
Dear Parents,
Tree Planting Alert! The K–3rd grade students have approximately 30 cottonwood saplings thriving in the greenhouse, plus several more that children have been nurturing at home. We are scheduled to plant the saplings the week after Spring Break, on the afternoon of Friday, March 18th.
If hiking to Croton Spring packing a shovel and a couple of saplings sounds like an amazing adventure you wouldn't want to miss, consider yourself cordially invited to join the class and become a part of this historical event.
Thank you and many hugs,
Pat

Tamarisk, also called salt cedar, is a tree native to North Africa, the Mediterranean, and the Middle East. It was imported about 150 years ago to be used as a windbreak and a method of controlling soil erosion. As with many introduced species, this plant not only thrived, it took over. Tamarisk has replaced thousands of acres of riparian habitat throughout the Southwest, eliminating the native plants and causing the animals that depended on the native plants to move on or die. In the 1980's the park restoration team began working to rid the park of this invasive tree. Croton Spring is one of the areas that has been reclaimed, and while native grasses and shrubs have returned, cottonwoods and willows have not. Ten young Citizen Heroes are now on the case.

"Seat belts, Everyone!"

"Yes, Ms. Frizzle."

Magic School Bus fans, all, we were off on another escapade as the Cottonwood Caravan began the ten-mile drive to the Croton Spring trailhead. Our magic school bus was crowded with children, their backpacks, and dozens of verdant, flourishing saplings. Precious cargo.

Dr. Sirotnak was helping us again. He led us in his truck packed with shovels, spades, buckets, and the additional saplings that we couldn't squeeze into the bus. Behind us came three or four private vehicles carrying parents and other volunteers willing to contribute time, as well as the considerable effort needed to carry trees and equipment over a rugged, ¾-mile trail to the wash where the saplings were to be planted.

"Water? Hats? Sunscreen? Gloves?

"Check! Check! Check! Check!"

"Cottonwoods?"

"Check!"

Croton Spring Trailhead

Then we were off down the sometimes steep, always rocky trail with our thirty-nine cottonwood saplings and all the necessities for planting them, including moms, dads, younger siblings, a group of park visitors, and a feature writer from a local newspaper.

Once into the wash, Dr. Sirotnak designated a prime planting area about 50 yards long and gave us some planting tips and a demonstration. Then we set to work. As each tree was planted Dr. Sirotnak entered its location into his Global Positioning System along with the name of the child who had planted it. When the students return to picnic under the cottonwoods with their grandchildren they will be able to locate the trees they planted. Forward planning at its finest.

Each child/adult team planted three trees. The six "orphan trees" were planted by the whole group and entered as "adopted" in the GPS record. In the event that a child's personal trees do not survive, he or she can picnic under one of the adopted trees. All the bases have been covered.

After the holes were dug and the trees settled into position, the children dipped water from the pools in the wash and poured it into the basins they made around each of their trees. With care, the saplings were straightened and the sand around the tiny trunks was patted down and adjusted. Then more water was added. Finally, hot and tired, but happy, the cottonwood crew collected the tools, the buckets, and the empty gallon pots, gathered up the backpacks, bid goodbye to the trees, and began the hike back to the vehicles waiting at the trailhead. The green leaves of thirty-nine saplings danced and waved behind us. Mission accomplished.

Mission Accomplished

CHAPTER 15

Changing Directions As the Beat Goes On

W hen John and I embarked on this West Texas adventure three years ago we had been in downsize mode for several years. We had planned to return to San Antonio when we left the park, and visions of a small River Walk condo danced in our heads.

Those visions no longer dance for me. Tucked into the quiet spaces between the flurry of school and home activities tiny secrets have been surfacing. Specks of information. Puzzle pieces. Riddles. Revelations. I've lined them up, rearranged, connected the dots, and acknowledged that concealed beneath the excitement of my headlong dashes to that next home, next job, next adventure, a part of me has longed for permanence, yearned for place. In the niche where dreams dwell and honesty lies hidden, my life, my essence, my being, everything that is me, has felt temporary, transitory, and unreal. Behind the laughter and the smiles I have spent a lifetime longing for a *real* life, *my* real life. I have ached for it to begin.

This West Texas desert is my permanence, is my place. From its sunsets, its silence, and its solitude my real life is emerging. Buried emotions pulled me here. Acknowledged emotions beg me to stay.

If it were possible, John and I would not leave our little house in the park. But one cannot live in the park unless one works in the park, remember? And the work, although we love it, is slowing us down. And the children, although we adore them, are increasing their pace. Distressing, but inevitable, we know it is time to retire. Again. Teaching young children is a young person's job.

We bought twelve acres in a subdivision near Alpine and began planning the small house we would build there. I have friends and family members who never miss a home show, visit open house events, read *Architectural Digest*, hang out at Home Depot, clip house photos from magazines, and plan dream homes. I am not one of these people. Designing and building a home is not something I had hoped to do. Designing and building a home is something I had hoped *never* to do. We engaged an architect, but the process proceeded slowly.

When people make the decisions to buy property, build a home, reset-tle themselves, and reorder their lives, one would suppose thorough thought, conscientious consideration, and prudent planning have informed their decisions. One would, in fact, presume these people knew what they were doing. Not necessarily.

We changed our plans. Again. John sent an update to our family and friends. He titled his message "Completely Unhinged!"

> Most people are satisfied to celebrate Easter with a chocolate bunny and a boiled egg or two, but not Pat and John P. Seawell. Oh, no. Not us. We celebrated Easter by buying a new, twenty-two acre home site.
>
> It all began Friday when Pat got a call from her friend Amy. "Have you started construction yet?" was the question that followed "Hello." Returning from a New Mexico trip via Alpine, Amy and her husband had visited a development that Pat and I hadn't bothered to look at because the area isn't too attractive from the road. We didn't realize that the portion being sold is in the middle of an 11,000 acre ranch and the views in that particular area are spectacular.
>
> We had already purchased twelve acres elsewhere, but we made an appointment for Saturday just to look around, just to see the thirty acres Amy and Jeff liked.
>
> Two hours after our arrival we had signed a contract. Besides the scenic beauty, the higher altitude (5,000 feet), the wildlife, and the rocks (Pat's requirement), we like the privacy, the underground utilities, and the fact that the development is on a working ranch. Homeowners get an agricultural exemption on the portion of their land not fenced in for the house site. The result is that we will pay the lowest real estate taxes we have ever paid.
>
> Words cannot express Pat's delight at the idea of living on a ranch again. When she married a soldier instead of a cowboy, she thought she had forfeited her ranch aspirations forever. Now we'll have the best of worlds — the rewards of a ranch without the hard work. In addition to her love for wildlife and wide open spaces, I've now learned that Pat has a special place in her heart for cows, especially the black variety that populate this property. She tells me these are the animals that fed and clothed her, bought her shoes, and sent her to college.
>
> For those of you who have suspected it all along, I submit this latest property-purchasing incident as proof that the Seawells are, indeed, unstable. But look for yourselves and see if you, too, wouldn't go crazy for this place: www.sierralarana.com JPS

Having exhausted myself with dog-training in a keelboat, tree-planting in a creek bed, and life-altering relocation decisions and revisions, I sought solace. Serenity. A place to unwind. I could use a hike in the Chisos.

A year ago I went on an overnight "backpacking for women" trek sponsored by the Big Bend Natural History Association and led by my friend and colleague, Melissa. The plan was to hike to a campsite on the South Rim of the Chisos Mountains, set up camp, enjoy the sunset, prepare and eat dinner, stargaze, then retire to the tents. My friend, Amy, came out from San Antonio to participate in this event.

Melissa has lived, taught, hiked, and backpacked in this park for the past seventeen years. Her strength and stamina are legendary, but this was the first time she had led a group of novice backpackers, and she misjudged the abilities of some of us.

Two of the adventurers were young and energetic. They were able to set and keep a pace that would have insured their arrival at the designated campsite on schedule.

But then there was Charlene (who was celebrating her 70th birthday with this trip) and me. We mature Americans found marching seven miles almost straight up over rough, rocky terrain with heavy packs on our backs rather challenging. The pace we set got us about halfway to the South Rim by nightfall.

And, somewhere in between, but much closer to the "youngsters" than the "older ladies," was Amy. The pace she set had her hiking alone.

A couple of hours into the trip Melissa's group of five was strung out over four or more miles along the trail. And Melissa was hiking back and forth among her charges. I begged her to stop returning to check on Charlene and me. I assured her we would be fine. But she is too conscientious to agree to such a proposal.

On Charlene and I trekked, and on. By the time we reached Boot Canyon, a particularly dicey area that includes crossing back and forth over a stream via slippery, moss-covered boulders, we had to use our flashlights to spot the trail. Night comes early in the canyons.

Meanwhile, up on the Rim, Melissa had declared a slow hikers emergency and had helped the youngsters set up camp at the first campsite they reached (a mile short of the campsite she had reserved for this expedition).

By then it was getting dark on the Rim, and Amy was still somewhere alone on the trail. Well, not exactly alone. She was in the company of the bears, the mountain lions, the bobcats, and all the other Chisos creatures of the night.

Once Melissa had the two youngest women settled, she headed back down the trail, met Amy, hiked with her to the campsite, then started back down the mountain to find Charlene and me, the oldest members of her expedition.

On Charlene and I trekked, and on. Charlene a tiny, little lady packing a 35-pound pack; me a large, robust lady packing a 55-pound pack.

By this time it was pitch dark and the three city dwellers back at the campsite began hearing strange noises in the woods. How much adrenaline does it take to create an adventure?

Ever calm and cheerful, Melissa finally located us, but it was after nine o'clock by the time she got us to the emergency campsite. She had inspired us to keep moving and had helped pack some of our load the last couple of miles.

It had taken Charlene and me ten hours to walk seven miles. Melissa had spent ten hours walking as well, but with all her backtracking she had probably clocked thirty miles. The legendary Melissa.

Tents were pitched, dinner was eaten, then everyone collapsed into their sleeping bags. There was to be no stargazing that night!

John thought that after what he called "your grueling death march" I had learned my lesson. But, no! Last weekend, I did it again! So did Charlene! So did Amy! ("What," John asked, "is wrong with you people?") The new backpackers who joined us on this trek were seven women who work together in a bank near Ft. Worth.

I may not have learned any lessons last year, but Melissa did. This year she reserved a different campsite, making the initial trek 4½ miles rather than 7. We set up camp early in the afternoon, then hiked the rest of the way to the South Rim without our backpacks. This year Melissa and I carried 2-way radios so we could keep in touch (although after she got the youngsters settled, she still felt compelled to hike back down the trail and help Charlene and me carry our stuff).

John weighed my pack before the trip. Sixty pounds. In addition to the essentials, I was packing appetizers for the whole group and a big box of homemade pralines for dessert. I had these goodies in an insulated container along with a frozen Polar Pack to keep them cool. John's prediction was that my generosity would probably lead to my demise.

But I survived the trek up the mountain, had a great time hiking the Colima Trail the next day, and made it home safely that evening. Then it was off to school the next morning. John was surprised that I made it, but I manage because of the snail's pace at which I move along the trail. In spite of my heavy pack, this trip was easier because I used my new carbon fiber trekking poles. Now I'm convinced that backpacking is all about proper equipment. For next year's adventure I will purchase a lighter-than-air backpack and a featherweight tent. I expect by the time I celebrate my 70th birthday on the Grand Canyon Rim-to-Rim Trail, that hike will be a walk in the park. John says I'm crazy, but he admires my tenacity.

Once down from the mountains, there were projects on the desert floor that needed tending. Last month when I walked away from the thirty-nine little cottonwoods in the wash at Croton Spring, I was not abandoning them. I knew that nature would take its course, but I planned to support our saplings as well as I could. When Dr. Sirotnak gave me a copy of the GPS printout, I made copies for the Citizen Heroes. They marked their special trees and the adopted trees, and I encouraged them to visit their trees with their families. I suggested they bring buckets, water their trees, water as many of the other trees as they could. And just to make certain the trees got attention, I made weekly treks to check on them myself. Sometimes a "volunteer" would come with me; sometimes I went alone.

South Rim Survivors

It was easy to water the cottonwoods at first because there were still several ponds in the wash. Even without help I could dip water from the ponds and irrigate the saplings in less than thirty minutes. It was a pleasant and satisfying task.

But week by week there were fewer trees to water. Despite my efforts, some of the saplings did not thrive. Their leaves shriveled and fell, their small trunks dried. Other saplings got disturbed by wildlife. I would find their exposed roots withering in the sun. Some saplings simply disappeared. Vanished without a trace.

By mid-April the ponds were dry. Twenty-three of the original thirty-nine trees were still thriving so I would pack six gallons of water from home down to the trees, then hike to a nearby earthen stock tank built during the ranching era and procure a few gallons more. But this stock tank water, although wet, was stagnant and smelly, and tramping through the tall grasses and weeds to get to it was probably dangerous and certainly no fun. I needed a better plan.

When I discussed the problem with Shirley she suggested that in lieu of PE one day a week I drive my class to the Croton Spring trailhead and take them on the ¾-mile hike to the wash. If my ten students and I each packed some water, all the cottonwoods would get a weekly drink. Of course parents and other volunteers would be welcome to help us.

The children were receptive to the plan. They take their stewardship seriously, and they understood that the saplings needed their help until the summer rains began. Besides, all activities involving riding in the school bus appealed to their sense of adventure.

With many new endeavors there is a period of adjustment, a learning curve. Such it was with our irrigating project. For our first trip I filled the gallon and half-gallon milk jugs the children had brought for carrying the water and packed them in the bus before the children arrived. I didn't count the jugs, I just filled them. Immediately after flag ceremony we climbed on the bus and headed to Croton Spring.

At the trailhead the children began transferring some of the jugs to their backpacks and choosing other jugs to carry in their hands. A gallon of water weighs eight pounds and in the dispersal flurry I didn't notice that many of the children were over-estimating their strength. It wasn't until we were halfway to the wash and were just reaching the top of the second, the steepest, hill that I got a clue. Lauren, who was walking in front of me, began a slow-motion topple over backward. I grabbed her backpack and helped her stand upright.

"Lauren, what do you have in here?"

"Mmmm, two gallons of water?"

"Halt! Everybody halt! Let's rest. Put your jugs down. Take off your backpacks."

I inventoried. Most of the children were carrying two gallons of water in their packs and a half-gallon jug in each hand.

"Guys and Gals, we're carrying way too much water! We're breaking our backs! Let's reassess."

Once we had redistributed and downsized our loads we ended up with many extra jugs of water. Do we leave them sitting beside the trail? Do we take them back to the bus? Do we make a return trip and carry them down to the wash? Do we chance getting back to school late for our second period class? As we debated how to handle our dilemma, we heard noises behind us. We turned to see a wondrous sight just cresting the first hill.

"Moms!"

"Super-moms!"

"Super-moms to the rescue!"

They were calling, waving, hiking at breakneck speed. And, they were wearing empty backpacks.

Our PE class made several more trips to Croton Spring before school was out, but never one that was more exciting than the first. Etched on our retinas forever is the vision of those super-moms flying over the hill. Those super-moms coming to our rescue.

As the school year wound down, we made time for one more activity. A favorite folk tale, *Stone Soup*, is the last story in our first grade reading series. After the children read it and several additional versions of the same tale, we celebrate the completion of the reading series with a party, a stone soup gala. Among other things, this party involves searching the playground for the perfect stones (one for each first grader and each kindergartner), writing the shopping list for the other ingredients, writing party invitations for all the other little kids, creating party decorations, practicing oral readings to present to our guests, discussing kitchen hygiene and safety, chopping vegetables, reviewing hostess manners and genteel eating behavior, studying table settings, and preparing soup. This year's party included dessert, the 500 Word Cake. Mr. John P. Seawell and his bright little readers had made great progress.

The second and third grade guests applauded the achievements of the first graders, graciously accepted second helpings of the delicious soup (and the 500 Word cake!), and enjoyed reminiscing about the stone soup parties they had hosted all those many months ago. Ah, traditions. They unite us and give us insight.

These stone soup parties were evidence that my youngsters were getting older, growing up. Are they prepared for a successful future? Are they prepared for moving on? How will they fare once they graduate from this tiny school?

High school was only a vague concept for most of my young students, but Tanya mentioned high school often. I assumed it was because she had transferred from Terlingua where the elementary school and the high school are located just a few yards apart. However, I was baffled when she announced early in her first grade year that she would probably go to jail when she was in high school.

I hear many odd statements from my young students. I realize they don't always know what they're talking about, and I didn't actually believe Tanya's high school career would include a jail sentence. Yet I found the casual way she mentioned going to jail alarming.

We discussed the issue and I learned that her sixteen-year-old half-brother was temporarily living with her family while awaiting placement in an alternative school. Tanya had equated this alternative school with "going to jail" and had accepted this situation as a normal high school occurrence. I knocked myself out explaining all the ways in which it wasn't!

Throughout the year I encouraged Tanya, along with all my other students, to work hard, do their best, and think about a career they might want to pursue when they grew older.

Recently my K–3rd grade students were discussing where they would go to college and Lauren reminded us that she would attend the University of Texas so she could become an astronomer and work at McDonald Observatory. Tanya's hand went up immediately.

"I'm going with Lauren."

She wasn't exactly sure what astronomers were or what they did, but she was going with Lauren. The rest of the children accepted this decision without question.

Tanya's leap from going to jail to becoming an astronomer was a broad one, even for a first grader, and I wanted to support her new plan. Most children make dozens of career changes before they reach college, and I expect Tanya will do the same. But a seed had been planted, and I wanted to nurture it and help it grow.

Tanya had not yet transferred to San Vicente ISD last year when we took our field trip to McDonald Observatory; however, when a child makes the decision to become an astronomer, the least I can do is make sure that that child gets to visit an observatory. Especially if that child is bright, eager, and loves learning. Especially if that child's favorite subject is math and she often asks for extra math homework.

Tanya's decision inspired me to write one of my "famous letters." (I've been doing this since childhood and my letters are legendary for getting results.) This time I wrote to the director of McDonald Observatory. I told him the story of my two young astronomers – Lauren, the second grader who decided on astronomy as a career while doing research in preparation for her field trip to the observatory last year, and Tanya, the first grader who decided recently to "go with Lauren" instead of going to jail.

I asked the observatory director if an invitation to a "future astronomer's day" could be arranged so I could legitimately single out my two young students for a visit. I said such a visit would make both little girls very happy and would reinforce Tanya's new aspiration.

Once again, my plea brought even better results than I had hoped for. Within days, we received a special invitation, and yesterday I took Lauren and Tanya to Fort Davis for their visit to the observatory. Lauren's mom went along as the second adult.

Other than the official invitation, the only thing I had asked for was a short greeting from "someone/anyone" on our arrival. I had explained that the other adult and I were prepared to show the girls around.

However, instead of a greeting followed by a self-guided visit, we got a personal, morning-long tour conducted by the observatory superintendent and his wife. This was followed by being treated to lunch at the observatory restaurant.

In addition to a private showing of a film about sun activity, our little group was driven up the hills in an official UT sedan to see the research telescopes. Tourists and school groups' heads turned as the VIP vehicle zipped around. Perhaps they were wondering who the visiting dignitaries could be. The girls even got to see the astronomers' dormitory, cafeteria, and work areas.

Lauren took on the role of big sister. "Look, Tanya, this is where we'll do our research. See, these will be our computers."

In the afternoon the education director took over and showed the girls the smaller telescopes in the viewing area near the visitor center and even allowed them to engage the mechanism that automatically turns and adjusts the telescopes.

The girls had a marvelous, magic-packed day, and I can't help but think that a lasting impression has been made on little Tanya – whether she becomes an astronomer or not.

"It will be so much fun when you two are astronomers and come to visit us."

"But Dr. Seawell, you'll be old then. You'll come creeping to the door with a walker."

"Well … possibly. If that's the case, you and Tanya could cook dinner for us."

"Dr. Seawell! Astronomers don't do cooking!"

"Oh. Well. Pardon me. I did not know that."

"Don't worry, Dr. Seawell. It'll be all right. We'll just pick up a pizza on our way to your house."

"Great idea, Lauren. We all like pizza."

San Vicente ISD
Big Bend National Park, TX 79834
May 30, 2005

David L. Lambert, Director
McDonald Observatory
The University of Texas at Austin
Austin, TX 78712-1083

Dear Dr. Lambert,

Thank you for making it possible for Lauren and Tanya to have a magnificent tour of McDonald Observatory. Marc Wetzel enchanted them before and after he taught other school groups, and Mr. and Mrs. Peterman devoted several hours of their day to the future astronomers. Although they may be too young to realize the significance of being given such attention, I trust that the visit will have a lasting impact on these little students. Despite their excitement and short attention spans, subsequent questions they've asked and conversations we've had have let me know they were absorbing a great deal of information.

On a personal note, my husband and I have recently purchased property near Alpine. One of the joys of this property is that we can see the domes of both the 82" and the 107" telescopes from our future home site. The young astronomers are happy that the teacher who will have been with them from kindergarten through second and third grade will be able to see where they are working when they "grow up." Lauren's details of her future career now include mornings when she and Tanya pick up a pizza at the Astronomer's Lodge and drive to our house for a sunrise supper on our front porch. This is to be followed by a nice nap in our guest room.

Once more, Dr. Lambert, thank you. I continue to be astounded by the time and effort you and your staff put into educating children.

Sincerely,
Pat Seawell

Teaching the same children for more than one year has advantages and disadvantages. Disadvantages include selfish teachers who become overprotective and possessive of their students. I am one of these. Jonathan, Gabriel, Alex, Alicia, and Jessica would be moving to 4th grade Spanish and social studies next year. After teaching most of them for three years, the thought of them becoming "big kids" was almost too much to bear.

But I would have Anna, Tanya, Don, Lauren and Apryl for one more year. I had witnessed the beginning of the academic journeys of all these children. For two years I had watched the progress Anna and Tanya made, rejoiced at their leaps and bounds, glimpsed their bright prospects and possibilities. I had watched the energy and effort Don exerted in kindergarten. His success was building and I was cheering for him. Lauren and Apryl would be with me for a fourth year of Spanish and social studies. And I'd still have all the girls for PE.

There. Pollyanna has *many* reasons to be happy. It just took a minute.

But I would miss my little kids, my gang of ten. We had had a thousand golden moments and during the last month of school they gave me one more. Sweet and sentimental. Indulge me.

We had been studying natural resources and were reading about the California gold rush and the 49ers. ("No, Jonathan, the *original* 49ers, not the football team.") Alex had learned the correct gold panning technique at a science fair in Alaska, and although he hadn't yet hit the mother lode, he had had experience panning for gold in both Alaska and Colorado. He brought his authentic placer mining pan in for us to examine and taught us proper panning technique.

Suddenly I remembered the dozen aqua-colored plastic cereal bowls stored in the cabinet at the back of the room.

"Boys and Girls, let's go outside and pan for gold!"

There are no streams anywhere near the school, but we have imaginations. We lined up along the little dry drainage ditch between the track and the tennis court. The kids scooped up bowls of dirt from the ditch, I added water to their bowls from a gallon jug, and they began swirling. It was a muddy process at first, with squeals, but I kept adding water and they kept swirling. Little red rocks, little white rocks, little black rocks appeared in the bottoms of the bowls. And then ... little gold-colored rocks were spotted.

Now the children got serious. Gold nuggets! We needed more water! I stepped to the faucet a few feet away and as I stood refilling the jug, I glanced back at my students.

The children stood with their backs to me, shoulder to shoulder, along the drainage ditch. A desert in front and to the left of them, a mountain range to the right of them, and a blinding white sun above them. They were laughing, giggling, ooing, and ahhing. I heard their excitement. I heard their joy.

Love is a time, a place, and ten precious children who drew me here and gave me reasons to stay. They gave me reasons to stay until I understood that this quiet chunk of Texas is home.

CHAPTER 16

The Great Train Robbery

For months John had been planning our summer vacation, our get-away, our first holiday in three years. It was to be a trip aboard the luxurious and recently restored American Orient Express. He had booked the largest, loveliest compartment, made arrangements for a kitty sitter, and located a temporary home for Mandy.

What do people who live in a national park want to see on vacation? Why, five other national parks, of course. From the comfort of a train. No driving, no searching for restaurants, no lugging baggage around. We would visit five spectacular parks in seven days. The trip of a lifetime.

On the appointed day, at the appointed hour, we met with the other eager passengers in a hotel in Albuquerque. Activities began with a festive buffet. Fruits, cheeses, meats, breads, and wines. Then we were given a pre-trip briefing.

In retrospect, there were clues. The man who presented the briefing mentioned the million dollars spent on restoring each train car, but reminded us that the cars were sixty years old and solicited our patience; we were to be driven to the train at a scheduled hour, but the briefing and the buffet continued long beyond that time; the train personnel were preoccupied with intense and frantic phone calls; the buses that were to transport us to the depot coughed and idled long in the driveway.

But at last we were informed that we would be moving to the train, that it would be leaving the station at four o'clock rather than two, and that a few last-minute adjustments were being made to the air-conditioning system. John and I exchanged an excited hug even though air-conditioning systems requiring adjustments caused a hint of unease.

When a metal box sits for several hours in the June sun of an Albuquerque afternoon, it becomes hot inside. So does a metal train car. The red rose on the table in our compartment had lowered its forlorn little head and dropped its petals. The champagne bottle, sad and defeated, slumped in a bucket of warm water, its refreshing chill a faded memory.

The compartment itself was tiny, dark, coffin-like. Turning on lights gave it a creepy, eerie glow, but raising the window shade let in sunshine making it hotter. By the time I unpacked our bags and stowed our stuff, I was one with the red rose and the champagne bottle.

The third time John called to inquire about our air conditioning we were invited to visit the club car where champagne was being served and the air-conditioning was functioning. We began the fourteen-car journey to the club car. The only thing more ominous than the hot cars through which we trekked was the sight of the men between the cars. They wore tool belts and were grappling with yards and yards of gray wire.

Ever optimistic and confident, I was still making light of the situation. But my dear John P. Seawell was becoming less and less amused.

When we reached the club car we noted that most of the other passengers in the fourteen cars had reached it before we had. With grace and style we pushed, shoved, and bumped our way to the bar, collected our champagne, and huddled together in our limited space. This packed club car was a fire marshal's nightmare, but close encounters spark conversations. We sipped champagne and chatted. Chatted and sipped champagne.

From time to time we were told our departure was eminent, and that when the train began moving, the air-conditioning problems would cease. The malfunctions, you see, were the result of the train standing still.

Cool air was pouring into the club car while the train was standing still. Cool air had been pouring into two of the fourteen cars through which we had traversed while the train was standing still. And what about those tool belts and all that gray wire? At six o'clock dinner began in the dining car so we headed that way.

A few diners sat at tables, stoic, glassy-eyed. We noted the chefs with shiny, flushed faces and the wait people with sweat dripping off their brows. Our appetites vanished. We moved on.

When we reached our compartment John presented two options. We could get off the train, take a taxi to our car, and crash in a cool hotel room. Or, we could flirt with the specter of a seven-day journey through the Great American West during the last week of June ...in a train with an air-conditioning system that needed adjustments.

"You planned this trip. You made the arrangements. You choose."

"I'll help you re-pack."

I should have been a pair of ragged claws
Scuttling across the floors of silent seas.

We heard that the American Orient Express left the station just before eight. News of a trainload of pilgrims perishing from heat stroke or asphyxiation never reached us. I've been told that air-conditioning systems work well once a train is moving. Could be.

By eight o'clock we were showered, relaxed, eating pizza in bed, and watching a CNBC special about Meg Whitman and eBay. I invited John to a couple or three national parks. Studied a map. Said I'd drive him. Coaxed and cajoled. Called it the trip of a lifetime. But home was what he wanted. Pick up our Mandy. Reunite with our kitties. Home.

My woe was not about the train trip. My woe was about my boy. Disappointed. Disillusioned. Anticipation thwarted. Expectations dashed.

I doubt our experience was normal. I think we just had a bad train day and for that I am sorry. I just hate it when my boy gets glum.

But John and I have spent a long time together, most of our lives. In four decades we've learned to weather storms. This is only a small gale. We'll chuckle about it in the future and move on to other travels, other trips. However, I do have serious suspicions that none of our future adventures will involve a locomotive.

We had been home from the non-vacation for a few days and John was beginning to cheer up. Then at eight o'clock on the morning of July 3 all the power in the park went off. At ten the power company reported they still had not located the problem.

"That's it! We're out of here!"

"And where will we be going?"

"Someplace that's air-conditioned. Any place! The first place!"

It was just after noon when we reached Marathon. The hotel was full, but La Casa Jardin was vacant. A cancellation. The only vacancy in town. John booked it, but we couldn't check in until four.

"So, what's La Casa Jardin?"

"It's a free-standing building across the track from the hotel. That's all I know."

"And it's air-conditioned?"

"Harrumph!"

"Let's see, 4th of July weekend, Alpine High School Reunion covering a decade of graduates, some festival in Ft. Davis, half a million bikers on holiday, a rodeo at Sul Ross. Cheer up, Sweetheart. We're really, really lucky. We've got La Casa Jardin and it's air-conditioned!"

We drove to Alpine for a Dairy Queen fest. Few things are as effective at lifting one's spirits as consuming hundreds of empty calories. Besides, a vanilla cone is Mandy's favorite treat. She was loving this outing. Her bed, her pillow, her private air-conditioner vent blowing full blast, and now a vanilla cone!

La Casa Jardin is an attractive room with a cold stone floor, a carport, a covered patio, and an extremely efficient air-conditioner. As its name promised, it was in a garden. Mandy and I were delighted. Apple trees. Butterflies.

"We girls are enjoying this adventure!"

"Harrumph!"

At six we left Mandy snoozing on the cold floor and crossed the track for a drink and dinner at the hotel. Moments after we toasted to the return of power to PJ, the lights in the White Buffalo Bar went out. Marathon had lost power.

"Not to worry. We'll have gazpacho, a salad, dessert. In the patio. See, they're already lighting candles. It'll be romantic."

"Harrumph!"

The hotel staff bustled about firing up the outside grill, but John wasn't hungry.

"Salad, whatever."

Then we got great news – the power was off only on this side of the track. Mandy's comfort at La Casa Jardin had not been compromised.

By the time we finished our candlelit dinner John's mood had lifted. The tiny kitten faces that kept popping out through the periwinkles under the apricot tree had enchanted him and soothed his frazzled soul. Back in our icy room he had just relaxed in front of the TV when La Casa Jardin's side of the track lost power.

"Sweetheart, remember, you have to be flexible to live in West Texas."

"Harrumph!"

"Goodnight, dear."

We took an extended road trip through the tri-county area the next day, contacting PJ every hour for power status updates. At two in the afternoon we were cleared to start home.

For the rest of the summer we were blessed with electrical power. I tended my peppers and tomatoes, caught grasshoppers for my friend Shelley, peeled the 72 bonus words off my classroom wall and added them to the 72 already on the ceiling, read books in the ramada with Mandy snoozing at my feet.

And I watered the cottonwoods. I needed helpers, and I recruited them in the most shameless manner. I was not particular. I was not proud. If a body could heft a jug of water over rough terrain he or she was mine. No one was exempted. No one was safe.

At the end of July we still had fifteen healthy cottonwoods. At the beginning of August the rains came. And came.

Five baby cottonwoods survived the flood of '05. The Citizen Heroes and I like to imagine that the other ten trees re-established themselves and are thriving somewhere along the way to the Gulf of Mexico. Of course we remembered that Ms. Forsythe said even one nice cottonwood at Croton Spring would improve the area. Besides, this is a project without an end. We've learned how to sprout cottonwood cuttings. We'll make more!

CHAPTER 17

Myxomycetes, Marriage, and Other Events Requiring Courage

School has begun. We are off and running again. Anna and Tanya are our second graders, Don is our first grader, and twice weekly we have our pre-kindergarteners. Since we had not had any pre-k children last year, and only one the year before, I had almost forgotten how much three four-year-olds can liven up a morning. Mr. John P. Seawell may request a raise.

On the first day of school the first grader and second graders got right back to reading, writing, and arithmetic. As always, science class is hands-on with projects and experiments, and since the Texas Legislature has designated August 26 as Women's Independence Day and has mandated that students be made aware of women's efforts to gain equality, deciding on our first social studies venture was easy.

I began preparing the class for Women's Independence Day by reading a short biography of Susan B. Anthony and playing a video that outlined her contributions. I had screened the video and although it was meant for older students and seemed quite dry, I told my class we would watch a few minutes of it just to get a flavor of the times. I suggested they notice the more formal use of language and manner of speaking as well as the differences in clothing and hair styles. I was prepared to stop the video the moment they became restless, but we all took notes and the video held their attention until the end.

When I explained that through the year we would learn more about American women's journey toward equality and their contributions to our society, the girls became concerned because there were so few examples of notable women in our textbook.

To address both the legislature's mandate and the girls' concern, as well to provide my class with a long-term project, I downloaded a list of 100 Famous American Women from the Internet. From that list each student chose a few names and did some preliminary research. (Don, my first grader, the youngest child in the class, and the only boy, went along with this salute to women. We females didn't give him a choice.)

After their preliminary investigations, each student selected a single person to learn about and "serious" research began. Tanya chose Susan B.

Anthony, Anna chose Pocahontas, Don chose Sacagawea, Apryl chose Georgia O'Keeffe, and Lauren chose Christa McAuliff. With back-to-school exuberance the children have now begun filling their research carrels with materials about their chosen subjects.

Our total student enrollment this is year fourteen, and with her usual zest for projects both wonderful and weird, Melissa has organized a major school-wide, K–8th grade long-term science adventure. Soon, while moisture from the summer rains still lingers in places in the park, we will begin our study of myxomycetes.

Our study of what? Nope, not a plant, not an animal. Not a fungi, nor an archaea, and *clearly* not a bacteria. Yet myxomycetes are living things; living things with their very own kingdom. The kingdom is protista, and, surprise! It is the least understood of the six kingdoms of life. And surprise! Myxomycetes are commonly called *slime molds*.

During the ten-year period from 1989-99, researchers collected seventy species of myxomycetes in Big Bend National Park. This summer Melissa participated in a slime mold study conducted in the Great Smoky Mountains National Park and she signed us on to participate in a nationwide myxomycetes research project. Big Bend National Park will be one of twenty areas involved in this study. We are to collect and analyze data from several areas of the park and submit our findings to the director of the project.

When Shirley dropped by our classroom this week she found that preparation for the slime mold study is running full throttle in the first and second grade science class. Anna and Tanya actually quizzed her to see how much she knew about the classification system, and were awed and impressed when she answered all their questions correctly. Using the mnemonic "King Philip came over from great Spain," courtesy of Melissa, they have memorized the seven levels scientists use to classify organisms. We have also been practicing using microscopes and magnifying loupes.

On September 2nd we will have our first field trip involving the slime mold project. Yesterday we had a whole-school organizational meeting to decide on data collection sites. During the meeting our students also received their team assignments, viewed a myxomycetes power point presentation, and received instruction on collection techniques. The students seem excited about participating in a nationwide research project and are looking forward to conducting field work.

John is settling into his piece of the scholastic puzzle this year by helping me with the first and second graders two mornings a week; however, his chief responsibility is leading the pre-k children on their public school journeys the two mornings per week they are at school.

Allison, Anna and Lauren's little sister, has been "volunteering" in our classroom with her mom once a week for two years; Wyatt, Jessica's little brother, has spent many after-school hours playing in our room; and Elena, although a recent arrival, attended pre-school last year in Colorado. Given this background, all three children are comfortable and confident at school. The little girls are delighted to be here, Wyatt is thrilled. Almost eight months younger than the girls, Wyatt often expresses his enthusiasm physically by clapping his hands, jumping up and down, and laughing. This little boy can hardly contain his happiness, and his joy is contagious.

Mr. John P. Seawell does an exceptional job of shepherding these three bright, cheerful, four-year-olds. I outline plans for him which include the usual early childhood activities. Together he and the children sing songs, do alphabet and number puzzles, create art projects, play games, and use their imaginations in any number of ways. John tells me he can't vouch for how much they are learning, but they are all having a wonderful time. It is a joy to watch my husband working with these enthusiastic little ones. From a person who was apprehensive about interacting with young children, he has evolved into a fine pre-k instructor. He keeps his little charges on track and in check, as would be expected of any former military officer, but he does it with a measure of patience and gentleness that I have never before seen him muster. Who is that very tall man teaching those four-year-olds? I am humbled by his calmness and compassion.

I am also grateful for the help John is getting this year from one of the pre-k parents. Scheduling and organizing a field trip for school children requires time and effort. Phone calls are made, messages are left, pre-trip visits are done, discussions with personnel at the trip site are held, discussions with personnel at the school are conducted, explanation letters to parents are written, permission forms are prepared, the list goes on. Field trips are not "jump onto the bus and go" affairs. When Elena's mother volunteered to organize some local field trips for the pre-k children, John and I were both delighted. She made all the arrangements, she and John are the adult supervisors, and most of the trips will be within walking distance of the school.

The post office, the recycle center, the climbing wall, and the park landfill are all loaded with educational possibilities and pre- and post-trip activities. This mom also arranged for the children to have a planting project with a park botanist and a painting project with a local artist. These field trips will enhance the pre-k program a hundred-fold, and the effort required to plan them is sincerely appreciated.

Because he was heartbroken over the outcome of our American Orient Express non-vacation, and because he has earned it, I'm sending John on a little trip. Next week he will leave for a three-week leaf-peeping tour. After a few days in New York City, he is scheduled for a 17-day cruise aboard his old ship, the *Seabourn Pride*. I am not any kind of a sailor, but John loves cruising and this will be his third trip aboard the *Pride*. This time he will travel around Long Island Sound, up the Hudson River, along the New England coast, through the Canadian Maritimes, and up the St. Lawrence Seaway to Quebec City. He will return to NYC with different stops along the way. He is looking forward to seeing some Broadway plays, eating some good lobster, and enjoying some fall foliage. We will follow his progress on our maps and communicate with him via email.

Meanwhile, back at the ranch, construction on our house is about to begin. It is hard to believe that this is our last year in the park. It has been a wonderful home, and we have loved being a part of this school and this group of people. We are excited about being retired again and having leisure time, but we will miss the children and the sense of community we've enjoyed in our little village.

The day after John's departure, all of the students, most of the teachers, Anna and Lauren's mother, Lisa, and their little sister, Allison, went out on our first expedition in search of slime mold.

Cattail Falls, a shadowy grotto of mosses and ferns at the base of a 60-foot waterfall, was our first data collection destination. We trekked the two miles to the falls with loupes suspended from our necks, and shears, collection bags, marking pens, identification photos, data sheets, notepads, water, and lunches in our backpacks.

Slime mold begins life as a microscopic spore, becomes a zygote, masses into a blob of plasmodium, then sprouts fruiting bodies. The fruiting bodies produce microscopic spores, thus the cycle begins again.

On hands and knees we searched for slime molds amid leaf litter and decaying bark. We peered at curious-looking items through our loupes, and we collected and labeled things we thought might be slime molds. Back in the classroom the big kids will mount and attempt to identify these samples. We also collected and labeled bits of leaf litter and decaying bark to culture in the lab. If the materials we culture contain slime mold spores they might produce zygotes, plasmodium, and fruiting bodies.

Apryl was our only casualty on this trip. Her scientific investigation was interrupted when she backed into a cactus. Lisa, our multi-talented parent volunteer, performed a delicate spine extraction procedure enabling Apryl to continue collecting data. Hazards in the field never dampen a true scientist's enthusiasm.

Back in our classroom the 1st–3rd grade social studies students had been plotting John's progress from New York City to Quebec City. He emailed us with details about his helicopter tour of Quebec City on the same day we read

"Quebec City Today" in our social studies book. His email told of two water-falls he had seen from the helicopter and we remembered that Cartier had explored the area in 1534 and found rapids and waterfalls blocking his path west. My students decided that Mr. John P. Seawell must have seen the same waterfalls that stopped Cartier's search for a direct route to China.

Seeking Slime Mold

The little kids have gone into fund-raising mode again. After hearing about Hurricane Katrina and reading about it online, they developed a list of activities to generate money to help the victims of this disaster. They raised $67.70 with their first activity, a Game Afternoon which was attended by most of the 1st–5th graders. During this event the children learned several new board games and also had fun playing some of their old favorites. The next fund-raiser on their list is a Sweet Bingo. This promises many delicious desserts and is being planned with the help of several of their moms.

While John was away, we began a study of family histories in social stud-ies class. Since America is a country of immigrants, each child investigated his or her own ancestry, collected maps of their countries of origin, and com-piled information for a short presentation to "take the mystery out of my his-tory." Anna and Lauren learned that their father's side of the family included immigrants from France, but the real bombshell came when they also learned that the French eat *snails*!

Thus began a strong attraction-repulsion with that particular culinary habit of the French. All the class members wanted to try what they had learned was escargot, yet they were sure that only Anna and Lauren, who, after all had French blood, would like them.

West Texas is not a great snail-eating area so I emailed John with a request that he procure some escargot before returning to PJ. On the morning he was to drive home from San Antonio, he picked up some cans of escargot, the shells to serve them in, and a freshly baked baguette.

The next afternoon we had "hors d'oeuvres at a French restaurant" during social studies class. The children had named our fancy restaurant "A Little Taste of France," and with their usual mania for making magic, they asked to go out the back door of the classroom so they could enter the restaurant through the front.

Affecting a French accent and recalling a phrase or two from a French class I had taken many decades ago, I greeted the guests at the door and guided them to their table like any competent maître d' would do. Then John, with a cup towel on his arm but no French accent, played the part of the waiter. Before the restaurant opened for business we had warmed the garlic butter and escargot in the classroom microwave, but we left the bread uncut so each child could pull off a piece.

Before the escargot was served, I gave instructions on how to remove a snail from its shell, dip it in the melted butter, and eat it with the bread. I also gave my usual spiel about how tastes for new foods sometimes have to be acquired over time and showed the children how to politely remove a snail from their mouths if their palates were not yet prepared for this exotic delicacy.

All our diners were courageous and tried the new food. Before long both the waiter and the maître d' were busy as child after child asked for another escargot, please, or more French bread. The five children managed to consume all eighteen escargot and the entire, extra-long baguette.

Later the children told John they had been apprehensive about taking the first bite. The news that they would be eating snails had been circulating throughout the school for days, and they had been teased by the big kids with things like, "Don't come to me for help if you get sick!" John said he could tell that the little kids felt proud of themselves for being so bold during their visit to the mythical Little Taste of France Restaurant.

John was back from his trip in time for a special day, our wedding anniversary. Ah, yes, marriage. It was never a part of my plan. Too independent. Too selfish. Too many ideas of my own.

"Marriage is a hard job," I had often explained to my secondary students on the occasion of my anniversary, "the second-hardest job in the world."

After I expounded on the difficulties and hardships of marriage – "because no one else is going to tell you this stuff and you deserve to know" – they would finally ask about the number one hardest job. Ah, ha! Then I'd launch into my lecture on the sacrifices and pains of parenting, make them weep, make them go home and thank their parents, make them ask forgiveness for all the anguish and grief they had caused. Oh, yes! Mine was a stirring lecture.

As for the difficulties and hardships of my own marriage, I had always known John P. Seawell and I would make a great *old* couple, but how, oh, how, would we be able to navigate this partnership through the trials of our youth? No longer a problem. No longer have to worry about our youth. And, I was right. John and I do make a great *old* couple.

Our anniversary inspired John to send an email to his friends. Short, but sweet. It's title? "Forty Years."

> Pat and I celebrate our fortieth wedding anniversary tomorrow. It's difficult to believe that that much time has passed – and even harder to believe that Pat has put up with me for all these years. There are a number of things in my life that I look back upon with pride, but none as much as the great honor Pat did me by agreeing to mingle our lives. Nothing can ever be as significant to me. JPS

Mid-October brings both our wedding anniversary and the annual visit of our London ISD guests. The 8th grade students are here for the first time, and it's nice to see the excitement in their young faces. Although the students' faces are new, their teachers are "old timers" and well known to all of us.

This year our children got a close up view of the impact of Hurricane Katrina; one of the London students was a refugee from New Orleans, a tall, polite, self-assured young man. The London students and our one eighth grader spent several days hiking, camping, and participating in natural science projects. As is the tradition, on their last evening we hosted a hamburger supper for them, followed by a dance in our gym. Since our school is so small, eighth grade students were imported from Terlingua to participate in the cookout and dance.

In the past it has usually taken awhile for the youngsters to work up the courage to begin dancing, but this year the young refugee from New Orleans got the ball rolling early by asking permission to have a dance contest. He then proceeded to organize the contest, getting even the shyest students involved. The dance floor stayed crowded, and it appeared that both our students and our guests were having a good time.

A few days after the London visit, an invitation was issued for five 3rd grade classes to participate in a state-wide video conference called the Invention Convention. The conference was based on one of the social studies TEKS: The student understands how individuals have created or invented new technology and affected life in communities around the world, past and present.

Since video conferencing is one way to connect my students with the larger academic community, I signed us up.

Five categories of innovation were to be addressed, and knowing Lauren's fascination with all things pertaining to blood and surgical procedures, I requested the medical vaccines category.

Rather than attempt to name all the individuals who have invented medical vaccines, I had my 1st–3rd graders focus on only one person, Jonas Salk. My students had never heard of the disease called polio, so we began our research by interviewing older members of the community and phoning grandparents. Then we shared the information we collected from these people.

In our library I found a memoir by Peg Kehert, a woman who had experienced polio as a twelve-year-old in the 1950's. She called her book *Small Steps: The Year I Got Polio.* I had planned to read a couple of chapters to the class and show them the photographs, but my four girls were mesmerized by this detailed account of a young girl's experience with a frightening disease, and I ended up reading the whole book to them. Don may not have identified as strongly with the protagonist, but he, too, found the story absorbing.

After Kehert's book, we read several short Jonas Salk biographies and did research online. We even looked into the live-virus vs. dead-virus controversy between Salk and Sabine.

"Now, Girls and Boy, we've learned a lot about polio and the vaccine Dr. Salk created that changed lives in communities around the world. We have ten minutes to share what we've learned with the other third grade classes. What ideas do you have for doing that?"

Without a pause Lauren went into movie director mode and the five children began moving furniture, creating a script, and putting into action the things they had learned. For two days they spent the forty-five minute social studies period creating a skit. They checked their books and Internet print-outs for facts and photos, occasionally they consulted me. I contributed by keying their script and making a copy for each child. On the third day, they began rehearsing. On the fourth day we timed their skit. Fifty-three minutes. Nobody ever said following the lead of the child would produce a short presentation!

"Your ideas are good, your facts are accurate. All you have to do now is pick out the most important points. Remember, you only have ten minutes to present your information."

The skit the children had created included a scene in which Tanya lay in an iron lung asking a nurse how much longer she would have to be confined. I had a butterfly protective custody cage big enough for Tanya. If we covered it with silver garbage bags and placed it on a cot it would look a lot like the iron lungs in our photos.

On the morning I brought the butterfly cage to school, it began raining during flag ceremony so we all stepped into my classroom.

"The iron lung!" my social studies children exclaimed in unison.

The nine older students stared at the uncovered cylindrical wire frame standing on end near my file cabinet.

"What's an iron lung?"

"It's for people who get polio," my social studies children exclaimed in unison.

"What's polio?"

Shirley told the older students they were lucky to know nothing about iron lungs and polio. Then she assured them they would get to see our presentation when we finished working on it.

We continued preparing for the Invention Convention, but with the rest of the student body, we also made three more trips into the field seeking slime. Pine Canyon was the site of our second investigation. Even though Melissa drove slowly along the primitive dirt road to the trailhead, the little kids enjoyed squealing as the bus crept over bumpy washes and slithered through roadside brush.

At the trailhead we did our final check for water, hats, lunch, and equipment, then pulled on our backpacks and set out through the rolling grasslands toward the canyon. The trail climbs steadily for a mile before entering the canyon where it continues to climb for another mile. I hiked behind the rest of the group at my usual snail's pace, but I knew I could depend on Apryl's older brother, Bryan, to supervise the three younger members of our team. Bryan is a 7th grader and the student leader of our team. He has learned how and where to collect data, and his manner of working with the younger children inspires their cooperation and confidence. Bryan would make sure our samples were collected, labeled, and stored properly. Without a worry or a trace of guilt I could dawdle along the trail.

From time to time a student or two would drop back and walk with me for a while or stop in the shade of an occasional tree to wait for me. On one such occasion as we rested, a small group of tourists stopped to visit with us. The students who were with me were delighted to give a full report about the scientific nature of our hike, and as related to the visitors, the work we are doing sounds extremely impressive.

Pine Canyon Trail becomes wooded once inside the canyon. First there are junipers, pinyons, and oaks. Then, as the elevation continues to increase, there are ponderosas, bigtooth maples, huge Texas madrones, and more oaks. I stood for a while attempting to comprehend this forest, this incredible, improbable forest, standing high on a sky island surrounded by a vast, dry and thirsty place. The air was cool and fragrant. The sun pushed variegated yellow shafts through the leaves. A beautiful California sister, a large butterfly rarely seen at lower elevations, patrolled the trail.

The trail ends at the base of a 200-foot igneous cliff that often glistens with seeps and always becomes a waterfall after rain. It was in this dramatic area, amid columbines and ferns, that the children searched for slime molds, then ate their lunches and clowned on the boulders at the cliff's base during their photo op.

Clowning in the Canyon

Tanya was our only casualty on this trip. Her scientific investigation was interrupted by the tender spot that was irritating her heel. A strategically placed Band-aid from my generous cache solved that problem, and she was able to hike back down the mountain without further medical intervention.

Rio Grande Village, an area along the river with a convenience store, a camp ground, and an RV park, was the site of our third slime mold field trip. In pre-park days, this area was farmed by using water diverted from the river. Miles of irrigation ditches from that time still crisscross the area, and on a gusty, gray day it was along some of these moist arteries that we searched.

We also collected samples on both sides of a lagoon known as the beaver pond, trooping back and forth across the boardwalk, bowed against the wind, and shrieking at its attempts to force us off our feet. By lunchtime it was raining so we appropriated the visitors' laundry facility connected to the convenience store and ate our sandwiches and chips with the comforting sound of clothes dryers humming in the background.

Alicia was our only casualty on this trip. Her scientific investigation was interrupted when she stepped backwards off the boardwalk and splashed into the beaver pond. Her teammates fished her out and she continued her search, wet and cold but unharmed and only slightly shaken.

Our final slime mold survey site was along an old trail just above the Basin. On a crisp, sunny morning our three teams investigated three different sections along a steep and heavily vegetated ravine. We inched our way over exposed roots and under low-hanging branches. We scratched through decomposing leaf debris and pried up decaying tree bark. As always, we squinted through our loupes, referred to photos in our field guides, analyzed, deduced, conferred, and collected. At noon the teams convened at the head of the ravine, and beneath gnarled, ancient oaks amid intriguing rock outcrops we sat and ate our lunches.

I was the only casualty on this trip. My scientific investigation was over and I was hiking back down the mountain when I stepped on loose gravel and slid to the ground. Jessica, who had slowed down to walk with me, was as startled as I was.

"Dr. Seawell! I've never seen you on your back before!"

I stood up, took five more steps, and slid to the ground a second time.

"Jessica! Now you've seen me on my back twice! It's your lucky day!"

No clothing was ripped, no bruises were incurred, and I was able to reach the bus with no more plummeting incidents.

Between and after field trips we conducted our lab work – mounting specimens, studying specimens through microscopes, attempting to identify specimens, culturing specimens, and submitting our findings to the project director. We weren't able to identify all the samples we collected. Much of what we cultured never produced fruiting bodies. Some of the samples we submitted failed to be slime molds. Yet amid our mistakes and mix-ups, despite our blips and glitches, we had several successes. More importantly we had learned a great deal about the patience, persistence, and precision that defines the scientific process.

Mounting Specimens

Studying Specimens

Identifying Specimens

When our students revisit the collection sites next year they will do so with more skill, thus making a greater contribution to this national research project. But even though hundreds of taxonomists have gone into the field with more knowledge than these fourteen youngsters, no one has ever searched for myxomycetes with more diligence and enthusiasm.

Between slime mold field trips my social studies children continued working on their presentation for the Invention Convention. They were still in the editing stage when three new students from Montana enrolled in our school. They were brothers whose dad had transferred from Glacier National Park to take a seasonal job as the park mule packer/wrangler. Two of the boys were little kids. We needed a narrator, and second grader Garrett was an excellent reader. We needed a small boy, and kindergartner Buck was just the right height. Perfect. The editing continued. Now the skit was twenty minutes long.

"You've almost got it! Keep looking for the absolute, most important, points."

Finally, with our fifty-three minute play compressed to ten minutes, and with Shirley managing the camera and me helping move props, our small screen stars went live with their production about Dr. Salk and his invention of the polio vaccine.

I had a momentary bout of self-reproach when I saw how different our presentation was from the other four. Perhaps I should not have sought one of the five invitations. We are just a tiny class, the other schools have casts of thousands. There were only five slots available, maybe I was selfish to request one of them.

There were other differences. Our seven presenters are in kindergarten, first, second, and third grades rather than all being 3rd graders like the children in the other four schools.

Our content was different as well. Although I had finally given my group some editing help in order to meet the time constraints, our children presented a skit they themselves had written. It was complete with doctors in white lab coats and stethoscopes, a distraught mother with two sick and moaning children, medical exams and dreadful diagnoses, a benevolent nurse/receptionist, a child gasping from an iron lung, and, yes, even Dr. Salk himself, carefully examining slides with a microscope, then scrutinizing a set of glass test tubes in a wooden rack. All this activity was kept organized and on track by our very good narrator.

Dr. Salk was played by John's special friend, Don. He was decked out in a white coat, his pose while viewing the test tubes was exactly like a photo of Dr. Salk from one of the books we had read, and in an eloquent and weighty voice he delivered his own paraphrase of one of Dr. Salk's famous quotes, "There is no such thing as failure. You only fail if you give up too soon."

For the most part the other presentations were fine, and a great deal of work had been put into some of them, especially in terms of artistic backdrops and props. But there were many "talking heads" reading long lists of inventors and their inventions, and much of the reading was poorly done. I saw my students' eyes glaze over a time or two. Too much information.

I found the Q & A at the end of the presentations revealing. When the host of the conference called for feedback from the presenters only two comments were given. "Where is that *little* school?" and "I liked the one with all the doctors." I think children were responding to a skit written for kids by kids.

Later when we discussed the other presentations, the first thing one of my children asked was, "Dr. Seawell, why can't those other kids read?" A good question. I think it might have something to do with all the hours in kindergarten, first, and second grades when "those other kids" didn't have the opportunity to sit on the floor reading books – one on each side of their teacher.

Shirley had asked personnel at the Region 18 Education Service Center to video the conference for us and when we receive the video we will present it one afternoon for everyone to see. Then, at last, to the big kids will be revealed the mysteries of iron lungs and the miseries of polio.

By the time we participated in the Invention Convention, Garrett and Buck seemed always to have been a part of our class, and their presence benefited us all. Both boys were bright, outgoing, and well-mannered, but the characteristic that was most obvious, the characteristic that most clearly defined them, was their self-reliance. Both were independent little boys who sought their own solutions and searched for their own answers.

I took a long look at Garrett and Buck's behavior. My natural propensity to help my students, coupled with our student-teacher ratio, had made it easy for me to slip into an unintentional role. I answered questions, removed obstacles, solved dilemmas. I was always accessible, always available. Whoops! By turning myself into a Rescue 911 responder I was making it difficult for my students to become self-sufficient. Thanks for making this obvious to me, Boys. I'll take a step back, and we'll all learn something important from your example.

My little girls could keep up with Garrett in reading, but they were stunned when he began surpassing them in math. Suddenly they had to work faster and work smarter to hold their own. But the area in which Garrett created the greatest impact was PE. Soon after he enrolled he met the Presidential Physical Fitness Challenge for the mile run. The girls took notice. The girls got serious. This new second grader, this *boy*, was presenting them with challenges. They both took deep breaths and began putting forth more effort. Yet despite the shock waves he was creating, Garrett was a charming youngster, a pleasant classmate, and both girls were fond of him. Even with the arrival of serious competition in our classroom, harmony prevailed among the second graders.

Buck was a little bundle of energy and imagination. He was only six months older than our two pre-k girls, and he benefited from working with Mr. John P. Seawell's group two mornings a week. During these sessions he often acted as John's assistant, a role he found much to his liking. John dedicated one of his volunteer mornings to working with Buck one-on-one; I had some daily one-on-one time with him, and I was able to group him with Don during part of the day. John and I had come full circle. This time we were teaching five different levels, but even with the extra level I didn't feel *quite* as scattered as I had the first time I entered this multi-level classroom.

Our research project concerning famous American women had been in progress for several weeks when Garrett and Buck arrived so I hurried to help them catch up. It didn't take Garrett long to choose Amelia Earhart as his subject. He was fascinated by planes and flight, and he approached his investigation with eagerness and energy.

Buck's subject didn't present herself immediately, nor was she as famous. However, once we read a bit about Florence Bascom, she became the ideal choice. The connection was geologic. Buck *loved* rocks. He picked them up on the playground and on his walk to school. He examined them and filled his pockets with them. He shared them with me and with his classmates, and, like a pebble-crazed Hansel, he dropped them along his trails through the classroom. After his classmates and I had all experienced incidents of stepping on Buck's rocks and sitting on Buck's rocks, I designated a special area in the classroom as the official collection site. On Fridays I'd help him sack up the week's cache to take home to show his family. Buck did *love* rocks.

So, also, did Florence Bascom. With geology as her field of study, she was the first female awarded a doctorate from Johns Hopkins University. She received her education sitting behind a curtain which separated her from her male counterparts. When she graduated in 1893 she did not cross the stage with her male classmates to accept her diploma. Take a look, Girls and Boys, here's a famous American woman who had to struggle for equality!

My students were wrapping up their famous American women research so it was time for the next step, power point presentations. But before I could teach the children this skill, I had to learn it myself. How hard could it be?

I leaned on the big kids. I begged them for tutorials. When they came by to help, I listened to their directions and took notes. When they left I did practice runs. For several afternoons I lurked outside the big kids' classroom and grabbed them when the dismissal bell rang. I listened again, took more notes, and did more practice runs. Finally I got it. I was certifiable.

I wrote out step-by-step directions for creating a power point slide. Then I paired the second and third grade children and asked one of the pair to read the directions aloud while their partner carried them out. After the first child created and stored a slide, the pair traded places. Keying the text took real concentration, but choosing background colors, transitions, and sound effects gave the children quite a thrill, and they did a fantastic job making their first slides together. When had they become so self-sufficient?

Another school semester was coming to an end when John suggested we try another train trip. Before my visions of a nightmare revisited became too vivid, he pulled a package from his jacket and handed it to me. It was a DVD based on the 1986 Caldecott winner, *The Polar Express*, by Chris Van Allsburg. Perfect. My students were familiar with the story and I knew they would enjoy the movie. Hence, on a cold, damp December morning I surprised the little kids by issuing red tickets to them as they left the gym after PE and inviting them to await the Polar Express at my classroom door. Meanwhile, John had turned half of our room into a coach car with chairs in a double column along the windows and the other half into a Pullman car with pillows in a double column on the floor. He had darkened the room, popped in a cinnamon-scented wall plug, turned on the twinkle lights, and rounded up a hole punch and a flashlight for the conductors.

The little kids were already lined up and giggling on the station platform when a couple of the big kids came flying through the breezeway.

"We don't have our tickets! Ms. Forsythe wants to know where we're supposed to get our tickets."

Gulp! Word travels fast in this little school. How silly of me to think the big kids would consider themselves *too* big for a magical journey.

"The ticket agent is on his way to your room right now! Hurry back over there so you won't miss him!"

The little kids shivered on the platform for a few minutes longer while the conductors hurried to set up a few more chairs, line up a few more pillows, and issue a few more train tickets. At last, with the whole student body assembled on the platform, tickets were punched by one conductor while another conductor escorted passengers to their car of choice. "All aboard" was called, the door was shut, and the magical journey began. Hot chocolate, warm banana/chocolate chip muffins, and silver bells were waiting at journey's end.

The next week the children were busy with their play, *Mr. Scrooge's Christmas*, their song flute performance, the school luncheon and their gift exchange. The fall semester ended with our honored traditions and good cheer. And with Tiny Tim's, "God bless us every one!"

Mr. Scrooge's Christmas

CHAPTER 18

My Neck Gets Smaller
and Additional Accomplishments

As soon as the holidays were over I began helping Buck and Don prepare their power point presentations. I wouldn't normally require power point presentations from kindergarteners and first graders. I'm not that zealous. But these younger children were in the same class, the same room, as the second and third graders. They wanted to participate. They *expected* to participate. Pick me! Pick me! I couldn't deny them. What would Frank Smith say? Besides, I'd promised all my students I'd key their reference pages for them and that's the only difficult part of a research project, right?

At the beginning of this assignment the students had generated a list of possible questions to answer about their famous women including dates and places of birth, childhood activities, education, interests, famous quotes, and the contribution each made to her community. For the last slide they were to give a personal comment such as why they had chosen their particular subject, why they admired her, or something important they had learned from her.

Using these questions as an outline the second and third graders had done their research and were preparing their power point presentations with very little help from me. I had suggested they each make five or six slides, but they begged to make more.

"This is supposed to be hard work. You girls and boy are having way too much fun."

"Just ten slides, Dr. Seawell. Please? Twelve, maybe?"

"Well, okay. Here, watch this. This is how you can change font styles and sizes. You might find this helpful."

"Cool! Let us try!"

So the second and third grade teams were flying along on their own, but I had to work one-on-one with the two youngest children. We would sit side-by-side at a computer; I would read a few paragraphs from their materials and ask if they thought they should say anything about that part. If their answer was yes, they would verbalize their statement, and I'd key it for them. Then they would take over and finish the slide by choosing the colors, design, transition, and sound. (The sound most often chosen by these two thrill seekers, these two little boys, was breaking glass. Alarming!)

Buck and I had downloaded all of his information from several Internet sites. Although his materials were limited to a few dozen pages, the information was adequate and included several photos of Frances Bascom to help us get a feel for her life and times. Occasionally the two of us would find a few minutes to work together while the other students were working in their teams. We proceeded slowly, but within a few weeks Buck had completed his slides and had replayed and rehearsed his presentation until he could read most of it and had memorized the rest.

Don's situation was different. His knowledge of Sacajawea was vast. He was bubbling with information. In addition to what he had learned during the two years we had immersed ourselves in the Lewis and Clark project, he had collected materials from the Internet and from our library. He also had a Sacajawea video which he had watched several times. Our problem was that we didn't have much one-on-one time. We would squeeze out a slide here and there, but as the deadline approached, he still had a long way to go.

Eventually we began working on his presentation for a few minutes every day after school. I would read, he would think about it and decide what to say, I would key, he would complete the slide. One afternoon as we sat so engaged, the room to ourselves, our chairs side-by-side, I began noticing that each time I took my turn at the keyboard Don seemed distracted. He wasn't looking at the computer monitor, he was leaning forward, twisting sideways in his chair, staring up at me. A distant region of my brain began wondering why I was being scrutinized, but my brain often wonders about the actions of young children, so I continued concentrating on the task at hand.

We completed one slide, hit "slide show" to check our progress, then began another slide. When I started keying again, Don resumed his staring.

Finally he reached his hand up under my chin and gently pressed the loose skin at my throat. It's normal for children to use their sense of touch when learning something new, but a closer region of my brain began wondering about this tactile investigation. What wheels were spinning in Don's head? What connections was he attempting to make? I kept keying. Don reached up to my throat again. This time his exploratory touch was firmer and included pressing the skin at several different points. At last his question came.

"Dr. Seawell, did your neck used to be bigger?"

Did my neck used to be bigger? Did my *neck* used to be *bigger*?

I grow old…I grow old…

I shall wear the bottoms of my trousers rolled.

"Don, maybe that's it. I've been wondering and wondering about that extra skin. Maybe my neck *did* used to be bigger… or maybe my skin has just gotten old and stretched out. You know, like a pair of old socks or something."

"Well, I think it used to be bigger."

"Well, I like your interesting idea."

"Well, I was just wondering about it."

"Well, I like hearing about your wondering."

Sacagawea was a teenager when she made her significant contribution to the opening of the Great American West. Despite her arduous, two-year journey, I'm quite certain there were no mysterious changes in her neck size. Besides, her infant, Pompy, was too young to wonder about it, anyway.

A few days after I received the troubling news that my neck had gotten smaller, my students' on-going love affair with dinosaurs was invigorated by one of Anna's NOVA reports. We visited the NOVA website, and then spent some time reading about paleontologists and the nature of their work.

After school that afternoon I rounded up the stray animal bones I had found in my classroom cabinets during an organizing spree and buried them, along with some small plastic dinosaurs, in a sandy area out by the greenhouse. The following day, armed with trowels and paint brushes, my five young paleontologists marched out to their dig and began working in their designated sectors.

Finding the plastic dinosaurs was fun, but extracting real "fossils" was exhilarating. For days the children kept the bones on their desks, inspecting them during free moments, guessing about their age and origins, and examining them with magnifying glasses. In one of her forays through our classroom Shirley suggested they imagine what the dinosaurs whose fossils they had found might look like and draw some pictures of them.

Not long after our dig we accepted an invitation to attend a presentation by Dr. Judith Sankey, a paleontologist from California State University at Stanislaus. The students asked to take their fossils along to be identified.

"Boys and Girls, you *do* know these aren't really dinosaur fossils, right?"

"Right, Dr. Seawell. We know we're just pretending."

"Yeah, Dr. Seawell, we know you buried them. We're just pretending."

"Well, okay. I just thought I should check."

"Dr. Seawell, we know real digs don't have little toy dinosaurs buried in them!"

"Well, okay. I was just making sure no one was confused."

"We're not confused. But the paleontologist might know what kind of bones these are."

"She might. She might even be able to tell you approximately how old they are."

"Let's give her the dinosaur pictures we've drawn."

"That would be thoughtful. I'm sure she would be pleased."

On lecture day, equipped with clipboards, paper, pencils, camera, bones, and dinosaur pictures, we walked down to park headquarters for the lecture. After the presentation and after the adults in attendance asked their questions, Dr. Sankey accepted the children's dinosaur pictures, then examined the "fossils" they presented to her. She told them she couldn't identify their findings, but she would try to tell them something about their age, and she explained the clues she would use to do this. She found one of the bones more interesting than the rest. After studying it and consulting with a colleague she told us the bone appeared to be that of some marine animal.

"I'm surprised to see this bone in the desert."

"I don't know where it came from. It's been in a cabinet in our classroom for years."

"Dr. Seawell just buried it so we could dig it up."

"We knew it wasn't a real dinosaur fossil."

"It's an interesting bone, just the same. Thank you for bringing it to show me."

Then Dr. Sankey continued visiting with my children, answering their questions, sharing her expertise. Although these students are much younger than those she normally teaches, what they lacked in paleontologic background they made up for in enthusiasm and she took the time to support their interest. This unexpected encounter with five-to-eight-year-olds was probably amusing for her, and clearly, it was enriching for them.

Almost every time we were invited to presentations at headquarters, I accepted. I felt these occasions were valuable in many ways. On the surface, it gave the children opportunities to practice some appropriate lecture behavior – attentiveness, note taking. True, the notes of a five-year-old may not be as comprehensive as those of an adult, but they are valuable nonetheless, and their value was acknowledged back in the classroom when we reviewed the lectures and shared our notes.

Attending these presentations gave my students opportunities to learn other things, as well. Of course they didn't always understand everything that was being reported. Neither did I! But beyond what they were hearing about such things as dinosaurs, birds, rocks, ants, frogs, volcanoes, and toads, they were discovering that scientific investigations are on-going; that new information is regularly being gathered and distributed; that people learn from experts in their fields; and, that the areas of study are many and varied. In short, they were learning to respect knowledge and those people who further knowledge. Because of the patience and generosity of the researchers in accepting and answering their questions, these young students were also beginning to appreciate their place in the community of learners, and this may have been their most valuable lesson of all.

Like youngsters in most schools, in addition to their academic pursuits, our students also have a few minutes every day for recess, unstructured outdoor play. For the past several weeks they have been devoting this free time to a new, all-encompassing activity. How should I describe it? City planning? Urban renewal? Architectural experimentation? A brave new world?

The latest project which has grabbed and is holding the children's attention grew from the region's rich and varied geologic history. Over the eons this area has been covered by a shallow sea, bathed in volcanic eruptions, and weathered by the tumults in between. As a result, the park is covered with rocks – all kinds of rocks: metamorphic, igneous, and sedimentary; big rocks, little rocks, flat rocks, and round ones. The school playground is no exception.

The children have always been aware of rocks. Gabriel, now a fourth grader, made his decision to become a geologist several years ago, and from all indications Buck, this year's kindergartner, will pursue some rock-related career, as well. But now *all* the K–5th graders have become obsessed with rocks. They are involved in a colossal project that seems to have swung out of their control and taken on a life of its own.

This rock-related fixation began when fourth grader Jessica started stacking rocks and sketching her conceptions of shelters that could be constructed with them. Her efforts caught the attention of her classmates, and soon all the children were spending their recess time searching for rocks of just the right size and shape, and using them to erect small shelters.

Most of the structures they have built are eight-to-ten inches high with interior spaces of about a square foot. Most face south to catch the winter sun and are created by fitting together and dry stacking flat rocks. A large flat rock is used for the roof, and the rounder, odd-shaped rocks are used to form walls for courtyards around the buildings. The young architects have completed about thirty of these little rock structures and the construction continues. Almost a fifth of our huge playground is now covered with these creations.

After only a few of the buildings were complete, the children perceived the need for rules and regulations. The town site was surveyed into a grid of lots drawn with sticks in the dirt. Streets were indicated and titles to the various lots were established. Then the children began selling properties to one another. The form of payment being – you guessed it! – rocks.

It wasn't long before government came to Stone Village, the children's name for the new metropolis. The first public building erected was a jail, complete with bars made of twigs for the windows. They also built a bank and a library. Defense needs were not overlooked; a walled fort was constructed. (It resembles Ft. Mandan, one of the forts built by the members of the Lewis and Clark expedition.) Taxes on land and buildings were assessed, and for those who couldn't or wouldn't pay, property was seized and tax auctions were held.

After establishing law, government, a monetary system, and taxation, the students have decided they need more cultural institutions to set the mini-society apart, so now they are making plans for developing their own language. I'm becoming somewhat anxious about my children. With all these profound and serious matters absorbing their recess time, when will they ever find time to play?

I am aware that I consistently describe my young scholars as bright, cooperative, happy, enthusiastic little beings. Flawless in every way. A teacher's dream. I am also aware that my rose-colored glasses have grown ever darker with time. A gerontologist once told me that as we age, we become more of what we've always been. At my age my optimism has probably reached critical mass. Just one of the advantages of living so long. However, despite the occasional argument, the occasional hurt feelings, the occasional tears, I find these children truly unusual in the way they accept and respect one another and in the patient and accommodating way the older children interact with the younger ones. I could fill pages with my analysis of this behavior, but suffice to say it reflects the values they bring from home and the advantages created by our small student population. Because we can operate more like a family than a bureaucracy, difficulties can be diffused before they develop. Then again, I could be wrong. Our unceasing cheerfulness may just be a result of all this fresh air and sunshine.

As the school days passed, we counted each one. This is a way to help young children grasp some ideas about time, space, and numbers. We marked the days by numbering paper arrows and taping them in sequence to the walls of our room. Reaching the 100th day of school is always cause for celebration. This year when we reached the 100th day we invited the 3rd and 4th graders to join us just before recess for a quick commemoration of the event.

Last year on the 100th day, we worked together in our social studies class to write 100 good wishes on slips of paper and we put them into a 100 Good Wishes bag. We opened the bag this year and each child read a few of his or her good wishes. Some of the wishes had to be re-wished (world peace, a cure for all diseases), but many of the wishes have become realities (stop spilling my milk, placing at the UIL meet, grandma coming for a visit). The children were especially amused by their last year's handwriting. They could see the improvement they have made in that area during the past twelve months.

By the 100th day, other long-term projects begin coming to fruition. Lauren, Jessica, Garrett, and Anna have all met the Presidential Challenge in the one-mile run. Now they are working as trainers to help their classmates qualify. They take this responsibility seriously and their trainees work hard to meet their weekly goals.

But all is not rosy in PE land. The K–4th grade class is up against an old nemesis, the shuttle run. In this event, students must sprint 30 feet, pick up a shuttlecock, return to their starting point, put the shuttlecock on the ground, sprint back to the 30 foot line, pick up a second shuttlecock, and then return to their starting point. And, at the Presidential level, all this dashing back and forth must be done in 11 seconds or less!

We have worked on the shuttle run all year, but we still haven't mastered it. I am suspicious that there are secret strategies for conquering this run, and this week I will beg for help in the parent letter. There must be coaches, athletes, and would-be athletes within our community who could come to the aid of our children.

This week we received an invitation to visit an excavation in Presidio that is being conducted by archeologists from the Center for Big Bend Studies at Sul Ross State University. The investigation is at the Millington site, a prehistoric to early historic village which is part of a larger area known as La Junta Archeological District. Archeological features uncovered with a backhoe by a city crew working at the edge of the site were the focus of the investigation.

Some 800 years ago people began living and farming in this region. Named *La Junta de los Ríos* (The Joining of the Rivers) by Spanish explorers, it is the place where the two largest rivers in the Chihuahuan desert meet. These are the Rio Conchos and the Rio Grande, and several villages were located along their banks. La Junta is the southeasternmost outpost of the ancient peoples of the American Southwest, and the area had become a cultural crossroads by the time the Spaniards arrived.

The first European to see and describe the villages of La Junta was Cabeza de Vaca. (In 1535. On that trek across southwest Texas with his three companions. After the shipwreck. Remember?) Beginning about forty-five years later the area was described several different times by members of various Spanish expeditions. By the 1680's missions were being established in the region; presidios (forts) were built beginning in the 1760's; and by the 1800's, La Junta was a major stopping point on the Chihuahuan Trail that linked Indianola, Texas, (that port of camel-importing fame), with Chihuahua City, Mexico.

Ever eager to see science in action, we accepted the invitation to visit the archeological excavation, did some quick Internet research, sent out field trip permission slips, and climbed on the bus at 7:30 the next morning. When we arrived at the site we were given a briefing, shown the excavation in progress, and taken on a short walking tour of the area.

Learning at La Junta

We learned that the region was first investigated by professional arche-ologists in the 1930's, and that it has been listed on the National Register of Historic Places since 1978. The most recent research is concentrated on sev-eral human burials and structural remnants exposed by the backhoe; and upon stone tools and pottery shards discovered at the site.

We had hoped for an opportunity to watch the archeologists and learn how they collect data and organize their findings, but what we got was even more rewarding. Our students were divided into four groups, shown how to search for and recognize artifacts and bits of charcoal and charred wood, then put to work at the screening trays.

During the next hour the children screened many buckets of dirt and sand. Although they found no pottery shards or residue from the manufacture of stone tools, they were thrilled each time they found small pieces of charred wood which they had learned came from ancient cooking fires.

The highlight of the screening project occurred when Lauren, who is enthralled by all things pertaining to blood, diseases, and the human body, found a bone. It was identified in the field by the physical anthropologist as a human finger bone, and it created much excitement and careful scrutiny among the children.

Fascinating Find

As they recovered them, the children turned their findings over to the archeologists and watched as they were bagged and properly labeled for analysis back at the lab. Their involvement in this project gave them an enormous sense of satisfaction. They were learning something about the ancient peoples who lived in this area, and they were playing a part in the process through which much of the information about these ancient peoples is gained.

This experience opened another door for our students, and we were grateful to the archeologists at the Center for Big Bend Studies for making this happen. Although none of my children have yet announced their decisions to become archeologists, the seeds have been sown, and they may, over time, sprout and grow.

As the last semester of our last year in the park continued, we found yet another occasion to celebrate.

"Hooray for you, Don! You've done it! You've learned to read the 25 most important words in the English language! What treat would you like for your Word Party?"

"Strawberry cake with chocolate icing. That's my favorite."

"Strawberry cake? Don, I'm not sure if I know how to make a strawberry cake."

"Dr. Seawell! It's *easy*! You just get a box of cake and put water in it and pop it in the oven."

"Oh. Well, that doesn't sound too difficult. I bet I can do it."

"It's *easy*!"

Oh, my. Don has worked so hard to learn these words. He deserves his favorite dessert. But where am I going to find a strawberry cake mix 100 miles from a supermarket? I don't even know if they make strawberry cake mix.

The Study Butte Store stands outside the west gate of the park amid buttes and mine tailings. A long church pew on the porch serves as a "new-to-you" exchange point. People leave clothing, household items, books, and sundry treasures on the church pew. Other people look through the stuff and take what they want. No need for a middle-man or woman. In south county this system works, and the flow of goods onto and off the Study Butte porch is smooth and constant.

The tiny store itself is crammed with an astonishing assortment of items. Need a fresh pineapple? Pliers? Pampers? Pickles? A toilet plunger? How about a bottle of chardonnay? An avocado or some clothes pins? A night light or a frozen turkey loaf? A box of strawberry cake mix! A can of chocolate frosting! The Study Butte Store rules! Kudos to the proprietor who delivers the service and the vendors who deliver the goods.

The strawberry cake with chocolate frosting was enjoyed by both the K–2nd graders and the dignitaries Don invited to his party. Among others, his guest list included his mom, Ms. Coleman, and Mr. John P. Seawell, that patient, patient volunteer who had worked so faithfully to help him learn to read the twenty-five most frequently used words in the English language. A goal had been reached. An achievement was celebrated. Sunshine saturated our world. And a little boy was happy.

CHAPTER 19

Hail and Farewell

O ne of the things that seemed most remarkable to me when I began teaching at San Vicente Elementary was something that happens after school. From 3:30 to 4:00 most weekday afternoons, most of the little kids can be found on the school playground. The unusual thing about this is that it is their moms or dads who take the time to sit on the playground bench and supervise them. Where else in this rushed and busy world are parents choosing to watch their children *play*? Do these children have any idea how lucky they are? Do these parents have any idea how rare their behavior is? Unstructured. Unorganized. Time to play. A precious gift.

Not every day, but often, Anna uses her play time in a different way. While the other children rip and roar around outside, she comes into our classroom and asks to "do my art." Then she assembles her supplies and works for the next thirty minutes in her focused, concentrated way.

Over the years princesses have given way to cheetahs, to marine mammals, to toads. Earthworms have given way to butterflies, to parakeets, to fish. Occasionally she recreates photos from the science books, pictures from the story books, drawings from the library books. She has also done many family portraits of herself and her two sisters.

As she has acquired spelling and penmanship skills, Anna sometimes writes stories instead of producing visual arts. But, artist or author, the little, round, red table in the back of our classroom is where her creativity often flows, and her works-in-progress cubby is never empty.

Although Anna and I engage in countless conversations during the day, these after-school sessions are quiet times. We work. Silent and still. We rarely exchange a word. Although we sit across the room from each other, our spirits are linked. We are Texas two-steppin' across the same dance floor, and we glide with a lighthearted lilt.

When the Famous American Women power point presentations were completed, stored on CD's, and the CD's safely secured in the children's research carrels, we began the next phase of the project. I had asked the children to begin noticing the women in Panther Junction who were making contributions to our community. We talked about their own mothers first and discussed their contributions, then we focused on the other women we knew.

Our plan was that each child would honor his or her mother and one additional woman at an afternoon tea party. The children would introduce their guests and give some information about the contributions they were making. Then the students would make their power point presentations, and finally tea and refreshments would be served.

The children sent out their invitations and I arranged with the honorees a time when they could be interviewed about the work they do. We were going to do the interviews by phone, so the children created a list of "talking points," brushed up on phone manners, and role played conducting interviews.

We practiced greeting guests at the door and leading them to their seats. We rehearsed the introductions we would make. We reviewed our power point presentations. Then we made no-cook orange ball delicacies to add to the refreshments that Shirley had volunteered to provide. Tea Party day arrived, and we were ready.

All our work came together as each child stood before the audience with his or her two guests, introduced them, and told about their contributions.

Then it was time to dazzle the honorees. The children took turns going to the laptop, inserting their CD, going through the several steps necessary to project their slide show on the large screen we had set up for the occasion, and reading their texts aloud.

The presentations themselves were well done, but the audience seemed even more impressed with the children's technical expertise. Even five-year-old Buck, who is just beginning to read, was able to manage on his own.

Refreshments followed, and Shirley had prepared an elaborate assortment of selections, a true "high tea." Everyone in attendance was especially entranced with the chocolate fountain which flowed with delicious coverings for the fresh fruit and marshmallows that were served.

After all the famous women departed, the big kids were invited to see the little kids' presentations. And, yes, afterward the refreshment table was reopened and the chocolate fountain continued to flow.

As the year winds down and our new house builds up, John and I are sometimes shocked at the thought of leaving our wonderful little school where, just like Lake Woebegone, all the children are above average, and all the people friendly and helpful. It will not be easy, but a recent exchange I had with our seventh grader points out that we've made the right decision.

Bryan asked, "Do you really have to leave?"

"Yes. It's time. I can't remember all your names anymore."

"But Dr. Seawell, there are only seventeen of us!"

"Right, Bryan! My point exactly!"

Our last spring in the park was dotted with happy events, but there also came a great sadness. In early March, we lost our beloved little Newfoundland girl. We had always known that Mandy would not have a long life. She is the second Newfy we have had who was born with sub-aortic stenosis, a congenital heart defect in which fibrous tissue develops in or near the aortic valve. This tissue narrows the valve and compromises the flow of blood as the dog grows. In 2002 a veterinary cardiologist at Texas A&M University told us that our twelve-week-old puppy would probably not live to see her third birthday. At that time the procedure to correct the problem was still at the experimental stage and she could not recommend it.

But five months ago we celebrated Mandy's fourth birthday and I suppose we thought we had somehow beaten the odds. After all, Mandy was rather small for a Newfoundland, we had kept her weight in a healthy range, and her problem had been detected early and was being treated with daily medication.

Yesterday John made the eight-hour round trip to Midland to get a supply of her food and favorite chews, and just two weeks ago he took her to Alpine for her annual vaccinations. We just weren't prepared to lose her now.

The redeeming feature of her malady is that, throughout her life, she suffered no symptoms. Last night she was sleeping, as she always did, in the hallway outside our bedroom with her head curled around the door frame into the room so she could be a part of the pack. At 11:00 John let her out as usual with the "go powder your nose" suggestion. When she came back in, we all went to sleep. The evening could not have been more normal.

At 1:30 we were awakened by a strange little whimper. Mandy was lying in her usual place and I thought she was having a bad dream. She whimpered again and I got up to reassure her. But as I reached her she made what sounded like a little gasp.

I knelt and put my hand on her shoulder. Then her breathing stopped, and she was gone. She never lifted her head. It was all over in less than a minute, and as sad as we are, we are grateful that she didn't suffer for long, if at all.

Mandy – Amanda In Pilgrim's Clothing because she was born on Thanksgiving Day and was black with a small white bowtie and white "buckles" on her front toes – will be missed not only by John and me, but also by her friends in the park. Besides playing the Newfoundland Seaman during our two-year Lewis and Clark project, she was an everyday part of school and neighborhood life. Many of the children loved her, as did many of the adults as well.

John always took Mandy on a special morning stroll through the neighborhood after I left for school, even though he had just finished a two-mile walk with me on the school track. Like most Newfoundlands, Mandy never met a human or an animal she didn't like, and she enjoyed nothing so much as stopping to greet passers-by. Many were the mornings that Apryl would dash into my classroom before school to wash Newfy slobber off her hands and the top of her head. ("But I *want* to be kissed by Mandy, Dr. Seawell!")

We are grateful to have had this joyful little girl with us for over four years, and we are glad she got to see the new house we are building and wander through it. We loved her. Our hearts are broken. We will miss her always.

Mandy's death was difficult for all the children, but especially for Don. He lives right across the street from us and was available to give her hugs almost every time she stepped out the front door. He brought tears to my eyes when he immortalized her in the autobiography he dictated to me, and he spent many after-school minutes searching for just the right clip art to complete the pages.

One of my friends is gone. Her name is Mandy. She was fun to play with, but she was heavy and strong. She was a Newfoundland dog.

We put Mandy in the Lewis and Clark play. She died on March 9, 2006. We all liked to play with Mandy, but now she is gone.

Of the many projects I've initiated with my students during my teaching years, the activities that involve them with writing have been the most important, the most powerful, the most worthwhile. When I began journaling with my high school students in 1971, I was stunned at the impact our weekly private dialogues created. The purpose of the assignment was to keep me updated on their individual reading, and I taped a list of thirty open-ended questions onto the inside cover of their spiral notebooks to help them do that. They were to begin their entries with any one of the questions and after writing their response, they were to complete the page with anything else they wanted to write.

It was not a complicated assignment. If they encountered brain freeze after responding to the reading question they were to fill the rest of the page with their favorite variations of "I can't think of anything else to write about today." I promised that their entries would be confidential, and explained if they wrote about something that needed to be handled by their counselor or their parents, I would come to them first. (And when this happened, they often asked me to schedule the meeting and come along.)

Each week I collected the journals, read every page of each one, and wrote comments in the margins. I never gave advice, but I often asked questions.

Did reading and commenting in 100+ journals every week take awhile? Yes. Did coming home with a stack of journals to read and comment in every night of the week make John P. Seawell roll his eyes? Yes. Was reading and responding to their journals the most significant thing I did for my students? Yes.

Reading the journals was a humbling experience. The students were so grateful that someone, *anyone*, was taking the time to listen to their ideas, opinions, hopes, wishes, dreams. And sometimes their fears. Often, in the course of explaining a problem they had, they would work out a solution; often in the course of explaining a fear they had, they would gain courage. And often, at the end of the page, they would write, "Thank you for reading this."

Beginning with that first year of journaling with students, as I went from school to school, from grade level to grade level, the journal was the heart of my class. Of course we covered the requirements, met the standards, completed the essentials. But the journal was the heart. Writing is a way of seeing, learning, understanding, gaining insight. Writing opens paths along which to wander, along which to explore.

This year writing has been popular with all my students. We write books. We publish them. Real books. Hardback covers. Shirley found the system; Lisa, our multi-talented volunteer, taught us how to use the program; all my students became authors; and I just sat back and cheered. Last week I even wrote and published my own book. It's about the Citizen Heroes and their riparian restoration.

Oh, yes, indeed. The Cottonwood Project is alive and well in the school greenhouse. The 24 cuttings the K–4th grade students set in pots a few weeks ago are putting on leaves. When they have developed good root systems we will plant these saplings at Croton Spring. Although only five of the little trees we planted in this location last year have survived, we have learned a great deal about growing cottonwoods and we are applying what we've learned to this year's experiment.

As we continued rolling toward the end of the school year, I realized how proud I was of the progress my students had made in PE. They had set high goals for themselves at the beginning of the year and they had worked toward these goals with diligence and dedication. They had become strong, powerful little kids. When Melissa's weight room conversation turned to organizing the park team for the Relay for Life, I wondered if my children might like to get involved. Participation in such a public event would be an opportunity for them to become part of a bigger world and would perhaps inspire in them a life-long commitment to exercise and good health.

The Relay for Life is conducted every April on the Sul Ross campus. Through this activity the people of Alpine and the surrounding area participate in a national fund- raising event sponsored by the American Cancer Society. The Relay consists of 14 hours of continuous running in relay to raise money for cancer research. Park personnel take part through their team, the Paisanos (Spanish for "fellow countryman," the word commonly used along the U.S.-Mexican border for the bird known as the Greater Roadrunner). Could our students form their own team?

Many phone calls and emails later, the Relay chair agreed to allow our children to participate. Since the relay was run throughout the night, there had never been a request for a children's team before. But it had been decided that the children would be responsible for the first hour of the relay only, and their team would be counted as one member of the park adult team. Thus, the Paisanitos (little fellow countrymen ... and women) team was born.

I explained the purpose of the relay and the way it worked to the children, then I asked if they would be interested in participating in this activity. Of course! Another great adventure!

We located the relay batons in the PE shed and the children began practicing hand-off techniques. We ordered Relay for Life T-shirts and started collecting money for a worthy cause.

Since the field trip to Alpine would last until well into Friday night, participation was optional. Only those children who volunteered and whose parents were amenable participated. At the final count we had seven children on the Paisanitos team – one pre-ker, one 2nd grader, two 3rd graders, and three 4th graders. Shirley and Lisa accompanied the Paisanitos and me on our bus ride to Alpine on the afternoon of the event. We were joined later by Lisa's husband and two more sets of parents who drove to the event after completing their work day.

Several people in the park had made donations in the name of the Paisanitos and many members of Lauren, Anna, and Allison's large extended family had sent checks to sponsor their girls. Thanks to the generosity of all these donors, the seven Little Roadrunners had raised $695 to contribute to the American Cancer Society.

The Paisanitos arrived at the track in high spirits, and after settling their backpacks and assorted gear at the Paisano headquarters tent and eating a snack, they asked permission to run a practice lap around the track. Then away they sprinted in their matching T-shirts. Next, with almost an hour left before the scheduled events began, the children started creating their own entertainment.

The theme of this year's relay was, "Lights, Camera, Action," so the children had made and brought with them megaphones and a snapping, ruler-topped sign like those used to mark motion picture takes. For her contribution, Melissa brought along a director's chair. With all this film equipment available, the children decided to make a movie. So, for the next half hour they entertained themselves with shouts of "Quiet on the set," "Cut," and "That take will be in the blooper reel!" as they took turns being movie directors.

After their last film was finished, I walked the children over to the huge snack tent where participants in the relay, identified by the wrists bands they had been issued, could get fruit, cookies, water, and other refreshments. My ground rules were one piece of fruit, one cookie, and one water bottle per child, but Apryl negotiated for a large dill pickle in lieu of fruit. The children were thrilled to be recognized as participants and to be given "free stuff."

By the time the Paisanitos finished their snacks, the relay opened with a march around the track by area cancer survivors. The children cheered them on with encouraging shouts through their megaphones. Then each relay team walked around the track. The Paisanitos walked with the Paisanos, and the children had the honor of pulling the team's mascot, a six-foot papier mache road runner mounted on a red wagon.

After these procedures, the running phase of the relay began. Each team had been given a placard with a number on it to be worn by the member who was on the track. Since the Paisanitos were scheduled to run during the first hour, they began taking turns running a lap around the quarter-mile track, then handing off the number placard to the next runner before walking a cool-down lap.

Five-year-old Allison was the last of the seven Paisanitos to have a turn. Her mother had planned to run with her, but when her time came Allison grabbed the number placard and took off like a rocket. Lisa, young and in good shape, tried her best, but she never even came close to catching up. Allison tore around the track wearing bright red Crocs on her little feet because a blister she had gotten on a long hike the day before prevented her from wearing her running shoes. (In case their shooting star has faded into oblivion, Crocs are rubber, clog-like shoes that remind me of the ones Koreans were wearing forty years ago.) Both the Paisanos and Paisanitos shouted and cheered for Allison, awed by her amazing speed. The child was inspiring!

All the children ran hard when their turns came, and those adults from the park who had not seen them run before were astonished. These young athletes are in excellent shape; running in relay as a team embodied their idea of glory; and, the cheers of the crowd spurred them to even greater efforts.

In between laps while they waited for their next turn, the children amused themselves in the broad-jump sand pit near the team tent. Since rocky soil dominates in the park, the smooth, soft sand was a tempting treat. Craters, tunnels, and volcanoes quickly took shape in the sand.

I had estimated that each child would run a total of three laps before the Paisanitos' hour was up. At the end of the hour the number placard was to be passed to one of the adult team members. Easier said than done! The children took no notice of their summons to stop at three laps. They were on a streak, and they didn't want to give up the number placard or the limelight! Finally, after most of them had run a full mile, I insisted that they stop, and the Paisanitos' part of the relay was over.

Meanwhile, Shirley had taken pizza orders and gone to the local Pizza Hut to reserve a table for the young runners and their parents. Unlike most American youngsters, the park children don't have the opportunity to visit such places often; consequently, a trip to a fast food restaurant was almost as exciting to them as the relay itself.

At last I tore the children away from the track and the sand pit, got them cleaned up, on the school bus, and off to the Pizza Hut. As we walked through the door our pizzas were just being set on the table. The parents were amazed at how perfectly Shirley's advance planning had worked out. "After over thirty-six years in the education business, I've been to the rodeo before," was her response.

By the time the feast was finished it was almost 10 p.m. and time to begin the two-hour drive back to the park. I had suggested that the children bring pillows for the trip home, and they had done that and more. Pillows, blankets, and stuffed animals littered the bus.

"Seat belts, Everyone!"

"Yes, Miss Frizzle!"

The children viewed the return trip through the middle of the night as a combination of the Magic School Bus and the Polar Express, but before long exhaustion took its toll, excitement was replaced by sleep, and I was left with only Shirley and Lisa to help me spot deer, javelina, and kamikaze bunnies along the road as we made our way back to the park.

It was midnight when our little group got home. I dropped the children off at their houses, often having to wake them and help them collect their possessions. Another long field trip was over. My last one. But I couldn't dwell on that. Too difficult to drive a bus with tears in my eyes.

The final six weeks of school brought some changes to our class. It was hard to say goodbye to Garrett and Buck when they headed back to Montana, but just a few days before they left we welcomed a new first grader, Tristan. He and his family have returned to the park after their stay in Alaska. Tristan's older sister is an 8th grade graduate of San Vicente.

John and I have been surprised by the number of park service personnel who divide their time between this park and parks in Alaska. They like the contrast. They refer to Big Bend National Park as Baked Alaska.

Tristan slid easily into our class. He is a bright, cooperative little boy with a good sense of humor and good classroom manners. As with Don, math is his favorite subject, so the two boys soldier through their assignments because math games await the successful completion of their work. Rather than sit at their individual computers, the boys find it more satisfying to play games together at one computer. Although I sometimes have to calm their excitement, playing together seems to increase their level of engagement, and without doubt, it increases their level of fun.

The week we said good-bye to Garrett and Buck, we welcomed another new student. Kassandra is a second grader and a sweeter, more loving child you will never meet; however, her transition to our tiny class was not so easy. She had spent her school years in classes of traditional public school size in a town southwest of San Antonio. Anna and Tanya were welcoming and friendly, but for the first few days Kassandra had crashed upon an alien planet, a stranger in a strange academic land.

The problem was that the other two second graders were reading at a grade or more above level, using vocabulary words from college entrance exams, and requesting "a little Mozart, please," as they zipped along in math. Kassandra is a conscientious student, and a solid, on-level, second grader. But in her new school she had some frustrating moments. There were even a few tears.

It was important for Kassandra to know that she was okay, important for Anna and Tanya to know that Kassandra was okay. The three girls and I discussed the situation. We talked about the differences in their classroom experiences and how students in a class of two might make more rapid progress than students in a class of twenty-two. It was a serious, thoughtful discussion in which all three girls participated and gained insight. When Kassandra said she wanted to "catch up," Anna and Tanya offered suggestions.

"Dr. Seawell could help you for a little while after school every day."

"Your mom could help you practice your math facts."

"You could take the story tapes home and read with them so you'll get faster."

"You could take extra math sheets home and practice."

"These are good suggestions, Kassandra. It would mean a lot of extra work. What do you think about doing extra work?"

"I want to do it!"

Now that my three second graders were clear about our circumstances, I met with Kassandra's mom. It was easy for her to see how two little girls, sitting one on each side of their teacher for two years, might have made rapid progress. She understood Kassandra's dilemma and was eager to help her adjust to this new situation.

We implemented most of the suggestions Anna and Tanya had made, I gave her mom some specific home activities, and Kassandra began her campaign to pull alongside her new classmates. Soon I discovered that story writing was an area in which she could shine. She wrote with care and attention to detail. When she learned that she could publish her stories with our special book-binding program, she developed many book ideas and often spent after-school time searching for the perfect clip art to enhance her pages. Writing and publishing stories became her joy and her reward as she worked to strengthen her reading and math skills.

Following our mid-May tradition, we traveled to Terlingua for the Spring Fiesta. As always, the children demonstrated what they had learned in dancing, gymnastics, and music. We had also sent displays of their art work and writing samples to be exhibited during the fiesta.

The morning went well as the children strutted their stuff; however, by afternoon the weather had grown oppressive, even by Terlingua standards. In lieu of giving the younger children an extended recess on such a searing day, the Terlingua teachers chose to take their students into their air-conditioned classrooms and show them a movie.

The Second Grade Gals

My five were invited to join the Terlingua second grade class, and the movie they watched was an animated and lively well-known children's story. At the movie's conclusion, the Terlingua teacher complimented me on the attentive behavior of my first and second graders. It was a generous comment, and I appreciated it, but as I drove our little bus back to the park, I had to smile. It was true. My students had no trouble paying attention to a spirited, bubbly children's story. These were the same children who had been able to focus for forty-five minutes almost a year earlier on a slow-moving, pedantic video about the life and times of Susan B. Anthony!

I never mean to bore my students. Not with Susan B. or anything else. It is in the spirit of being thorough that I subject them to a few dull, plodding experiences. I don't want them to miss anything important. In elementary classrooms I am always haunted by the specter of inadvertently skipping something vital.

During the first years of John's retirement, I initiated a pre-k program in the district in which I was teaching. I threw myself into organizing the curriculum and teaching the four-year-olds with a frenzy that startled my husband and gave him cause for alarm. Each morning as he bid me goodbye he would whisper, "Remember, you don't have to teach them everything. You're not the only teacher they're ever going to have."

But things had been different at San Vicente. I *had* been the only teacher several of my children had ever had. I had been their only teacher for four years. Had I given them enough? Had I taught them everything they needed to know? The idea of releasing them, of sending them on to become "big kids," unnerved me. Were they prepared? Were they ready? Would they be successful when I let them go?

Wait a minute. I still had the summer months. Weren't the children still mine for the summer months? Of course they were. In two months we could learn a little more.

"Girls! I have a great idea! A summer diary! We can write about the places we go and the books we read and anything else we think of. Then we'll get together just before school starts next year and share our diaries with each other. It'll be fun."

"Good idea, Dr. Seawell. Maybe we should get together at your new house."

"Excellent plan!"

"Maybe we should have a sleepover at your new house."

"Most excellent plan!"

"Maybe we should invite all the other girls."

"Superb idea! Let's plan the whole project and write our invitations."

"We should make the diaries for everyone. We can use everyone's favorite color for the folders."

Recess arrived and the second graders shared their plan with the 3rd and 4th grade girls.

"What about us, Dr. Seawell? What about the boys?"

"Gabriel, of course! The boys!"

"But, Dr. Seawell, boys don't write diaries."

"They don't?"

"Boys write journals."

"Of course! I knew that!"

This project was working out beyond my most selfish dreams. *All* my children would be "little kids" for two more months. After that I could do it. After that I could let them fly.

As my days at San Vicente continued dwindling down, the storm clouds behind my eyes grew denser. Although my mind knew concluding my teaching career was the right decision, my heart wasn't anywhere near embracing the idea. As we headed toward June, thoughts that this was my last year had to be held at bay.

Graduation came, along with the end-of-school awards. The children's many academic achievements were recognized, followed by the Fitness Awards. Every one of my PE students had reached National or Presidential status. They had done the work, but I was the one peacock proud.

Then it was over. Report cards were finished. Books were checked in. Electronic equipment was returned to the technology room. I peeled the bonus words off the classroom wall. And off the ceiling. I made a final survey of the room, the room that had vibrated with laughter, and learning, and love. Tears were splashing when I stepped outside and locked the door. Last time forever.

CHAPTER 20

Keeping a Secret

O n the 9th of June, 2006, Mr. John P. Seawell sent his final email from the park. His subject line was "The Big Surprise." This is what he wrote:

The planning had been going on for months. We would have a surprise party for Pat. My chief co-conspirator, and the person who did the bulk of the work, was Lisa, mother of Allison, Anna, and Lauren. Lisa's girls have formed the nucleus of Pat's classes for the four years she has taught in the park.

Using my experience as a military intelligence officer, I knew that in order to keep anything secret, there must be a deception plan – an alternate, plausible scenario that will distract attention from the real secret. In Pat's case, we felt that she would expect *something* to be done for her upon her departure, so we constructed a luncheon in Terlingua. Her colleagues would give her a nice gift, everyone would say goodbye, and we felt she would buy into the deception.

Meanwhile, our friend Shelia arrived from North Carolina. She had been a seventh grade student of Pat's in Northern Virginia and is now a partner in a law firm in Charlotte. The cover for her visit was that her secretary was taking her vacation that week.

Lisa had worked out an elaborate plot to get Pat to the community center on the evening of the party. Meanwhile, Pat had her own ideas about what to do on party day, and her arrangements created some complications in an otherwise well-oiled plan.

First, Pat decided to show Shelia the beloved cottonwoods her kids had planted and she called Lisa to see if she and the girls wanted to go along (a great way of getting extra water to the trees!). Lisa declined, but couldn't come up with an excuse to keep the girls at home, so she reviewed the secrecy vow with them and held her breath that they wouldn't slip and let the cat out of the bag.

Next, Pat decided we should take Shelia to dinner at the Starlight. Then she called Shirley and invited her to go along. After a prolonged giggle, Shirley accepted, but invented some story requiring that she take her own car and meet us there.

The closest call had come a few nights earlier. Pat and I were watching a movie in bed and I was nodding off when she asked, "Did you get any interesting email today?" Without thinking I blurted out that Lisa had written she would need to fly to Colorado this week, but she wouldn't leave PJ until after the party.

Before Pat could even respond with the predictable, "What party?" I was wide awake and thinking furiously. I decided to give up the deception party so I said, "I'm sorry, this is supposed to be a secret, but the school is having a luncheon for you in Terlingua Saturday. Please, *please*, act surprised." After a few good-natured jibes about never trusting me with secrets, she bought it.

Then there was the call from our friend John, the retired Border Patrol veteran. He phoned to tell Pat that he and his wife would not be able to attend her party. He didn't know it was a surprise! Fortunately, Pat passed the phone to me before he could blurt it out, so the secret was safe.

With these near disasters survived, Lisa made her call on the night of the party, and we proceeded to the community center. I told Pat that I wanted to take Shelia in to see what the community center looked like. I know, a bit lame. ("Sweetheart, Shelia has seen a big rectangular room before.") But after rolling her eyes at Shelia, Pat went along with it, as she often goes along with things I want to do that seem idiotic to her.

When she walked into the room, Pat was totally surprised. All of Lisa's hard work, and that of so many others, had paid off. After hugs all around, a couple of margaritas, and a wonderful Mexican food dinner, Lisa started the presentation.

The centerpiece was a beautiful scrapbook filled with photos and artwork. It also contained letters from Pat's Big Bend students, past and present, telling what they remembered most about her. Interspersed among these priceless mementos, Lisa had written a wonderful commentary, which summarized each of Pat's four years.

Lisa and many others had put hundreds of hours into the scrapbook. They had been able to contact all but one of Pat's former students who had left the park and are now scattered from Alaska to Hawaii to Indiana to several different towns in Texas. The most amazing thing to me is that all these children had known about the surprise for months and had kept quiet about it. During the presentation the students stepped forward, one by one, and read their letter and a letter from one of the former students who now lives elsewhere.

Pat is thrilled with the scrapbook. It is a wonderful souvenir of our years in the park and will have a special place in our home, and in our hearts, for the rest of our lives. JPS

While John was writing his email, I added an entry to my journal. This will be the entry I share with my students when they come for the sleepovers.

June 9, 2006
Dear Summer Diary,
What a day! It began with a trip to Croton Spring to water the cottonwoods and ended with a beautiful surprise!

The surprise began when Ms. Spier called and asked if I could stop by the party she was helping with at the community center. She wanted me to pick up her house key so I could feed Anna's fish while the family was in Colorado.

Mr. John P. Seawell insisted he and our friend Shelia go with me to get the key. He wanted Shelia to see the community center. How weird is that? It's a big, rectangular room!

When we got to the community center I hesitated. I didn't want to interrupt the farewell speeches so I opened the door a tiny bit and peeked in.

Just as I had imagined, everyone was seated and quiet. All the children were sitting together at the front table. That seemed strange. They always sit with their parents.

Then I saw Ms. Spier standing in the middle of the room and she waved for me to come in. ("Oh, good grief! I don't want to interrupt everything! Why doesn't she just come over here and hand me the key?")

Meanwhile, I noticed that all the kids had gargantuan grins on their faces. Evidently the speaker had just told an excellent joke.

Suddenly I realized Shelia and Mr. John P. Seawell were *pushing* me through the door. How rude! This whole situation was becoming embarrassing.

Next I noticed Ms. Coleman sitting at a table with a big smile on her face. What was she doing here? She should be driving toward Terlingua to meet us for dinner. Nothing about this scene was making sense.

By then Mr. Seawell and Shelia had successfully pushed me into the room, but I still didn't get it. Even though the children were laughing and shouting "Surprise!" I still didn't realize this party was for me.

When I finally understood what was happening, I was beyond surprised. How could they have kept this secret from me? Me? I was a middle school teacher for a hundred years. No one can keep a secret from me!

It was a beautiful, wonderful party, and the thoughtful, loving letters the students had written to me were so touching they made me cry. Happy tears. The children, the adults, and the scrapbook merged to create an evening beyond compare. The surprise party of June 8, 2006 was a rare and precious gift that I'll cherish for the rest of my days.

During our last weeks in the park I kept my precious scrapbook on the coffee table, read and reread the letters, smiled at the photos, enjoyed the art work. The following is an excerpt from the scrapbook, written by Lisa and read by her at the party.

Into the West Texas Sunset

The years, months, and weeks are now down to days left in Big Bend. Walls in Alpine are going up, while books on shelves, items in desks, and pictures on walls in the classroom are coming down. The desk fairy has made her last appearance and Ted, the imaginary playmate, has taught his last computer game. The end of Year Four has come.

And so Dr. Seawell and Mr. John P. Seawell are moving on – up actually, just ever so slightly north of us ... yet much of them will remain here in the park with the children they have taught and the lives they have touched.

Albert Einstein said, "Imagination is more important than knowledge. Knowledge is limited. Imagination encircles the world." In this author's mind, there can be no better mantra by which to teach. We have seen in Pat the ability to inspire creativity, to help imagine those unheard of galaxies, to encourage the desire to take those established paradigms one step further...

As parents we tend to look at the big picture of reading, writing, and arithmetic. We look at these young faces and try to ensure that each and every child knows they have the potential to be our future leaders, scientists, role models, and peacemakers.

And yet, what was important to these children? Read the letters they wrote. "I remember you in your big floppy hat and I gave you a hug..." "You took the time to sit with me and explain things to me when I didn't understand." "You helped not just me, but everyone, become better people in the world." "Dr. Seawell is ... someone to talk to when I'm down, and an all around great friend." "I liked writing in my journal and getting the funny little notes that were always kind and encouraging." "I could talk on and on, but the best part is she is a nice person." "I will do what you taught me and set an example for others..." "You have been my teacher all my life ... and you will be in my heart always."

Off you go into the West Texas sunset, Dr. Pat and Mr. John P. Seawell – happy trails. Lisa Spier

Dear Dr. Seawell,

My favorite memory with you is when you invited me to go water the cottonwood trees at Croton Springs. I really had fun with you. I almost gave up carrying those heavy gallon jugs, but luckily you helped me make it to the creek. I can always count on you.

The most important thing you taught me is to help people who have trouble doing things. I will do what you taught me. I will even set an example for others.

You changed my life by becoming my friend and helping solve my problems. For example, you helped me make new friends. Without you the school won't be the same. The whole school will miss you.

Sincerely,
Your friend, Scott

Please don't leve, please. I have hade you as a teacher all my life and in my head past memorys about you are fulding my mind. Like learning to read. And the stinky bean process. You had told us that every seed has a baby plant inside. So we put some bean seeds in water and in about three days they stunk. And as the seeds spilt more and more the smell got worse and worse. We begged you to stop experimenting you agreed. Even though you're moving I want you to know you will be in my heart forever.

Love Anna

Dear Dr. Seawell,

My favorite memory with you is when you invited me to go water the cotton wood trees at Croton Springs. I really had fun with you. I almost gave up carrying those heavy gallon jugs, but luckily you helped me make it to the creek. I can always count on you.

The most important thing you taught me is to help people who have trouble doing things. I will do what you taught me. I will even set an example for others.

You changed my life by becoming my friend and helping solve my problems. For example, you helped me make new friends. Without you the school won't be the same. The whole school will miss you.

Sincerely,
Your friend, Scott

Please don't leve, please. I have hade you ds a teacher all my life andin my head past memorys about you are fulding my mind. Like leaming to read. And the stinky bean process. You had told us that every seed has a baby plant inside

So We put some bean seeds in water and in about three days they stunk. And as the seeds spilt more and more the smell got worse and worse. We begged you to stop experimenting you agreed. Even though Youre moving I want you to know you will be in my heart forever.

love anna

You shall know the truth and the truth shall make you free. Here is my truth: I was born with an expectation, a certainty. Something wonderful was to happen, was supposed to happen. Something wonderful that was *intended* for me.

Undefined. Unclear. Indefinite. Indistinct. An expectation without form, a certainty without face. Yet it persisted, insisted, pestered, and plagued. So…I waited. Something wonderful was intended for me.

With age came insight, came understanding, came acceptance.

For I have known them all already, known them all –
Have known the evenings, mornings, afternoons,
I have measured out my life with coffee spoons…

In youth I was charmed by the hope of something wonderful, beguiled. Hope gave me dreams; whispered enchantment. Hope also supported, guided, pushed, propelled, nurtured optimism, and cushioned my journey to maturity. I acknowledged hope's essential role, and tucked the whims of my youth into memory. Gently. With tenderness.

Then I stumbled upon a time, and a place, and children who can see camel tracks in a canyon and find gold nuggets in a ditch.

This was my kismet. *This* was the magic intended for me. I spent a long time waiting. But I found it. After my neck got smaller and my hair turned gray.

One of Our Courageous Croton Spring Cottonwoods, October 2012

REFERENCES

Abbey, E. (1968). *Desert solitaire A season in the wilderness.* New York: Touchtone.

Ambrose, S. E. (1996). *Undaunted courage.* New York: Simon & Schuster.

Baum, D. (2008, February). Texas camel corps. Retrieved February 25, 2008, from http://www.texascamelcorps.com

Bissonette, J. A. (1982). Ecology and social behavior of the collared peccary in Big Bend National Park, Texas. Washington, DC: US Department of the Interior/National Park Service.

Boren, M. (2008, winter/spring). Big Bend Natural History Association. *The Paisano. 28(1),* 2.

Boyd, E. J. (1995). *Noble brutes: Camels on the American frontier.* Plano, Texas: Wordward Press.

Cloud, W. A. (2008). Senior Project Archaeologist, Center for Big Bend Studies, Sul Ross State University, Alpine, Texas. Personal communication.

Cloud, W. A., *et al.* (2007, December). La junta de los rios: Villagers of the Chihuahuan Desert. Retrieved May 7, 2008, from http://www.texasbeyondhistory.net

Collyer, S. (2005, April). Teaching kids about resource restoration, one small tree at a time. *The Big Bend Gazette, 5*(4), 26-27, 28.

Conover, A. (2001, March 1). Hunting slime molds They're not animals and they're not plants, and biologists want to know a lot more about them. *Smithsonian, 31*(12), 26-30.

Davila, V. (2007). Superintendent, National Park Service. Wind Cave, South Dakota. Personal communication.

Dean, R. (2007). Environmental Education Coordinator, National Park Service. Big Bend National Park, Texas. Personal communication.

Emmett, C. (1969). *Texas camel tales.* Austin: Steck-Vaughn.

Evans, D. S., & Mulholland, J. D. (1986). *Big and bright A history of the McDonald Observatory.* Austin: University of Texas Press.

Flippo, M. (2007). Supervisory Park Ranger, National Park Service. Big Bend National Park, Texas. Personal communication.

Henderson, A. K. (2002). *Tenderfoot Teacher Letters from the Big Bend 1952-1954.* Fort Worth, Texas: TCU Press.

Kimball, A. C. (1996). *Big Bend guide Travel tips and suggested itineraries.* Wimberley, Texas: Sun Country Publications.

Lesley, L. B., Ed. (1929, 2006). *Uncle Sam's Camels The Journal of May Humphreys Stacey Supplemented by the Report of Edward Fitzgerald Beale (1857-1858).* San Marino, CA: Huntington Library Press.

Lindfors, J. W. (1987). *Children's language and learning, second edition.* Englewood Cliffs, New Jersey: Prentice-Hall, Inc.

Nelson, K. (1992). A *road guide to the geology of Big Bend National Park.* Big Bend National Park, Texas: Big Bend Natural History Association.

Nokes, J. (2001). *How to grow native plants of Texas and the Southwest.* Austin: University of Texas Press.

Parent, L., & Potoski, J. N. (2006). *Big Bend National Park.* Austin: University of Texas Press.

Reid, J. (2004). *Rio Grande.* Austin: University of Texas Press.

Richards, H. & D. (1997). *Newfoundlands today.* New York: Howell Book House.

Robertson, E. C., & Gohn, K. (nd). Florence Bascom – Pioneering geologist. *USGS science for a changing world.* Retrieved on March 7, 2008 from http://www.usgs.gov/125/articles/bascom.html

Schneider, J. S. (nd). A life of firsts: Florence Bascom. gsa.org./gsat/gt98feb8_9.pdf

Scobee, B. (1947). *Old Fort Davis.* San Antonio: The Naylor Company.

Shriners Hospital for Children – Galveston. (2007, November 12). Care Specialists. Retrieved on February 25, 2008 from http://shrinershq.org/Hospitals/Galveston

Sibley, D. (1996). *The North American Bird Guide.* New York: Knopf.

Skiles, R. (2007). Wildlife Biologist, National Park Service, Big Bend National Park, Texas. Personal communication.

Smith, F. (1973). *Psycholinguists and reading.* Twelve easy ways to make learning to read difficult (*and one difficult way to make it easy). Frank Smith, ed. New York: Holt, Rinehart & Winston, Inc.

Spearing, D. (1991). *Roadside geology of Texas.* Missoula, Montana: Mountain Press Publishing Company.

Spier, M. (2007). Chief Ranger, National Park Service. Big Bend National Park, Texas. Personal communication.

Sorlier, C., Ed. (1979). *Chagall by Chagall.* Translator John Shepley. New York: Harry N. Abrams.

Texas Parks & Wildlife. (2002). Mountain lions in Texas. Austin: Texas Parks & Wildlife, Wildlife Division.

Tiffany, L. H., & Knaphus, G. (2001). Myxomycetes of the Big Bend National Park, Texas. *Journal of Iowa Academic Science, 108*(3), 98-102.

Tucker, A. B., (2008). *Ghost Schools of the Big Bend.* Brownwood, Texas: Howard Payne University Press.

Tyler, R. C. (2003). The Big Bend a history of the last Texas Frontier. College Station, TX: Texas A&M University Press.

VandenBurg, T. (2007). Supervisory Park Ranger, Division of Interpretation, National Park Service. Glacier Bay National Park and Preserve, Alaska. Personal communication.

Verhovek, S. H. (1994, December 9). Another day, another 89 miles to school. *The New York Times.*

Verhovek, S. H. (1996, May 27). End near for 179-mile bus trip to high school. *The New York Times.*

Wauer, R. (2002). *Butterflies of West Texas parks and preserves.* Lubbock, Texas: Texas Tech University Press.

Wauer, R. (1996). *A field guide to birds of the Big Bend, second edition.* Austin, Texas: Texas Monthly Press.

West, S. (2000). *Northern Chihuahuan Desert wildflowers.* Helena, Montana: Falcon Publishing, Inc.

Wolford, G. (2007). *Texas Mountain Trail Region.* Austin: Texas Historical Commission.

Yancey, D. (1995). *Camels for Uncle Sam.* Dallas, Texas: Hendrick-Long Publishing Co.

http://www.nps.gov/archive/whsa/tamarisk.htm

http://www.nps.gov/bibe/planyourvisit/basin.htm

http://www.tpwd.state.tx.us/publications/nonpwdpubs/introducing_mammals/javelinas

http://www.uen.org/K-2educator/word_lists.shtml

CPSIA information can be obtained
at www.ICGtesting.com
Printed in the USA
FSOW03n0847200815
10136FS